Costume Jewelry

1

1. A rare 1940s Nettie Rosenstein butterfly fur clip, in vermeil sterling silver, with enamel and diamanté, signed. 4in (10cm) long **E**

2. A 1940s Coro "Quivering Camelias" Duette, in gilt metal with colorless and emerald rhinestones and enamel, signed with patent numbers. 3in (7.5cm) long **D**

MILLER'S
Costume Jewelry

2

JUDITH MILLER

Miller's Costume Jewelry
by Judith Miller

First published in Great Britain in 2010 by Miller's,
a division of Mitchell Beazley,
imprints of Octopus Publishing Group Ltd,
Endeavour House, 189 Shaftesbury Avenue, London WC2 8JY.
An Hachette Livre Company
www.hatchettelivre.co.uk
www.octopusbooks.co.uk
www.millersonline.com

Distributed in the US and Canada by Octopus Books USA
c/o Hachette Book Group USA
237 Park Avenue South, New York, NY 10017

ISBN 978 1 84533 563 2

A CIP record of this book is available from the British Library and the Library of Congress.

Set in Caslon and Univers
Printed and bound in China

Publishing Manager: **Julie Brooke**
Editorial Director: **Tracey Smith**
Design: **Mark Kan**
Art Director and Jacket Design: **Pene Parker**
Deputy Art Director: **Yasia Williams-Leedham**
Chief contributors: **Carolyn Madden, Alycen Mitchell, Katy Armstrong**
Editors: **Alexandra Stetter, Lesley Malkin**
Editorial Assistant: **Katy Armstrong**
Proof Reader: **Ruth Baldwin**
Indexer: **Isobel McLean**
Production Controller: **Susan Meldrum**

Value codes
Throughout this book the value codes used at the end of each caption correspond to the
approximate value of the item. These are broad price ranges and should be seen only as a guide
to the value of the piece, as prices for costume jewelry vary depending on the condition of the
item, geographical location, and market trends. The codes are interpreted as follows:

A	Less than $40 / £20		**H**	$800–900 / £500–600
B	$40–80 / £20–50		**I**	$900–1,100 / £600–700
C	$80–$150 / £50–100		**J**	$1,100–1,250 / £700–800
D	$150–350 / £100–200		**K**	$1,250–$1,400 / £800–900
E	$350–500 / £200–300		**L**	$1,400–1,600 / £900–1,000
F	$500–650 / £300–400		**M**	More than $1,600 / £1,000
G	$650–800 / £400–500			

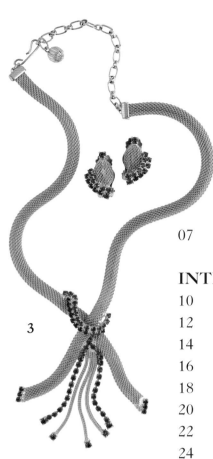

CONTENTS

07   Foreword

INTRODUCTION
10   Ancient Times
12   Renaissance
14   Early 18th Century
16   Late 18th Century
18   Early 19th Century
20   Late 19th Century
22   Art Nouveau
24   Arts & Crafts
26   Art Deco
30   1940s and 1950s
32   1960s and 1970s
34   1980s and 1990s
36   Into the 21st century

MAJOR DESIGNERS
40   Trifari
52   Miriam Haskell
62   Stanley Hagler
72   Coro & Corocraft
80   Christian Dior
86   Elsa Schiaparelli
92   Marcel Boucher
98   Joseff of Hollywood
104   Chanel
108   Theodor Fahrner
110   Weiss
114   Kramer
118   Vendôme

122   Lisner
126   Kenneth Jay Lane
130   Butler & Wilson
134   Hobé
136   Schreiner
138   Eisenberg
140   Mazer & Jomaz
142   Hattie Carnegie
144   Har
146   Lea Stein
148   Coppola e Toppo
150   Matisse & Renior

CLASSIC DESIGNERS
154   ACME, Alcozer, Art
156   Avon, Beaujewels
158   Jakob Bengel, Bogoff,
        Bond Boyd
160   Cadoro, Carolee, Castlecliff,
        Alice Caviness
162   Ciner, Sarah Coventry,
        Cristobal
164   DeLizza & Elster
166   Lily Daché, Danecraft,
        Robert De Mario,
        DeRosa
168   Eugene, Florenza,
        Givenchy
170   Gripoix, Grosse,
        Hollycraft,
        Harry Iskin

3. A Hobé-style necklace and earrings set, in gold-tone mesh with lilac and deep pink chaton-cut rhinestones. Necklace 17.5in (44cm) long **C**

4. A 1950s Miriam Haskell bracelet, in rose pink with gold painted ivy leaves and diamanté on clasp. 7.5in (19cm) long **E**

5

GALLERIES

200   Austrian Jewelry
202   Plastic Jewelry
208   Christmas Tree Pins
212   Czech Jewelry
214   Double clips
216   Jelly Bellies
218   Unsigned gems

FUTURE DESIGNERS

230   Hanna Bernhard,
       Bijoux Heart
232   Alexis Bittar, Lara Bohinc
234   Eddie Borgo, Sabrina Dehoff
236   Erickson Beamon,
       Dana Lorenz
238   Mawi, Simon Mower
240   St Erasmus, Tatty Devine
242   Marion Vidal, Scott Wilson

246   **Dealers**
248   **Glossary**
250   **Marks**
252   **Index**
256   **Acknowledgments**

172   Christian Lacroix,
       Karl Lagerfeld, Lanvin
174   Judy Lee, Marvella,
       McClelland Barclay
176   Iradj Moini, Monet,
       Mimi di Niscemi
178   Napier
180   Panetta, Pennino Brothers,
       Rebajes
182   Regency
184   Réja, Robert
186   Nettie Rosenstein,
       Rousselet,
       Yves Saint Laurent
188   Sandor, Selro & Selini
190   Sherman
192   Adele Simpson,
       Hervé van der Straeten,
       Tortolani, Vogue
194   Larry Vrba
196   Warner, Vivienne Westwood,
       Whiting & Davis

5. A Victorian shield pin,
in 15ct gold, with enamel, and
silver and rose-cut diamond
flower. 2in (5cm) long **F**

6. A mid-1910s Art Nouveau
pendant, in silver, with faux
emeralds. 2in (5.5cm) long **D**

7. A pair of 1940s Trifari flower
earrings, designed by Alfred
Philippe, in sterling silver, with
invisible-set caliber-cut petals and
green and clear rhinestones. 1.25in
(3cm) long **D**

6

FOREWORD

My love affair with costume jewelry probably began as a child playing with my mum's jewelry box in the late 1950s. The look of these sparkly multi-colored glass pins, earrings, and necklaces was so much more attractive to a child than the rather restrained pieces of precious jewelry. And not just to a child. In the past few years the appeal of dazzling diamanté has grown, and the value of these pieces has exploded.

I find when I wear my Joseff of Hollywood Russian-gold "moon pin with ruff," I attract many admiring glances and comments—particularly when people notice that the eyes actually move! That is one of the appeals of costume jewelry—it doesn't take itself too seriously. There is a sense of humor in many of the pieces. There is also the fact that many of the pieces are small works of art. The designer did not have the inherent value of the diamonds, rubies, and emeralds, and had to instead work with multi-faceted, multi-colored pieces of glass and stones to create a desirable object. The craftsmanship in top-quality costume jewelry is certainly equal to that of precious jewelry.

When 20th century costume jewelry was created it was designed to fit every budget and the same is true today. If you find Schiaparelli and Chanel out of your budget, check out some of the minor designers or unsigned pieces. Search out yard sales and thrift shops. I have bought earrings in a brocante in the Dordogne, France; pins in thrift shops in Edinburgh, Scotland; and some wonderful parures and pins in a great shop in Galveston, Texas. I have bought online, and at antiques and collectibles fairs. One of the great advantages of costume jewelry is that it is so accessible. Don't forget your granny or great aunt may well have some gems tucked away in the back of the chest of drawers.

It is wonderful to be able to wear your collection. And in the words of Kenneth J. Lane in *Faking It*, "Wearing costume jewelry is like wearing glass slippers. You can feel like you're going to the ball, even if you're not."

Introduction

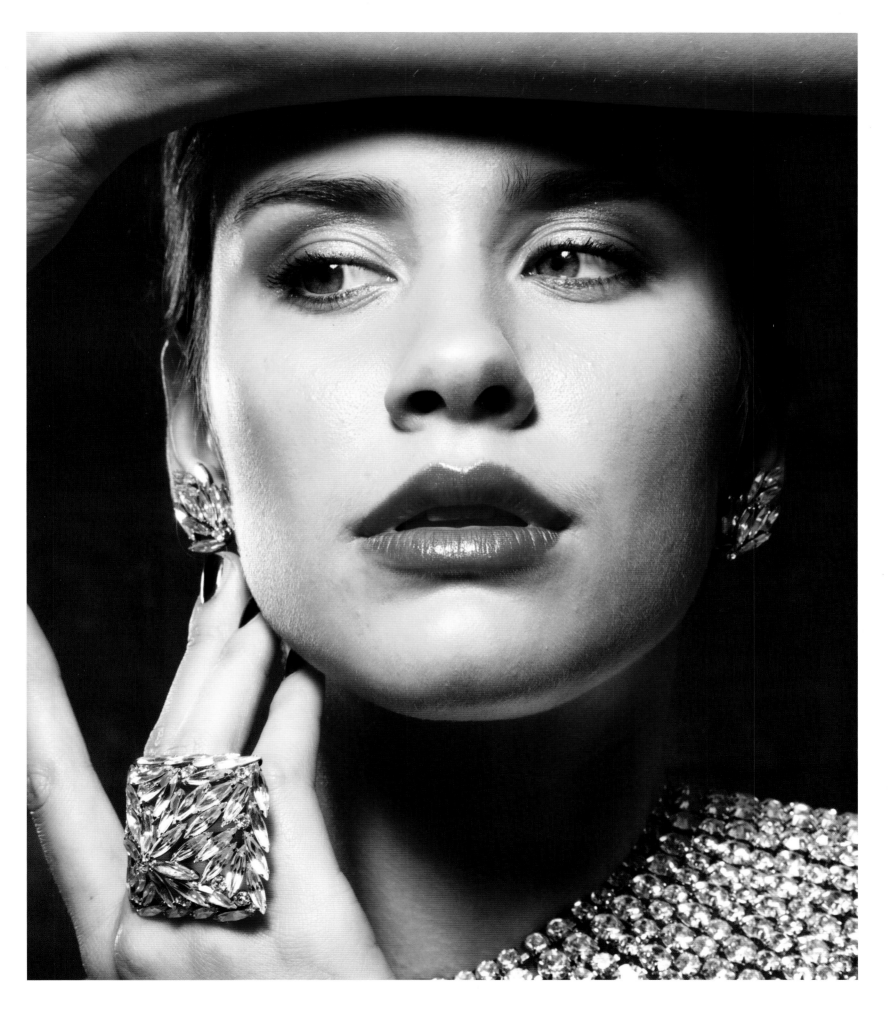

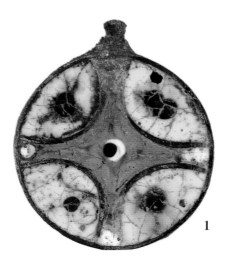

1

ANCIENT TIMES

The term costume jewelry only came into common parlance in the early 20th century. Initially it was used to describe the imitation jewels couturiers created to coordinate with the outfits they designed, which were then known as costumes—hence costume jewelry. Made from materials with little intrinsic value such as glass, base metals, and plastic, this kind of jewelry was a fashion accessory, meant to be cast aside as a new style came into vogue. The phenomenal popularity costume jewelry currently enjoys can be attributed to its endless novelty and outfit-enhancing qualities. Since costume jewelry is predominantly mass-produced to meet widespread consumer demand, it is often thought of as a modern invention, but forms have been made since ancient times. In fact, many examples of what is now considered costume jewelry played a vital and integral role in the development of all jewelry.

The world's oldest-known pieces of jewelry—shell beads found in caves in South Africa and Israel—are thought to be 75,000 and 100,000 years old respectively. Deliberately pierced for use as pendants or in necklaces, these finds offer some of the earliest evidence of human aesthetic and symbolic expression. Scientists believe humans originally began adorning themselves with leaves, berries, feathers, animal teeth, and shells as a by-product of their search for food. These rudimentary personal ornaments literally signified a successful hunt or fruit-gathering expedition. As our ancestors evolved, they began seeking out rare materials and fashioning them into increasingly sophisticated forms of jewelry. Some pieces conveyed status, kinship, or membership of a wider social group. Others were worn as amulets that were believed to grant supernatural powers or ward off evil. Jewelry could be used to display wealth or employed as currency in trading. Evidence suggests we started making metal jewelry about 7,000 years ago. However, pieces made from gold and silver, especially with colored stones, did not become common for another 2,000 years.

The Ancient World

The Egyptians were among the most renowned goldsmiths of the ancient world, but they also made jewelry from humbler materials such as enamel, glass, earthenware, wood, bone, amber, coral, and jet. Their most popular motifs were scarabs and the eye of the god Horus. On religious occasions, they wore intricate garland collars fashioned from blossoms, leaves, and berries. The ancient Egyptians were the first people to make imitation gemstones out of glass. Colors were imbued with deep meaning for them: green, for example, symbolized growing crops and fertility. As a result, they frequently preferred using vividly colored glass to precious stones. A significant proportion of their pieces were made to accompany the dead to the afterlife. Many Egyptian techniques spread to neighboring Phoenicia, which was also a center of jewelry production. This famous seafaring civilization had trading partners in locations from the Mediterranean to the Far East, and the Phoenicians brought Egyptian techniques to southern Europe around 500 BC.

Trade in modest items of jewelry was thriving by the Roman period. The most common items of jewelry worn by the Romans were pins for fastening clothing. They often fashioned pieces from bronze, bone, and glass, and ceramic beads were glazed to look like cornelian or turquoise. Imitation stones were a Roman specialty: glass was carved or molded with intaglio designs to make it resemble engraved gems. Glassworkers capitalized on the Roman love of pearls, producing imitations by lining glass beads with iridescent gold and silver foil. In fact their versions were so good that "Roman pearls" is still a byword for quality simulants. Many of these were intended to deceive: glass replicas were frequently passed off as highly desirable gems. These became such a problem that the first century philosopher and writer Pliny the Elder was moved to offer pointers on how to detect them. He said to watch out for warmth to the touch, air bubbles, and a soft easy-to-chip form—sound advice.

Early Middle Ages

As Christianity spread throughout the Roman Empire, craftsmen began incorporating images of Christ and the Virgin Mary into traditional Roman jewelry designs, including those made of inexpensive materials like bronze and glass. Christian symbols such as the cross and the tree of life became widespread.

The Romans were losing control of Western Europe and tribes such as the Goths were coming to the fore. In 324 AD, Constantinople became the new Christian capital of the Eastern Roman or Byzantine Empire. Jewelry design took a new direction and became more delicate, with the emphasis on gold-leaf work, pierced openwork, and filigree designs. Although there are fewer historical records compared with Roman times and the centuries that followed, the early Middle Ages were a period of great cultural achievement, as archeological excavations have demonstrated. Jewelry produced by the Saxons, Celts, and Vikings was equal to anything made by Roman jewelers, both technically and artistically. However, unlike their counterparts in Byzantium, these craftsman preferred solid metal mounts, cloisonné enamel decoration, and intricately set stones—typically garnets.

1. A rare Roman disk pendant, with enameled design in turquoise, white and yellow. 14in (35cm) diam **F**

2. A Byzantine cross, in bronze, with empty setting for a gemstone. c700–800AD 1.25in (3cm) long **C**

3. An Egyptian hair ring, in carnelian. c1200BC 0.5in (1.5cm) diam **C**

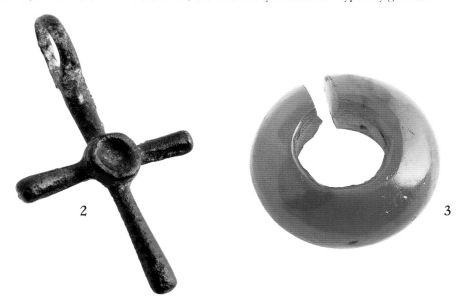

1

RENAISSANCE
MEDIEVAL THROUGH TO 1730

During the later Middle Ages enameling was the most popular form of decoration on jewelry. People favored images of patron saints, to whom they prayed for their powers of intercession, and these were portrayed on hat badges and other jewels. Jewelers continued to mix precious and semi-precious stones with glass imitations. Most gems were simply polished rather than cut, and set in high foil-backed cup-like cabochon settings. Glass itself had become a rare commodity and was often to be found in the caskets in which the rich stored valuable goods.

Jewelry fraud was an extensive problem throughout the medieval era. By the early 13th century, many European states had introduced legislation to combat deception: substituting glass or cheaper stones such as amethysts for costly gems such as sapphires was forbidden, as was setting precious gems in cheap silver. However, contemporary documents and surviving pieces of jewelry suggest enforcement of these laws was lax.

During the later medieval era, earrings and bracelets fell out of favor as a result of the fashion for elaborate headdresses and long sleeves. The wealthy of both sexes wore pins, rings, clock clasps, collars, chains, girdles, and coronets. More ordinary members of society adorned themselves with silver, amber, and mother-of-pearl buttons, and with spangles of beaten gold and silver.

The late 13th century saw laws to curb ostentatious display, especially common among prosperous merchants and artisans. These laws—known as sumptuary laws—dictated what people of various social positions could wear. In France, for example, townspeople were not allowed to wear girdles or coronets made of pearls, gems, gold, or silver. Although widely disregarded, these laws were retained until the 17th century to ensure that people did not dress "above their station," and to reduce spending on the import of foreign goods.

A rebirth
The Renaissance was a period of dramatic artistic and scientific progress brought about by the rediscovery of Classical antiquity. It began in 14th-century Italy and spread throughout Europe over the next two centuries. The era is famed for its sculptural jewelry, inspired by Roman imagery. Mermaids, cupids, and heraldic symbols were fashioned from gold and embellished with colorful enamel and gems. These pieces were incredibly costly to make and were worn only by the very upper echelons of society.

2

In the 16th century, women began to wear more jewelry than men. The garments and coiffures of noblewomen were covered with pearls and gems, and they often wore several necklaces, chains, and pendants together and several rings on each finger. Inevitably such lavish finery was supplemented with imitation jewels. Venice, an important glassmaking center during the Renaissance, became renowned for its imitation pearls and gems. A lady's numerous "false" pieces were made for court events or portrait sittings in order to enhance her family's wealth and rank. From their enameled sculptural forms to their chased-gilt backs, they were exact replicas of real pieces, as surviving examples indicate.

17th century

The use of sculptural forms gradually declined in the 17th century, and gemstones started to dominate design. There was also less emphasis on enamel decoration. The girandole—three pendants suspended from a bow—was one of the most popular designs. The French began to set fashions in jewelry, a lead they would maintain until the mid-20th century.

Pearl jewelry had been worn in extravagant abundance since the late Renaissance and by the 17th century no fashionable woman would be seen without real or imitation pearls. The finest imitations were made by Jaquin of Paris, who weighted glass beads with wax before giving them an iridescent coating made from a mixture of fish scales. His faux pearls were so highly acclaimed that he received a royal warrant from Louis XIV.

By the end of the 17th century glittering gems began to eclipse the ubiquitous pearl. Although precious stones, especially diamonds, were still great rarities, improved trade with the East made them more readily available in Europe. The discovery of diamonds in Brazil in the 1720s further increased their availability. More plentiful supplies granted jewelers the freedom to experiment with cuts that enhanced a diamond's sparkle and clarity. Gem setting was improving, too: metal settings surrounding stones were now barely visible, and foiling—the art of using thin sheets of tinted metal to intensify the color of stones in closed-back settings—reached new levels of refinement. Jewelers also started to set diamonds in silver rather than gold to avoid the yellowing effect of gold's reflected glow.

In this period most costume jewelry was copied from the precious gems of the time.

1. A 16thC French Henri III portrait medallion, in gilded bronze with engraving, opening to reveal compartment, inscribed "HENRICVS III D G FRANCORVM ET POLANIAE REX 1584." 4.25in (11cm) long **M**

2. A bow pendant, in gold, with rubies and diamonds. c1560–1640 2in (5cm) long **M**

3. A Netherlandish swan pendant, in gold, with enamel, pearl and stones. c1590 3.75in (9.5cm) long **M**

3

1

EARLY 18TH CENTURY

In the early 18th century, brighter lighting from new beeswax candles meant an increasing number of important social events, such as balls, could take place after dark. This added to the demand for sparkling jewels that shimmered attractively in candlelight. A distinction developed between simpler pieces of jewelry worn with everyday clothing and the brilliant splendor that accessorized formal dress for evening occasions.

The obsession with rich glitter emanated from the luxury-loving French court, which soon influenced taste throughout the rest of Europe. The Industrial Revolution was also gathering momentum in the early 18th century, leading to greater prosperity among the middle classes. Keen to display their financial success and new standing in society, they aspired to the glamorous splendor of the aristocracy. Dressing impressively required a profusion of sparkling stones, yet diamonds were relatively scarce and extremely expensive. The solution came in the form of a new glass imitation—paste.

Satisfying demand with paste

The lead glass used for making paste stones was developed by British craftsmen in the late 17th century. This hard, brilliant glass could be cut and polished to produce "gems" with a convincing sparkle. In the 1730s, Parisian jeweler Georges Frédéric Strass began widely promoting pastes as a substitute for precious stones—particularly diamonds. Strass's paste jewels were of an exceptionally high standard, and his sumptuous creations were a great success with French courtiers, which gave them additional cachet.

Although Strass was the most famous paste jeweler of the day, he had many competitors, as wealthy people throughout Europe rapidly began to emulate the latest French fashion. Quite apart from their dazzling brilliance, paste jewels held another appeal: they were safe to take on journeys. The well-to-do were beginning to travel more despite the trepidations of the road and the menace of highwaymen. With paste jewelry in their trunks, travelers could look their best when required without risking losing a fortune.

Popular motifs and fashionable pieces

Jewelers in the 18th century used similar motifs for both real and paste jewelry. Girandole designs were still in demand; ribbons and bows were also very popular. There was great enthusiasm for designs drawn from nature such as birds, butterflies, and flowers. Giardinetti—a type of multi-colored floral jewel whose name means "little garden"—reflected this passion.

1 An early Georgian memorial pendant, with enamel Latin inscription and clear stone over hair scroll, obituary to reverse. 1.25in (3cm) long **M**

2

The most stylish pieces were bold and extravagant. Some of these jewels were mounted on springs so they swayed when in motion. Women stuck feather-like headpieces called aigrettes in their towering wigs; large stomacher ornaments adorned the front of their dresses; and they wore slides threaded on ribbons about their throats and wrists. Matching suites of jewelry known as parures became more common as the century progressed.

In the latter half of the 18th century, jewelers were increasingly enthralled by themes from Classical antiquity which were influencing architecture and the decorative arts in general. Imagery including arrows, trophies, crescents, and stars became popular. Jewelers replicated the diadems and bandeaux Roman matrons wore on their brows, and Spartan necklaces featuring graduated stones or pastes called rivières were much admired.

Men's finery

Jewelry was still a vital part of men's dress during the 18th century. In fact men enjoyed wearing sparkling jewelry as much as women at the time, as demonstrated by plenty of surviving pieces set with glittering pastes. Ornamental shoe buckles were the height of fashion; pins were used to keep cravats in place; suits were trimmed with quantities of decorative buttons. Miniatures and lockets dangled from ribbons around necks, and it was stylish to wear a pocket watch and chain hung with your keys and the seal you used to identify a document.

By the end of the 18th century, fine paste pieces had gained widespread acceptance as a distinct form of jewelry in their own right. Uninhibited by scarcity of materials or expense, 18th century jewelers cut and set pastes in ways unimaginable with precious stones, and their exceptionally fine workmanship ensured that paste pieces were costly enough to be regarded as exclusive luxuries. Paste creations were sold by jewelers alongside real jewels—a practice that continued into the early 20th century.

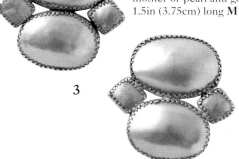
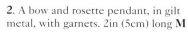

3

2. A bow and rosette pendant, in gilt metal, with garnets. 2in (5cm) long **M**

3. A pair of Queen Anne earrings, in mother-of-pearl and gold-plate. c1700 1.5in (3.75cm) long **M**

1

LATE 18TH CENTURY

Paste jewels were not the only alternatives to the precious gems and metals that were so popular in the 18th century: advances in technology made new materials increasingly available for use in jewelry. Highly attractive as well as affordable, these stylish novelties were worn by monied society.

Around 1720, Christopher Pinchbeck, a prominent London watchmaker, developed an alloy of copper and zinc that successfully mimicked gold. The beauty of pinchbeck—as it became known—was that it retained its warm golden color without tarnishing. Although it was a humble material, the highest level of craftsmanship went into fashioning it into accessories. In fact, its malleability meant it could be worked and decorated in exactly the same way as gold. Pinchbeck pieces were often set with pastes or embellished with royal-blue enamel. It was used for a variety of jewelry, but it was especially popular for chatelaines, a stylish yet practical accessory used by both sexes. Hung from the waist, it had clips from which the wearer could suspend items such as scent bottles, keys, watches, and bodkin cases.

The pinchbeck formula was soon widely imitated by other manufacturers in Britain and France. It remained popular until the mid-19th century, when it was gradually superseded by rolled gold and other gilt metals. At this point people started using the term "pinchbeck" to describe any yellow metal jewelry other than gold. As an unfortunate consequence, today gilt jewelry is often incorrectly said to be made of pinchbeck.

Cut steel

British metalworkers had begun producing faceted steel studs for decorative purposes in the 16th century. By the 1730s, Woodstock in Oxfordshire became renowned for its cut-steel trinkets such as scissors and mesh watch chains. It took great skill to make these pieces, and they were expensive as a result. Although cut-steel jewels sparkle delightfully—especially in candlelight—unlike paste jewels they were never seriously intended to simulate the diamond's remarkable glitter. Yet their twinkle caught the eye of fashion leaders and their popularity grew. By the mid-18th century, cut-steel jewelry was produced throughout Britain and France. Around this time jewelers began combining cut-steel studs with little stones of marcasite, a form of yellowish iron sulfide mineral that shines attractively when polished.

However cut steel only became a widespread alternative to gem-set jewelry in the 1760s, after a Birmingham industrialist named Matthew Boulton discovered a way to mechanize the manufacturing technique without compromising quality. Soon Boulton was exporting affordable cut-steel pieces, particularly buttons, throughout Europe. Cut steel would continue to be popular until the late 19th century, but few later examples were as well made.

Imitation intaglios and cameos

In the mid-18th century, the Scottish entrepreneur James Tassie began producing high-quality paste replicas of ancient engraved intaglios. The buried Roman towns of Pompeii (1748) and Herculaneum (1738) had just recently been rediscovered and the excavation of artifacts encouraged renewed interest in Classical architecture and design. As a result, "Tassie medallions," as they were called in the 18th century, rapidly caught on. Soon Tassie was commissioning new designs with a Neo-classical flavor from contemporary artists.

At first Tassie medallions were sold in sets, to be admired as miniature artworks in their own right. Catherine the Great famously ordered a set for the Russian royal collection. However, by the late 18th century, individual Tassie medallions were being mounted in rings, seals, pins, bracelets, necklaces, and buttons. Around the same time, the ceramics manufacturer Josiah Wedgwood started to make replicas of ancient cameos in his famous Jasperware. Typical images include characters and scenes from Classical mythology and contemporary literature. Wedgwood cameos were made in a variety of colors but white figures on a blue ground are by far the most familiar. Like Tassie medallions, Wedgwood cameos were originally sold in sets.

By the late 18th century Wedgwood had teamed up with Matthew Boulton to produce cameo-like jewelry such as pins, diadems, hair combs, and chatelaines with mounts made of cut steel, silver, and occasionally gold.

Tortoiseshell

Like ivory, horn, and shell, tortoiseshell is considered a natural plastic: it can be softened and molded into new shapes. Craftsmen in France were the first to start making accessories from tortoiseshell in the early 17th century. They developed a technique known as piqué for delicately inlaying the surface of tortoiseshell items with mother-of-pearl, silver, and gold. Common inlay patterns include geometric arrangements of stars, dots, and stripes. Floral sprays were also widely used.

In the late 17th and early 18th centuries, Huguenot craftsmen fleeing religious persecution in France spread the fashion for tortoiseshell piqué to Holland, Germany, and Britain. Tortoiseshell piqué jewelry such as pins, earrings, combs, buttons, and buckles remained popular throughout the 18th and 19th centuries.

1. A Victorian lion-head pin, in pinchbeck, with faux rubies, the rings stamped and hand-soldered together. c1850 **E**

2. A Georgian necklace, in silver, with faux garnet. c1780 16.25in (41.5cm) long **H**

1

EARLY 19TH CENTURY

At the end of the 18th century the fashion for clear, sparkling jewels began to wane. The French Revolution had a profound effect throughout Europe and no one wanted to be associated with the profligate extravagance of the "Ancient Régime". However, when Napoleon became emperor of France in 1804 he encouraged craftsmen to develop a new style befitting a glorious new leader. They looked to the Roman Empire for inspiration, and the result was a new "Empire" style. Inspired by authentic gold-work discovered in Roman archeological sites, they produced earrings, headpieces, bangles, and necklaces in gold, pinchbeck, and gilt which were accentuated with flamboyant combinations of multi-colored stones and pastes.

Berlin ironwork jewelry

The influence of the Empire style influenced reached Germany, one of the countries invaded by Napoleon's army. There, it helped to promote a fashion for ironwork jewelry, much of it made by Silesian armorers. As demand for metal armor declined, they applied their casting skills to making iron jewelry. They produced delicate openwork earrings, bracelets, necklaces, and combs inset with figured medallions finished with black lacquer.

In the early 1800s, a number of industrial manufacturers picked up on this technique—most notably the Royal Berlin Factory—hence the name Berlin ironwork. The restrained beauty of ironwork jewelry was embraced by Germany's fashion leaders. Iron's durability symbolizes unwavering support, and this jewelry's appeal reached new heights when the government began giving ironwork pieces to women who donated their costly jewels to fund the nation's battle for liberation. Many of these tokens of gratitude are were inscribed with sayings phrases such as "I gave gold for iron." After Napoleon's defeat, the popularity of ironwork jewelry went from strength to strength, and these arresting pieces were seen worn by women in many countries. Ironically, this jewelry was especially popular in France, where a number of manufacturers became renowned for their skill.

Mourning jewelry

The late 18th and early 19th centuries saw a growing obsession with the practise of wearing mourning jewelry in memory of dead relatives. This fervour would reach its zenith in the mid-19th century. Mourning jewelry has its origins in the medieval era, when the wealthy would bequeath a number of identical, inexpensive rings to kinsmen and associates as personal mementos. At that time, the well-to-do also wore macabre trinkets—shaped, for

2

1. A pair of Berlin ironwork floral earrings, with gilt highlights. c1820 2.25in (6cm) long **M**

2. A Victorian hair pin, in pinchbeck. c1860 2in (5cm) long **D**

3. A late Georgian oval-shaped shoe buckle, in steel and silver, with clear and sapphire pastes. c1820 2in (5cm) long **C**

example, like skulls—as reminders of human mortality. These customs gradually spread to the middle classes. By the second half of the 18th century it had become a convention to wear special pieces—principally rings—inscribed with the names and dates of deceased loved ones. Mourning rings from this period are usually oval or marquise-shaped and often feature a framed and glazed memorial picture decorated with pearls to symbolize tears, or enamel in the traditional mourning colours—black, white, and purple. As the 19th century progressed, the popularity of mourning rings declined in favour of commemorative pins and pendants. These were mainly mass-produced using a wide variety of inexpensive materials, including gilt with enamel, onyx, and glass.

Jewelers had begun to incorporate the deceased's hair into mourning jewelry in the 17th century. By the late 18th century, it was customary to place elaborate arrangements of hair in glazed compartments behind commemorative pendants, pins, and clasps. Hair jewelry became even more popular in the first half of the 19th century, when hair was woven into decorative items of every conceivable form, from earrings to watch chains. These pieces were not only used commemoratively but were also worn as a gesture of love or affection. Hair-work became a popular hobby for well-to-do young ladies, although the majority of surviving examples were made by professional hair-workers.

Vauxhall glass jewelry

The enthusiasm for glitter had not been completely extinguished. For people whose style exceeded their financial means, Vauxhall glass jewelry provided a relatively inexpensive solution. Manufacturers had been making this type of faceted glass jewelry since the 18th century. Its name derives from a mirror factory founded in the 17th century by the Duke of Buckingham in the Vauxhall area of London, although historians have yet to find any evidence that jewelry was ever actually made there.

Vauxhall jewelry came in colours such as burgundy, amethyst, white, and black. It was especially fashionable in the 1830s and 1840s, when it was often used in designs that looked like flowers or insects.

3

1

LATE 19TH CENTURY

B etween 1820 and 1840, Romanticism was at its height in European culture. This artistic movement emphasized emotions and sentimentality. Its most important elements were feelings for nature and an interest in the past—particularly the Middle Ages.

It became fashionable for gem-set jewelry to contain coded messages to loved ones. For example, there was a vogue for pieces set with rubies, emeralds, garnets, amethysts, rubies again, and diamonds—or their paste imitations—whose initial letters together form the word REGARD. Favored motifs like hearts, knots, love-birds, and hands of friendship were used to convey love and affection. Many of these pieces were made in pinchbeck or gilt lavishly decorated with floral filigree work.

Medieval themes began to permeate jewelry design. Scrolls, pointed Gothic arches, and intricate tracery were adapted from medieval architecture and incorporated into the design. Long chains, usually made of pinchbeck and similar to those seen in Tudor portraits, were incredibly fashionable. Crosses and other Christian emblems were worn on a wide scale for the first time since the Renaissance.

Subjects derived from nature were also typical of jewelry design of the period. Butterflies, insects, birds, flowers, and grape vines were very fashionable. The serpent with its tail in its mouth, signifying wisdom and eternal love, was another popular motif, especially for bangles.

A plethora of novelties

By the time Queen Victoria ascended the British throne in 1837, the industrialization of jewelry production was fully underway. Mass-production lowered the cost of making pieces available to most sectors of society and led to an extraordinary surge of novelty in design.

The popularity of Roman archeological-style gold jewelry endured. This resulted in the manufacture of gilt-metal copies on a previously unprecedented scale. Queen Victoria's holidays in the Highlands of Scotland started a fashion for Scottish pebble jewelry. These distinctive designs were made of engraved silver set with flat pieces of coloured agate arranged to imitate the tartan patterns used widely for fabrics.

In keeping with the Victorian fascination with nature, imagery such as birds' nests and branches covered in ivy became common. In fact, all manner of organic materials were transformed into jewelry, including horn, bone, nuts, even tiger's claws. Among the more outlandish fads were earrings and necklaces made from iridescent insects and stuffed humming birds. A passion for Japanese goods in the 1870s and 1880s sparked a craze for silver jewelry decorated with asymmetrical Oriental motifs.

Jet jewelry

Jet, a form of glossy black petrified wood similar to coal, had been carved into mourning jewels since the early 1800s. After Queen Victoria's husband Prince Albert died tragically young of typhoid in 1861, Britons took to wearing jet pieces in solidarity with their grieving monarch, giving a huge boost to jet's popularity.

Whitby in North Yorkshire, which had large jet deposits close by, was the center of the jet jewelry industry. Craftsmen carved and faceted jet to produce an extensive range of pieces, from rings and beads to buttons and hair ornaments.

Predominantly hand-carved, jet jewelry was relatively expensive. By the end of the 19th century, cheaper imitations were being mass-produced from materials such as vulcanite, a type of hardened rubber, and faceted black glass called French jet. Although people gradually stopped wearing mourning jewelry around 1900, shiny jet jewels, especially beads, remained fashionable until the 1920s.

Classical clarity

Throughout the 19th century, sparkling jewelry set with precious stones or fine pastes handcrafted by skilled jewelers remained stylish among the wealthy elite. By the 1830s, open-backed settings which allowed more light to pass through real and faux gems became more commonplace. As the century progressed, the techniques for stone cutting and polishing advanced to a great degree.

The opening of diamond mines in South Africa in the last quarter of the 19th century meant there was a steady supply of quality stones. This gave rise to the modern "brilliant"—a stone cut in such a way as to give an unparalleled sparkle. These marvellous diamonds were beautifully set-off by a mount made from a rare silvery-white metal called platinum which jewelers had only recently begun to employ.

Fashionable designs like such as swags, bows, and garlands harked back to the Neo-classicism of the 18th century. However, diamond jewelry from the 1890s and early 1900s tended to be lighter and more delicate-looking. Superb versions of these elegant jewels were also created in colorless pastes and silver.

Suffragette jewelry

As the 19th century drew to a close, women began actively striving for better rights, particularly for a voice in government. Women proudly wore jewelry expressing their support for the suffragette movement, which campaigned for votes for women. Suffragette pieces were immediately recognizable because they were decorated with green, white, and violet stones. The initial letter of each colour—G, W, V—echoed the suffragettes' demand of "Give women the vote."

1. A late 1830s jet anchor pin. 2in (5cm) long **C**

2. An Egyptian Revival necklace, in silver-gilt hung with mosaic insect and other charms. c1900–10 16in (40cm) long **E**

3. A Renaissance Revival parrot pendant, in gold, with diamond, enamel, and baroque pearl. 3.75in (9.5cm) long **M**

1

ART NOUVEAU

Towards the end of the 19th century there was a backlash against cheap, poor-quality jewelry and other mass-produced goods throughout Europe and the United States, led mainly by artists and the educated classes. Designers and artisans rejected machine manufacturing in favor of traditional handcrafting: they believed that a piece of jewelry should be appreciated for its fine workmanship and the creativity it expressed.

A new art for a new century

Art Nouveau was a new international style which got its name from a Parisian shop called Maison de l'Art Nouveau that was owned by the influential art dealer Samuel Bing. It was at its most pervasive in France but its influence was felt across the western hemisphere. Not only did the Art Nouveau movement unite the arts, it succeeded in revolutionizing design, too. The new style looked forward to the future rather than back to the past, and was the first modern look for the new 20th century.

Art Nouveau's most emblematic motif was a long, sinuous line, like a whiplash, which was used to represent everything from a plant's tendrils to a maiden's flowing hair or swirling robes. One of the movement's underlying themes was the ruthless beauty of nature. Mysterious, alluring, and sensual semi-clad sirens—known as femmes-fleur—dragonflies, orchids, bats, and mistletoe were all quintessential Art Nouveau images, as were peacocks and their feathers. The style introduced a moody, earthy palette of rich browns, greens, yellows, and harebell blues. Bold, sensual, even decadent—Art Nouveau jewelry was the complete opposite of the restrained good taste expressed by the gem-set pieces from the 1890s and early 1900s.

Resurgence of enamel decoration

Inspired by this burgeoning spirit, enameling techniques unseen for centuries were revived. Enamel is essentially a compound of powdered tinted glass fixed to the surface of jewelry by low-temperature firing. Plique-à-jour enamel has 15th-century origins but is predominantly associated with Art Nouveau jewelry.

Meaning "open to light," plique-à-jour is one of the most difficult forms of enamel decoration to master, and creates an effect similar to stained glass. This remarkable form of jewelry is produced by filling metal cells backed with copper foil with an enamel compound. The compound is fired, cooled, and hardened. The foil backing is then dissolved with acid to reveal the finished piece. Art Nouveau jewelers renowned for their plique-à-jour pieces include Georges Fouquet, Philippe Wolfers, and Lucien Gaillard.

Emphasis on materials with little intrinsic value

Many Art Nouveau jewelers preferred working in humble and more affordable materials such as ivory, horn, glass, copper, and silver. They produced pieces for their aesthetic properties rather than intrinsic worth, emphasizing their passionate belief that craftsmanship and artistry were more important than costly metals or precious gems. This reinforced an attitude to jewelry that grew throughout the 20th century: it was considered a personal adornment and fashion accessory rather than a signifier of wealth.

Jewelry by René Lalique

However, just because this jewelry was made from modest materials, it did not mean the results were inexpensive. René Lalique, the most influential jeweler of the Art Nouveau era, worked in plique-à-jour was his favorite medium, and was widely acclaimed for his exquisitely executed pieces. Lalique pioneered the combination of gold and costly stones with lesser materials such as moonstone, horn, pressed glass, ivory, steel, and aluminum. Although he was inspired by Neo-classical, Symbolist, and Oriental designs, nature was the main driving force behind his astonishingly original jewelry.

Many of his fantastic pieces were unique one-offs intended to be treated more like works of art than jewelry. A sinister and provocative half woman/half dragonfly ornament is probably his most famous design: even today, this spectacular piece has lost none of its power to shock. Lalique also created a number of pieces for Sarah Bernhardt, an internationally celebrated actress of the day, who was a great patron of Art Nouveau designers. Around 1914 Lalique stopped making jewelry altogether and applied his fertile imagination to manufacturing the beautiful molded glassware for which he is possibly better known today.

Spread of Art Nouveau style

High-end costume jewelry specialists including Piel Frères, Rouzé, and Mascaraud in Paris rapidly capitalized on the Art Nouveau trend and produced Art-Nouveau-style pieces for the stage and for couturiers. Their first-rate workmanship and designs at relatively affordable prices made "artistic" pieces more widely available, earning them praise in fashionable magazines of the period and thereby further promoting the style.

Art Nouveau designs stood out at the world's fair held in Paris in 1900, helping the style cross the Atlantic to the United States. The ubiquitous image of a mysterious maiden with her flowing hair and swirling robes captured the imagination of American silver manufacturers, who produced endless variations of this motif on silver pins and pendants on a commercial scale.

The largest of these firms was Gorham & Co. of Providence, Rhode Island. Gorham's "martelé" (hand-hammered) line was designed by William Codman. Nearby company Howard & Co. also produced notable jewelry, including belt buckles and pins. In Newark, New Jersey, Unger Bros. created heavily chased pieces with floral or foliate motifs, while La Pierre mixed silver with novelty materials, such as celluloid. Other important American makers of this period include Shiebler and Kerr & Co.

1. A belt buckle, in gilded brass, featuring maidens surrounded by flowers. c1900 4in (10cm) long **C**

2. A fan-shape pendant, in silver, with plique-à-jour and green and blue pastes, stamped "Th U" and "Sterling". 2in (5cm) high **F**

3. A Brandt mistletoe necklace, signed. 3.25in (8.5cm) high **M**

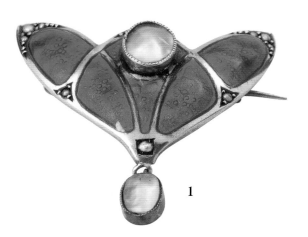

1

ARTS & CRAFTS

Many ideals of the Art Nouveau movement were also shared by Arts and Crafts jewelers in Britain, Northern Europe, and the United States. Both artistic movements had strong roots in mid-19th century Britain, and two leading British cultural figures of the day—the art critic John Ruskin and the designer and philosopher William Morris—articulated in print the dissatisfaction of many artists and craftsmen with industrialization and the shoddy goods it produced. Ruskin and Morris romanticized the medieval handicraft guilds, believing that these collectives maintained standards of workmanship and encouraged creativity among their members. They urged artists and designers to embrace their idealized pre-industrial vision and many took up the cause.

Made by hand

Just like Art Nouveau jewelers, Arts and Crafts jewelers produced finely wrought pieces, and their work featured similar undulating and entwined lines. Humbler materials like silver and enamel appealed to them more than costly rarities such as gold and emeralds. They were also drawn to the same enigmatic imagery as Art Nouveau jewelers—wistful maidens, Viking sailing ships, peacocks and their feathers.

Arts and Crafts jewelers such as C. R. Ashbee, Frank Gardner Hale, and Edward Everett Oakes differed from their Art Nouveau counterparts in that they emphatically stressed the fact that their pieces were entirely crafted by hand. For example, they deliberately left hammer marks on silver surfaces and produced grainy images in matt enamel in order to display the honesty and integrity of their work in these materials. Silver was the Arts and Crafts jewelers' metal of choice. They also liked using irregularly shaped pearls as well as simple cabochon-cut stones such as amethysts, moonstones, and opals which were placed in plain settings.

Arts and Crafts jewelers looked to Northern Europe's distant heritage for inspiration: the knotted patterns of Celtic goldsmiths and silversmiths in particular had a huge impact on their designs. Another major source of inspiration was jewelry from the Middle Ages, such as enamel figurative pendants. In contrast to the extreme sophistication of Art Nouveau jewelry designs, Arts and Crafts pieces tend to be simpler, lighter, and more naive. On the whole, they lack Art Nouveau jewelry's darkly sensuous qualities.

Although Arts and Crafts jewelry was made from inexpensive materials, the skill and artistry that went into these handcrafted pieces still put them out of many people's reach. However, several leading retailers and silver manufacturers of the day quickly recognized that the fresh simplicity of Arts and Crafts designs had wider appeal.

Liberty & Co.

Liberty's department store in London had been famous for importing exotic Oriental goods since the 1870s. By the end of the 19th century, the store was also commissioning stylish products with artistic merit from British designers and manufacturers.

A number of leading Arts and Crafts jewelers, including Jessie M. King and Arthur and Georgina Gaskin, created designs for Liberty. Although these pieces were produced using industrial technology by companies such as W. H. Haseler & Co. in Birmingham, they offered desirable Art and Crafts quality and looks without the expensive price. Archibald Knox was probably the best known of all the jewelers and silversmiths designing for Liberty. Drawing on his roots in the Isle of Man, he produced pins, buckles, and pendants with a strong Celtic flavor. His designs often feature a distinct whiplash motif and muted-colored enamels. Liberty's jewelry in the Arts and Crafts style proved such a success that the pieces were cheaply imitated for the mass market.

Murrle Bennett & Co.

Another London-based business to take note of the Arts and Crafts look was Murrle Bennett & Co., owned by German jeweler Ernst Mürrle. The company's jewelry was similar to Liberty's and was also available in the upmarket department store. Typical Murrle necklaces, pins, and pendants had gold or silver mounts and were set with blister pearls or turquoises. Like Liberty and Co., Ernst Mürrle had designs made to his specifications by industrial manufacturers who could be relied upon for quality, such as Theodor Fahrner in Pforzheim, Germany.

Kalo Shop

The Arts and Crafts design aesthetic was also successfully combined with industrial manufacturing techniques by the Kalo Shop in the United States. Clara Barack (later Barack Welles) founded the Chicago-based firm in 1900 and named it after the Greek word for beauty. She and her all-female design team (known as "Kalo girls") initially offered a variety of decorative items, but switched exclusively to copper and silver goods after Clara married amateur silversmith George Welles in 1905.

Barack hired Scandinavian metalworkers, under whose influence the jewelry soon developed an Arts and Crafts flavor. Stylized, geometric shapes and naturalistic forms, such as blossoms, oak and vine leaves, and acorns, were common. Many were embellished with semi-precious stones, and share a hammered surface with the work of C. R. Ashbee.

A number of notable Chicago jewelers and silversmiths such as Julius Randhal, Grant Wood, Matthias Hanack, and Emery Todd are associated with the Kalo Shop, which closed in 1970.

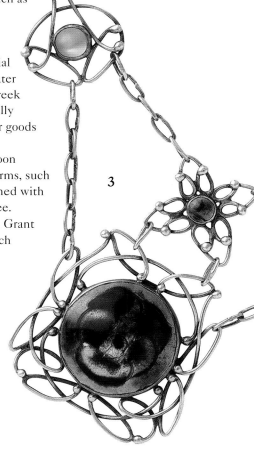

1. An insect-wing pin, in the style of James Fenton, in silver and blue/green enamel, with blister pearl and a drop pearl. c1900 1.5in (3.5cm) wide **E**

2. A shield-form pendant and "paper-clip" chain, designed by Frank Gardner Hale, in silver with garnet and bezel-set blister pearls, signed "F.G. Hale". c1915 Pendant 2in (5cm) long **M**

3. A Newlyn pansy necklace, in silver wirework, with enamel and moonstone, signed "Newlyn". Central plaque 2in (5cm) high **M**

ART DECO

By the end of World War I, a bold new style had begun to permeate all areas of design. It was sparked by the stunning costumes and sets of the Ballets Russes, the dance company formed by impresario Sergei Diaghilev that made a huge impact when it arrived in Paris in 1909. In the 1960s, this style became known as Art Deco, its name derived from the international exhibition of decorative arts held in Paris in 1925 that helped spread this style.

Art Deco is most commonly associated with primary colors and strong geometric forms. Jewelers of the period produced dazzling pieces based on circles, squares, and triangles.

Chanel's influence

More than any other fashion designer, Coco Chanel is credited with persuading women to dress in a more practical—almost masculine—style. During World War I, women had taken on new roles outside the home. This trend continued throughout the 1920s and 1930s, with women playing a more active part in politics, business, and sport. The flappers, with their short hair and short skirts, typified this newfound emancipation, and Chanel's clothes suited their new, more independent lifestyles.

Costume jewelry, especially long ropes of faux pearls, was an important element of Chanel's elegant, understated look. She did not copy trends in real jewelry: her costume jewels were undeniably fake, and she often mixed real and faux together. Apart from her signature pearls, she was known for her long gilt chains and richly colored "poured glass" jewelry with a vaguely Eastern flavor. Although only wealthy women could afford Chanel's couture pieces, the chic image she promoted encouraged many women to personalize their outfits with fake jewels.

Bakelite jewelry

"Plastics" have been made since ancient times. The word can describe any material that can be molded, from tortoiseshell to chemical resins. The first synthetic plastic was invented in 1907. Called Bakelite after its inventor Leo Baekeland, its name has become a catch-all term for many early manmade materials.

Until the late 1920s, plastics were predominantly employed to imitate other materials, such as the tortoiseshell and ivory used for hair combs and belt buckles. This was the period when phenolic resin plastics first became available. These improved plastics combined sturdiness with greater translucency, and could also be easily tinted in bright colors such as amber yellow, cherry red, jade green, and jet black. The low cost of these manmade materials left designers and manufacturers free to experiment in whatever way they wanted. Costume

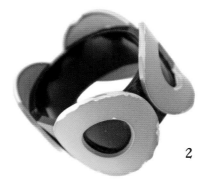

2

jewelry firms were quick to spot that these innovative materials could be cast, shaped, and carved into exciting new forms of jewelry.

During the late 1920s and 1930s, this exciting new material inspired the creation of unprecedented designs. European costume jewelers working with plastics produced some daring and highly original pieces based on simple cubes and other geometric shapes. These stark, abstract designs were relieved with metal accents made from brass or chrome, another modern material. The Europeans' contemporaries in the United States also produced striking geometric designs, but they preferred to use plastic by itself.

In the interwar years, it was fashionable to wear a lot of bangles, many of which were made of plastic that had been molded and carved in a wide variety of stylish designs. Chunky hinged bangles which opened up into two halves were a noteworthy favorite.

Witty plastic novelties

The rise of plastics coincided with the Wall Street stock market crash of 1929 and the terrible economic depression that followed. While people had less disposable income, they were still willing to spend small sums on cheery novelties, such as inexpensive plastic jewelry that offered some diversion from current uncertainties and hardship.

During the Depression many costume jewelry firms produced an array of fun and witty plastic pieces inspired by modern phenomena such as jazz music, and new forms of adventure, such as travel by automobile, ship, or airplane. Figural pins shaped like caricature jazz musicians, hotel bellhops, and sailors in bell-bottoms were popular. So were cute pins that looked like all types of animals, from cats and Scottie dogs to parrots and swordfish. The Brazilian performer Carmen Miranda sparked a craze for tropical-style plastic neck-chains and pins decorated with dangling fruit charms.

The American influence

French designers, particularly Coco Chanel, may have made costume jewelry stylish, but the overwhelming majority of plastic pieces were manufactured in the United States, which by the 1930s was much more industrially advanced than Europe. As a consequence, Americans produced and wore more plastic bangles, pins, and necklaces than Europeans.

The plastic industry wasn't the only American business of the 1930s to benefit from a general desire for inexpensive diversions: visiting the cinema to see the latest Hollywood films was another popular form of escapism. As the decade unfolded, movie stars and their glamorous outfits began to make a huge impact on fashion.

Women copied their gowns and the way they attached chic clips to their dresses, coats, hats, and shoes. Mass-market manufacturers rushed to copy the costume jewelry worn by famous actresses such as Jean Harlow and Joan Crawford in major motion pictures. Leading costume jewelry firms such as Trifari added to their reputations by producing exclusive designs for the stars of stage and screen.

3

1. A 1930s Krementz necklace, in sterling silver, with faceted carnelian, onyx and pale citrine stones, signed. 16.5in (40.5cm) long **G**

2. A bangle, in green and black painted Lucite. 3.25in (8cm) diam **D**

3. A 1930s American Modernist ring, in gold, with bezel-set coral and black onyx. 1in (2.5cm) long **M**

Hollywood antiques

Towards the end of the 1930s, Hollywood's popularization of historic costume dramas began to have a dramatic effect on American costume jewelry design. Old-fashioned motifs such as bows, insects, and crowns that harked back to the 19th century were revived. Costume jewelry manufacturers re-worked nostalgic styles such as cameo pins, lockets on velvet ribbons, and pins decorated with pendent drops.

One costume jewelry firm in particular—Joseff of Hollywood—came to prominence with an exaggerated "antique" style. Founder Eugene Joseff was a leading supplier of costume jewelry to the major studios. His bold pieces were featured in films such as *A Star Is Born* and *Gone with the Wind*. In 1937 he launched a retail line to cater to popular demand for his jewelry. Joseff's pieces made a strong visual statement becayse they were made of rich matte gold metal. Joseff originally developed this attractive finish, known as "Russian gold," to reduce the reflective glare from gilt jewelry so it could be filmed more easily.

By the 1940s, American costume jewelry designers had largely abandoned Art Deco's dense sparkle of stones in favor of a warm yellow glow. The golden age of costume jewelry had arrived.

The all-white look

Typically, however, the Art Deco jewelry is closely identified with the "all-white" look of densely set sparkling diamonds. The latest setting techniques allowed jewelers of the day to pack stones so closely together the effect was like a glittering white carpet. This elegant look was occasionally set off with other materials such as onyx and coral.

Cutting techniques had improved enormously, and fancy new shapes such as square cuts and baguettes were eminently suited to fashionable geometric designs. Manufacturers of glass gems kept up with these latest developments in diamond faceting.

The best faceted glass gems came from manufacturer Daniel Swarovski in Austria, whose premises were near the river Rhine—which is how faux gems came to be known as rhinestones. In the 1890s, Swarovski invented a mechanized stone cutter. Until that time all glass gems had been cut by hand. The new invention made it possible for Swarovski to produce large quantities of fine-quality faceted glass gems with speed. By the 1920s the company was the main supplier of faceted glass gems to the costume jewelry trade.

To begin with, costume jewelers simply imitated trends in Art Deco diamond pieces. However, costume jewelry's popularity went from strength to strength during the interwar years, and manufacturers such as Eisenberg grew more confident, proudly producing pieces set with "rocks" frankly too large and too unusual in shape to be real.

4. Actress Pia Angeli wearing a Joseff necklace and earrings.

5. A 1930s Eisenberg Original sunburst fur clip, in sterling silver, with large aquamarine stone, signed. 2.5in (6.5cm) long **M**

6

Exotic jewels

Exotic goods, such as sumptuous jewels from far-off lands, were a major source of inspiration for Art Deco design. The taste for the exotic was fueled by a growth in adventurous holidays for the wealthy to Africa and India, and reached its height with the 1931 Exposition Coloniale in Paris. Black American Jazz Age musicians and the dancer Josephine Baker encouraged this fascination with tribal art and materials such as ivory. The results can be seen in pins inspired by tribal masks and carved faux ivory beads.

Makers of both precious and costume jewelry were notably struck by Moghul jewels. A key characteristic of these traditional Indian designs, known as "Tree of Life" jewels, was an abundant mix of carved, irregularly shaped rubies, emeralds, and sapphires. In turn, these opulent designs influenced the work of famous Parisian jewelers in the 1920s and 1930s.

Cartier and other illustrious firms combined colorful gems carved to resemble flowers and berries with faceted diamonds on bracelets, necklaces, and pins shaped like vases or baskets. These juicy-looking pieces were soon nicknamed tutti-frutti or fruit-salad jewelry. This attractive trend quickly spread to costume jewelry firms such as Trifari in the United States.

The discovery of Tutankhamen's tomb in 1922 ignited a worldwide fascination for all things ancient Egyptian. Imagery such as cobras, scarabs, sphinxes, and falcons became fashionable. These motifs, resurrected from ancient designs, were employed on jewelry set with faceted pastes. Jewelry designers frequently chose to mix ancient Egyptian themes with modern geometric forms, and often mimicked the inlaid gold pieces found in pharaohs' tombs in gilt, brass, and colorful enamels.

Fahrner's geometric designs

German manufacturer Fahrner produced some outstanding geometric Art Deco designs for costume jewelry. Based in Pforzheim, the center of the German jewelry industry, Fahrner had already developed a first-class reputation turning out good-quality silver jewelry in the Arts and Crafts style at the turn of the 20th century. By the 1920s, the company was producing stylish geometric bracelets, pendants, pins, and earrings. These silver pieces featured inexpensive stones such as blue chalcedony, onyx, and coral in unusual, cubic cabochon cuts. However, the hallmark of Fahrner's Art Deco designs was intricate marcasite detailing. Very popular throughout the interwar years, Fahrner's Art Deco pieces are still highly sought after today and have been widely reproduced.

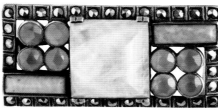

7

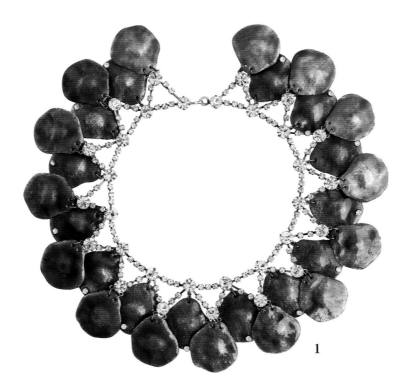

1

1940s &1950s

Hollywood inspired a demand for gorgeous gowns and costume jewelry. The movies also fed a desire for an exciting social life. They not only glamorized nights out on the town dining in restaurants or dancing at clubs, but also helped popularize a new way of entertaining at home—cocktail parties held in the early evening.

This more casual conviviality required less formal dressing—more Chanel-style "little black dress" than traditional eveningwear. It became all the rage to accessorize this simpler night-time look with amusing, eye-catching costume jewelry.

Jewelry for the people

Like her archrival Coco Chanel, the leading Parisian fashion designer Elsa Schiaparelli encouraged women to use costume jewelry as a fashion statement. Schiaparelli's dramatic style was the polar opposite of Chanel's understated elegance. Closely associated with the Surrealist artists and their provocative dream-inspired imagery, she designed clothing and jewelry full of shocking surprises.

In the 1930s Schiaparelli worked with artists and designers such as Salvador Dali, Jean Cocteau, and Jean Schlumberger to produce unexpected designs including telephone earrings, pea-pod necklaces, and lantern pins that actually lit up. However, it is the jewelry she designed in New York City in the 1950s that brought her work to the masses. Her abstract and naturalistic designs used unusual iridescent "fantasy" paste stones and glittering rhinestones which were often copied but never bettered.

At the same time, Miriam Haskell was also building a reputation among stylish women for her daring pieces. Haskell creations were prized for their aesthetic properties in much the same way that precious jewels were prized for their rarity. Well-known show-business figures such as Joan Crawford were enthusiastic customers. Haskell's groundbreaking designs were ideal for that "day into evening" transformation. She had developed a singular style unique to costume jewelry, giving her pieces an elaborate, three-dimensional quality that was almost baroque. Like Chanel and Schiaparelli, Haskell helped give costume jewelry prestige.

1. An Elsa Schiaparelli lava rock necklace, in gold-plate, with colorless rhinestones. c1940 16in (40.5cm) long **G**

2. Grace Kelly wearing a pair of Joseff of Hollywood pearl drop earrings in *High Society* (1956).

3. A Jomaz Moghul-style pin, with faux emerald and diamanté. 3in (7.5cm) long **E**

The development of the cocktail style

The outbreak of World War II led to America's isolation from Europe and shortages of imported raw materials such as rhinestones. By the time the United States entered the conflict in 1941, the government had imposed restrictions on base metals which were needed for the war effort.

Despite these adverse conditions, American costume jewelers thrived by substituting sterling silver for base metals and using new plastics such as Lucite in place of cabochon-cut

pastes. Without European trends to influence their designs, US jewelers started to produce the first completely American look. One of the most distinctive features of this American style was the lavish use of deep yellow vermeil, or silver gilt as it is also known. These new designs were often dominated by enormous stones. Another key characteristic was the use of jarring combinations of colored faux gems, for example aquamarine blue against ruby red.

These free-form pieces were more dynamic and streamlined than their Art Deco predecessors. One frequent source of inspiration was the machine in motion; another was abstracted design that looked like drapery. Bold sculptural bows and scrolls were also common. The new American style became known as cocktail jewelry, after the fashion for wearing it to cocktail parties and other dressy evening assignations. The style was exciting and assured: costume jewelry now set the trend while real pieces followed in its wake.

2

Quality and mass-production

Coro and Trifari were the pre-eminent American costume jewelers of the 1940s. Both firms originally found success imitating Art Deco precious jewels. Inspired by Cartier's designs, Coro was the first costume jewelry manufacturer to produce interlocking double clips that could be used together or separately. Called "Duettes," they became immensely popular. Meanwhile, Trifari—under chief designer Alfred Philippe—made its name producing good-quality costume jewelry versions of tutti-frutti pieces.

Coro and Trifari were in the vanguard of cocktail style. In the late 1940s and early 1950s, they took the fashion for dressy costume jewelry forward in a fun, figural direction. The most notable Coro designs of the period include pins shaped like hands, donkey carts, and angelfish, while Trifari became associated with "Jelly Belly" animal pins made from Lucite.

In the mid-1950s, Swarovski developed a special shimmering rhinestone for Christian Dior. The company called its new glass gems "aurora borealis" after the famous northern lights.

These iridescent rhinestones were also used by Weiss, the New York costume jewelers, to create a range of jewelry for evening wear which became very influential. Weiss's "aurora borealis" designs consisted of a glittering cascade of marquise- and brilliant-cut rhinestones in fantasy hues such as plum, smoky gray, and citrus orange. They were of first-rate quality and Weiss's ingenuity—for example, setting rhinestones upside down to make their shimmer more pronounced—earned the company accolades among its peers.

3

1

1960s & 1970s

The 1960s were a time of affluence, change, and technological progress. Youth culture dominated most fashion trends, and the formal, elegant attire of the older generation was superseded by the carefree casual clothes worn by the young, such as the mini skirt. Slim-fitting and brightly colored, they were a world away from the formality of previous decades.

Stepping away from reality

In the immediate post-war period, French fashion designer Christian Dior led a revolution in clothes for women. Introduced in 1947, Dior's famous "New Look" was alluringly luxurious after all the wartime austerity. It ushered in an era of prosperity and optimism. Just like his fashions, Dior's opulent-looking costume jewelry echoed his fascination with French history and antiques. He never simply copied historic jewelry, however, but gave historic forms a modern twist. For example, he liked the contrast between traditional settings and blatantly artificial, colored faux gems. This theme can be seen in the jewelry designed under creative director Marc Bohan, who led the label from 1960 to 1989. He successfully designed clothes and accessories which appealed to Dior's older clientele and new, younger buyers.

In contrast, American designer Stanley Hagler's necklaces, bracelets, and earrings bear little relationship to real jewels, but in their own way they were just as luxurious and extravagant as Dior's pieces. Hagler's remarkable creations were assembled entirely by hand from clusters of seed pearls, glass petals, and gilt. His design mentor was Miriam Haskell, whose company he worked for briefly in the late 1940s before starting his own business. Hagler pushed the boundaries of Haskell's ideas: not only were his designs far more complicated, he also preferred to use pearls in new fantasy colors such as coral, ultramarine, and honey brown.

From space age to disco

In the 1960s, the space age inspired costume jewelers to take a completely fresh approach to jewelry design. They experimented with manmade materials such as enamel, plastics, and mirror-like white metal to create futuristic pieces inspired by the possibilities of space travel and scientific research into the atom. These simple, geometric designs were often bold and brightly colored. Typical space-age pieces include wide bangles, dangling earrings, chunky rings, and square or circular pendants on chains. Novel and fun, these inexpensive pieces of jewelry were the ideal way to complete the youthful look of the era. Many used plastic or nylon filaments to great effect, as well as featuring colors which were far removed from anything seen in nature.

1. A pair of 1960s articulated hoop earrings. 2.25in (7.75cm) long **B**

2. A 1960s flower pin, in lime green nylon. 4in (10cm) long **B**

3. A Diane von Furstenberg necklace, in black and white enamel, marked "D.V.F." to reverse, with "snakechain". 1975 16in (40.5cm) long **D**

Costume jewelry styles were highly eclectic in the 1970s. The Massachusetts-based firm of Whiting & Davis had been renowned for manufacturing fine metal-mesh chains, handbags, and change purses since the beginning of the 20th century. In the 1970s, it caught the disco trend by making mesh jewelry to complement its bags. Other companies worked with new designers to add contemporary designs to their range. Trifari's association with Diane Love was particularly successful.

Throughout the decade, brightly colored plastics continued to be popular for beads, bangles, and pins made to look like flowers, but there was also a reaction against the type of cheap and cheerful jewelry that was intended to be discarded when it fell out of favor. The period saw a return to natural materials and traditional craftsmanship. Young artisan silversmiths produced their own simple pieces by hand in small workshops. The homespun look of wooden beads and bracelets became fashionable. Young men and women took to wearing leather thongs hung with feathers, shells, and ceramic amulets around their neck or wrist.

Hippy travelers opened Western eyes to exotic folk jewelry from the far corners of the globe. Inexpensive glass bangles and filigree silver pieces were imported in large quantities from India, and people wore long strands of brightly colored African beads. There was a vogue for bracelets, belt buckles, and other jewelry made by Native Americans from turquoise and silver. Greek puzzle rings made of silver were copied on a wide scale by mass-market manufacturers.

Reinterpreting the past

One of the most important figures in costume jewelry of the period was American designer Kenneth Jay Lane. He specialized in outrageous, outsized interpretations of precious jewelry. Lane's fantasy jewels often featured massive plastic cabochons in gaudy colors such as turquoise, coral red, and bright pink. His famous "big cat" pins were inspired by precious jewels designed by Cartier, and he also produced overtly fake versions of Van Cleef & Arpels's lion-head doorknockers.

In the early 1970s there was also growing interest in original Art Nouveau and Art Deco pieces which were inexpensive to buy. Stylish women began to collect vintage costume jewelry from the 19th and early 20th centuries, and it became fashionable to visit antique markets in search of Art Deco Bakelite bangles, late 19th century marcasite pins, and paste jewelry. As demand began to outstrip supply, a number of manufacturers started to produce copies of older costume jewelry designs. The time was ripe for a retro costume jewelry revival.

1

1980s & 1990s

The brash, shoulder-padded fashions that have come to epitomize the 1980s required bold "statement" jewelry to give them a feminine edge. Established designers rose to the challenge by reinterpreting old styles in showy gilt and bright poured glass, while new names provided their own take on the new look. The final effect was showy—and often outrageous—and it revived a fashion for jewelry that hadn't been seen since the 1950s.

Leading the revival

British costume jewelry company Butler & Wilson was at the forefront of the retro revival. Owners Nicky Butler and Simon Wilson originally sold vintage costume jewelry pieces from a stall at a London antiques market. In the 1970s they opened a shop selling a mixture of authentic and reproduction pieces. By 1980 they were designing their own line, taking inspiration from the vintage costume jewelry they admired.

Butler & Wilson became renowned for updating old designs and giving them a brash, glitzy twist. The company's diamanté-set salamanders, spiders, and cocktail-glass pins became costume jewelry classics. Another notable motif was a dancing couple made of black and clear rhinestones, with large paste stones representing their heads. Big and bold, these novelty designs were conversation starters on a par with many of the original costume jewels they sought to imitate.

At around the same time American Iradj Moini began designing jewelry for New York fashion designer Oscar de la Renta. With its clean lines, his costume jewelry manages to look simultaneously both contemporary and vintage. Moini's rhinestone-set creature pins in particular have a strong echo of the 1940s and 1950s about them. In contrast to the creature pins from the golden age of costume jewelry, his exotic creations are set with large rhinestones of varying size and shape.

Jewelry in the boom years

The 1980s saw the start of an economic boom. After battling to break the "glass ceiling," the invisible barrier that inhibited their progress up the career ladder, professional women were finally making their mark in the corporate world. With its exaggerated shoulder pads, the "power-suit" became the uniform of the career woman. This essentially masculine look was softened with showy costume jewelry—especially large earrings and pins. Many of these loud, proud pieces were produced by major figures in fashion of the time, such as Christian Lacroix, who pushed the boundaries of design to their limits: some of his earrings were so outrageously large and dangly they almost touched the shoulders.

2

After fashion designer Karl Lagerfeld took charge of the House of Chanel in 1982, he introduced a new generation to the great designer's original style. Lagerfeld was responsible for rejuvenating many of Coco Chanel's timeless classics, such as her famous suit, her "little black dress," her quilted handbag and, of course, her costume jewelry. In keeping with the 1980s aesthetic, Lagerfeld gave Chanel's favorite themes a larger-than-life quality by using gobstopper-sized pearls, gilt chains, and cabochon glass gems.

Some of the necklaces and bracelets he produced featured enormous pearls of almost cartoon proportions. He printed images of Chanel jewelry on fabric for clothing and scarves, and even used Chanel's interlocking "CC" insignia as a motif for earrings and pendants—thus sending up designer fashions of the 1980s and cleverly promoting the brand at the same time. He meant these exaggerated pieces of jewelry to be worn together in lavish profusion.

A punk interpretation

Vivienne Westwood, the original punk designer, first came to public attention in the late 1970s with her bondage trousers, safety-pin earrings, and ripped T-shirts accessorized with spiked leather dog-collars. Westwood was largely responsible for bringing punk's shocking new rebellious look into the mainstream.

Always provocative and iconoclastic, Westwood's costume jewelry designs frequently parody traditional pieces, such as those on show at the coronation of British monarchs. She produces crowns complete with velvet lining and faux ermine trim for evening wear and weddings, and is particularly partial to the orb—a large spherical ornament surmounted by a cross that symbolizes sovereignty. She has even employed this form on a range of pendants and earrings.

During the 1990s, women's fashion became more sombre and minimalistic. The emphasis was on body-conscious clothing. The ritzy costume jewelry of the 1980s—those large earrings and flashy pins—fell out of favor, and what costume jewelry was worn tended to be discreet. Designers such as Robert Lee Morris produced subtle pieces, which were more art than fashion.

Leather thongs and cords strung with drilled pebbles and little nuggets of metal became hugely popular, worn wrapped and draped around the neck and wrist. These ornaments reflected a new genre of handcrafted costume pieces produced by artisan jewelers, which often featured an unusual combination of materials, such as felt and beads; rubber and resins; lace and wire; papier-mâché and glass; and wood and rhinestones.

1. A pair of Celine button earrings, in gilt. 1.5cm (3.75cm) diam **C**
2. A Chanel Moghul-style pendant, in pâte-de-verre with rhinestones and faux pearls. c1980 Pendant 3in (7.5cm) long **E**
3. A late 1990s Robert Lee Morris necklace, in aluminum. 7in (17.75cm) long **C**

3

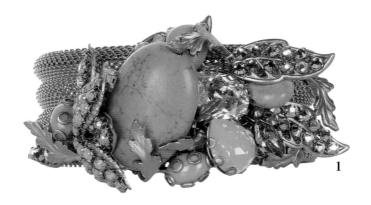

INTO THE 21ST CENTURY

The new millennium saw a renewed interest in vintage costume jewelry styles. Dainty pendant necklaces and matching earrings came into vogue, harking back to the turn of the 20th century. Pieces in the style of French jet were offered by mass-market retailers, and there was keen interest in traditional ranges from long-established costume jewelers such as Ciro and Fior from Britain and Kenneth Jay Lane in America. Established jewelers Erickson Beamon made their jewelry available to many more people by creating diffusion lines for retailers such as Target in the US and Debenhams in the UK.

Innovative new materials and styles have also emerged, such as Uli Raap's "Textile Jewelry", created from a fusion of jersey and rubber, or the work of German company Bless. Designers with a background in Industrial design, such as Lara Bohinc, brought new techniques, such as Computer Aided Design, to the field of costume jewelry design.

Events such as Swarovski Runway Rocks (2005), Coutts London Jewellery week (2008) and the "Jewels for Fashion" symposium held at Geneva's University of Art (2008) emphasized the continuing change in attitude towards jewelry. Where once it had appeared to play second fiddle to clothing in the fashion industry, it has since become a dominant voice.

The new-found appreciation of costume jewelry coincided with a trend for recycling and a worldwide recession that resulted in a renaissance and new respect for vintage finds. Consequently new and vintage jewelry has never been so sought after.

Tradition with a twist

Today a new generation of designers are working to combine traditional techniques with modern technology, and vintage gems with new materials to push the possibilities of costume jewelry forward. Jewelers, such as Tracy Graham of Bijoux Heart, use materials such as faux gems and Murano art glass beads to create extravagant pieces, which celebrate vintage style for 21st century wearers. Laurent Rivaud, who has designed jewelry for Vivienne Westwood since 1994, also creates his own antique-style pieces under the name "R". Pavé set with marcasites, and hung with coins, pearls, figurative elements such as bird skulls, and graduated beads, R jewelry is instantly recognizable and memorable.

Others jewelers like to push the boundaries of traditional forms of jewelry to create exciting contemporary pieces. American designer Philip Crangi created quadruple-sized rhinestone jewelry for Vera Wang's Fall Winter 2008 catwalk show, meanwhile London-based Mawi has transformed classics such as the pearl necklace into futuristic-looking designs, in which pearls become bullets and knots become box chains. Inspirations as diverse as antique jewelry and punk led to the creation of jewels that are the hallmark of 21st century style.

1. A Bijoux Heart bracelet, with vintage cabochons, crystals, and rose montées, on a mesh band. 6.5in (26cm) circ **J**

2. Michelle Obama at the White House Correspondents' Dinner, 2009, wearing a St. Erasmus necklace.

3. A Mawi "Claw Set Pearl" necklace, in gold-plate, with faux pearls. 16in (41cm) long **G**

Celebrity endorsement

There has been a long tradition of the wives of American presidents wearing costume jewelry on formal state occasions. First Lady Mamie Eisenhower, for example, wore Trifari pieces at her husband Dwight D. Eisenhower's Presidential Inaugural Gala in 1953 and again in 1957.

2

Michelle Obama has continued this tradition and is renowned for wearing exciting pieces by contemporary costume jewelers, such as St. Erasmus, Erickson Beamon, and Dana Lorenz. She also famously wore vintage costume pieces to her husband's inauguration and has been photographed wearing vintage costume jewelry by Schreiner, among other famous makers.

Mrs Obama is not the only famous face who has helped to make costume jewelry newsworthy again. Patricia Field, the stylist for the *Sex and the City* television series and movies, is well-known for mixing vintage and contemporary clothes and jewelry. Additionally, the star of the series, Sarah Jessica Parker continues the trend off screen when she attends fashion shoots and film premieres and has been credited with inspiring many others to do the same.

A range of choice

The thread that runs through the story of costume jewelry is the continuous quest for the most exciting new materials and ideas. Although some modern pieces are cheaply made, the better pieces should rise in value over the years to come, becoming good investments for the future. The incredible artistry and techniques that go into making some of these amazing pieces mean that no one today worries about wearing mere "imitations." The challenge lies in choosing from the extraordinary range of designs on offer to suit a personal style and look.

3

Trifari
Miriam Haskell
Stanley Hagler
Coro & Corocraft
Christian Dior
Elsa Schiaparelli
Marcel Boucher
Joseff of Hollywood
Chanel
Theodor Fahrner
Weiss
Kramer
Vendôme
Lisner
Kenneth Jay Lane
Butler & Wilson
Hobé
Schreiner
Eisenberg
Mazer & Jomaz
Hattie Carnegie
Har
Lea Stein
Copplo e Toppo
Matisse & Renoir

Major Designers

1

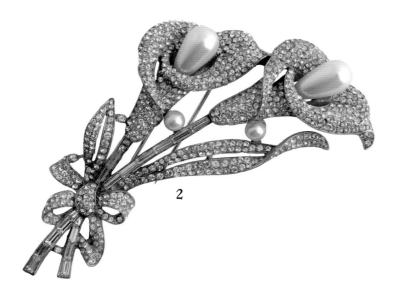

2

TRIFARI

Trifari is probably the most successful and best known costume jewelry manufacturer. Under the aegis of talented designer Alfred Philippe, the Italian-American company produced a vast range of finely crafted, innovative styles in the mid-20th century.

Born in Naples in 1883, Gustavo Trifari trained as a goldsmith under his grandfather. He emigrated from Italy to New York City in 1904 and worked with his uncle making costume jewelry. In 1910, they set up a company together called Trifari & Trifari, but Gustavo soon went his own way, establishing Trifari in 1912 to produce high-quality pieces. In 1917, Leo Krussman joined as sales manager and a year later, having achieved some commercial success, the company became Trifari & Krussman. Karl Fishel was hired as a salesman in 1923 and helped the company grow further. By 1925, it had become Trifari, Krussman & Fishel (TKF), but was still known as Trifari.

Trifari became a success story thanks to the quality and range of its jewelry. In the 1930s, the public's attention was captured by the company's designs for Broadway shows such as *Roberta*, and the Trifari pieces worn by many Hollywood and Broadway stars. Alfred Philippe had joined as head designer in 1930, taking Trifari to new heights with his imaginative designs and quality of production. It became the second largest costume jewelry firm in the United States, after Coro. Under Philippe, the company produced two of its most successful lines—"Crown" pins and "Jelly Bellies."

The "Crown" pins, produced from the late 1930s to the 1950s, included a special series for the coronation of Queen Elizabeth II in 1953. Some designs featured brightly colored cabochons, others used clear rhinestones for a sparkling, monochrome effect. Alfred Philippe's "Crown" designs from the 1940s feature large cabochons set on heavy vermeil silver, enhanced with rows of colorful rhinestones. These icons of design are avidly sought after and fetch high prices.

Appearing on the market in 1940, the "Jelly Bellies" had a Lucite "pearl" as their feature stone and were set in sterling silver or gold plate. The rarest designs, which include seals, roosters and poodles can command high prices.

Due to wartime metal restrictions, Trifari was obliged to use sterling silver, as opposed to base metals, from 1942. This tripled prices but did not have an impact on sales. After the war, Trifari attempted to revert to less expensive metals, but the market now demanded silver. To counter this, in 1947 the company introduced "Trifanium," a special alloy which it used to create cast settings. It was filed, polished, and plated before being set with "gems."

Key designs under Philippe's direction include enameled floral pins from the 1930s. Eye-catching patriotic pins from the 1940s, which promoted the war effort, feature American flags and eagles, and appeal to collectors both of patriotic and costume jewelry.

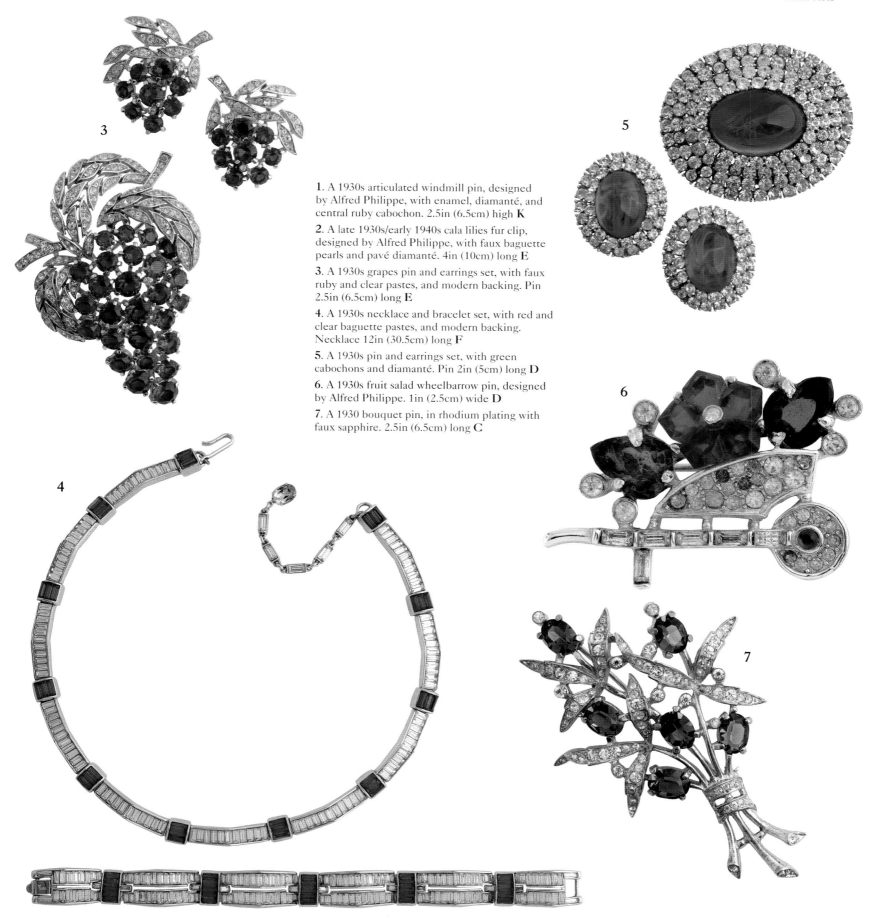

1. A 1930s articulated windmill pin, designed by Alfred Philippe, with enamel, diamanté, and central ruby cabochon. 2.5in (6.5cm) high **K**

2. A late 1930s/early 1940s cala lilies fur clip, designed by Alfred Philippe, with faux baguette pearls and pavé diamanté. 4in (10cm) long **E**

3. A 1930s grapes pin and earrings set, with faux ruby and clear pastes, and modern backing. Pin 2.5in (6.5cm) long **E**

4. A 1930s necklace and bracelet set, with red and clear baguette pastes, and modern backing. Necklace 12in (30.5cm) long **F**

5. A 1930s pin and earrings set, with green cabochons and diamanté. Pin 2in (5cm) long **D**

6. A 1930s fruit salad wheelbarrow pin, designed by Alfred Philippe. 1in (2.5cm) wide **D**

7. A 1930 bouquet pin, in rhodium plating with faux sapphire. 2.5in (6.5cm) long **C**

Also from the 1940s are Philippe's "Fruit Salad" or "Tutti Frutti" designs: glass stones molded in leaf or fruit shapes, usually in primary red, green, and blue but also in moonstone, coral, and turquoise, set into white metal and highlighted with pavé-set crystals. Philippe's "Fruit Salads" were inspired by Cartier's revival of the Egyptian "Tree of Life" style. Collectors seek out Trifari's fruit and vegetable pieces too, especially the miniature fruit pins, released from the late 1950s through the 1960s. Finished with matte gold- or rhodium plate, these pins were charming worn singly or highly effective in a group. In 1950, Alfred Philippe released a collection of patented designs, "Clair de Lune," featuring moonstones. He also created "Moghul" jewelry, a range of heavy pieces designed after the abstract forms of royal Indian jewelry, in ruby, sapphire, and emerald colors, set in gold.

During the 1950s, many companies were quick to emulate the successful lines of their rivals but in 1952, Trifari took Coro to court over design copyright infringement. Trifari won its legal battle against Coro in 1954, establishing copyright for costume jewelry designs as works of art and, from this point onward, Trifari pieces bore the copyright mark.

Trifari's success was so complete that Mamie Eisenhower, the new First Lady, broke with the tradition of wearing fine jewelry at the presidential inauguration, and commissioned costume jewelry designs from Philippe for the inaugural ball in 1953. To complement her pink satin gown studded with 2000 rhinestones, he designed an "Orientique" pearl choker, bracelet, and earrings. Mamie Eisenhower was delighted with the result and commissioned Trifari again for her second inaugural ball in 1957.

Through the 1950s and early 1960s, Trifari produced parures in textured gilded metal, set with pearls and rhinestones. They were ideal for daywear and sold in huge numbers. In 1964, Gustavo Trifari Jnr, Louis Krussman, and Carlton Fishel succeeded their fathers as owners of Trifari. Alfred Philippe retired in 1968, handing over to other designers such as André Boeuf. Diane Love designed for the company from 1971 to 1974. In 1975, the three sons sold Trifari to the Hallmark corporation. Liz Claiborne, Inc. has owned it since 2000.

Marks include "Jewels by Trifari," "TKF," and "Trifari." All pieces are marked. Those made after c1937 feature the crown motif, and those after 1952 bear a copyright symbol, too.

ALFRED PHILIPPE

Frenchman Alfred Philippe was Trifari's most influential designer. Philippe had previously designed pieces for William Scheer, who produced fine jewelry for Van Cleef & Arpels and Cartier. He drew on this experience, using the best materials and exacting methods, including the invisible setting technique. Developed for Van Cleef & Arpels by Philippe, this method was normally reserved for fine jewelry and required an extraordinary level of craftsmanship. It involved fixing stones from the back, so that from the front it appeared as if there were no mount.

Philippe's favorite materials included Swarovski crystals, which resulted in the company being nicknamed the "Diamanté Kings." Wartime restrictions meant that non-precious metals could not be used, so Philippe used sterling silver, often plated with gold.

His design flair led to the creation of market successes such as his "Crown" pins from the late 1930s to the 1950s, which led to the crown motif being incorporated into the company's logo from c1937, and the widely emulated Lucite "Jelly Bellies."

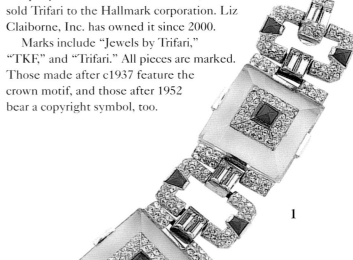

1

1. A late 1920s bracelet, with glue-set clear crystals and claw-set pyramid-cut sapphires, marked "TKF". F

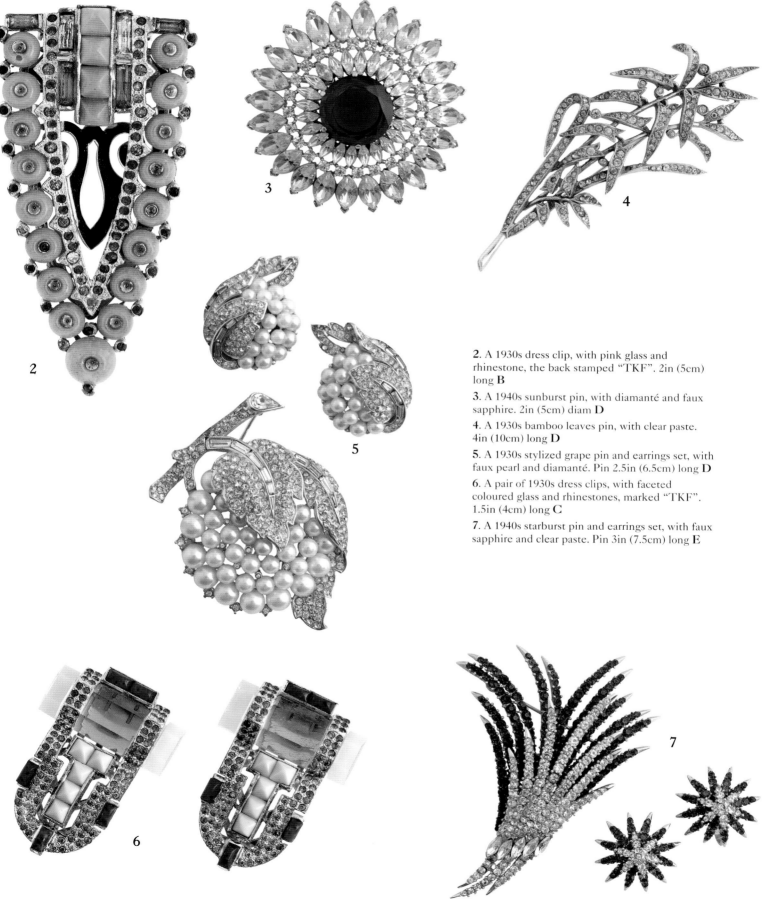

2. A 1930s dress clip, with pink glass and rhinestone, the back stamped "TKF". 2in (5cm) long **B**

3. A 1940s sunburst pin, with diamanté and faux sapphire. 2in (5cm) diam **D**

4. A 1930s bamboo leaves pin, with clear paste. 4in (10cm) long **D**

5. A 1930s stylized grape pin and earrings set, with faux pearl and diamanté. Pin 2.5in (6.5cm) long **D**

6. A pair of 1930s dress clips, with faceted coloured glass and rhinestones, marked "TKF". 1.5in (4cm) long **C**

7. A 1940s starburst pin and earrings set, with faux sapphire and clear paste. Pin 3in (7.5cm) long **E**

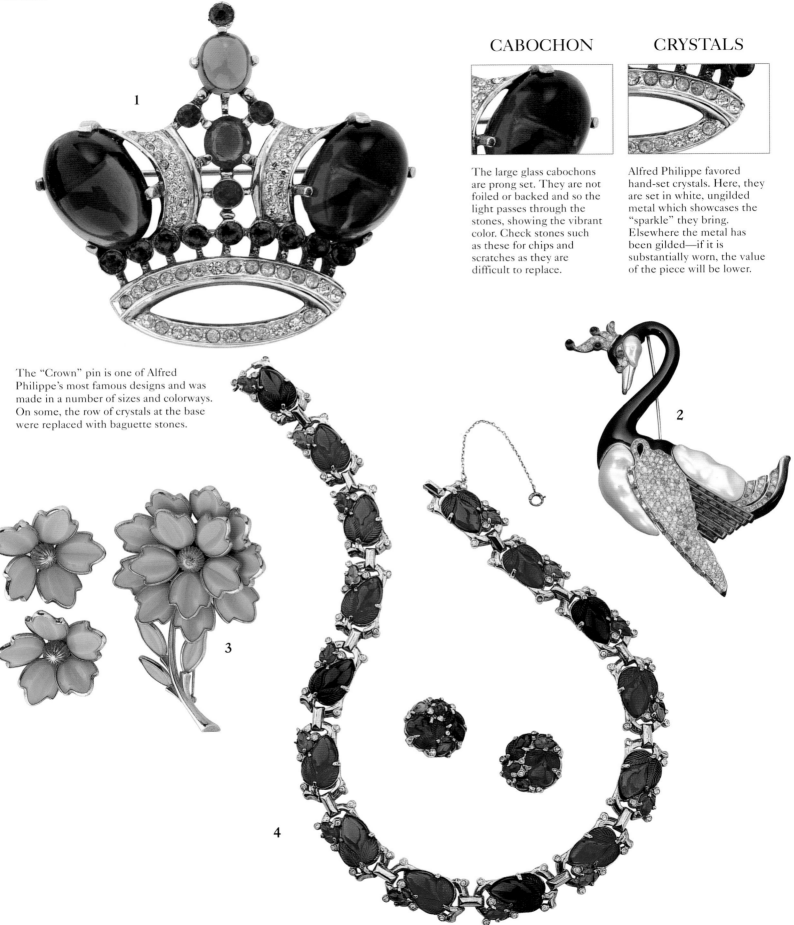

1

CABOCHON

The large glass cabochons are prong set. They are not foiled or backed and so the light passes through the stones, showing the vibrant color. Check stones such as these for chips and scratches as they are difficult to replace.

CRYSTALS

Alfred Philippe favored hand-set crystals. Here, they are set in white, ungilded metal which showcases the "sparkle" they bring. Elsewhere the metal has been gilded—if it is substantially worn, the value of the piece will be lower.

The "Crown" pin is one of Alfred Philippe's most famous designs and was made in a number of sizes and colorways. On some, the row of crystals at the base were replaced with baguette stones.

2

3

4

MAMIE EISENHOWER

First Lady Mamie Eisenhower helped to popularize and enhance the status of Trifari—and costume jewelry in general—when she wore specially commissioned designs by the firm for the 1953 and 1957 presidential inaugral balls. These parures were among the company's most pretigious commissions. However, it also made exclusive designs for Broadway musicals, such as *Roberta*, and for numerous film stars and other celebrities. Mamie Eisenhower's jewelry—the photograph above shows her wearing her 1957 ballgown by Nettie Rosenstein with the Trifari necklace and earrings—is now in the Smithsonian in Washington.

1. A Trifari first edition crown pin, in sterling silver, with prong-set glass cabochon and glue-set rhinestones. 1944 1.5in (4cm) long **D**

2. A Swan Lake pin, designed by David Mir. 1941 2.5in (6.5cm) long **M**

3. A late 1940s pin and earrings set, in pink glass. Earrings 1.25in (3cm) diam **D**

4. An early 1940s fruit salad necklace and earring set, designed by Alfred Philippe, in base metal, with prong-set molded stones and glue-set crystal rhinestones, the earrings marked "Trifari" to reverse. Earrings 0.75in (2cm) diam **E**

5. A mid-1950s Trifari fruit salad starburst pin, in Trifanium, with pastel stones and aurora borealis rhinestones. 2in (5cm) long **D**

6. A 1940s vase of flowers fur clip, in rose- and yellow-gold plate, with facet-cut amethyst pastes and diamanté. 2.5in (6.5cm) long **F**

7. A late 1940s necklace and earrings set, in gold-plate, with fan-shaped links, the hook stamped "Trifari." Necklace 16in (40.5cm) long **C**

1

The Swarovski crystals that form the central stigma and run up the poinsettia leaves are pavé set—packed so closely together that the metal setting is virtually hidden.

Alfred Philippe had previously worked for precious jewelers. Here, he used the invisible setting technique developed by Van Cleef & Arpels where dozens of faux rubies were set so closely together that they appeared to be one larger faceted stone.

2

1. A 1950s poinsettia pin, designed by Alfred Philippe, with invisible-set faux rubies and diamonds. 2.75in (7cm) diam **I**

2. One of a pair of late 1950s leaf earrings, with invisible-set faux emeralds and clear rhinestones. **C**

3. A mid-1950s leaf garland bracelet and earrings set, in Trifanium, with faux sapphire and emerald, marked "Trifari ©." 1in (2.5cm) long **C**

3

4. A 1950s Trifari pin and earrings set, with colorless and blue baguette-cut rhinestones, the backs stamped "TRIFARI PAT PEND." Pin 2.25 (5.5cm) high **D**

5. An early 1950s Pearl Belly turtle pin, designed by Alfred Philippe, with enamel, glue-set green cabochon eyes and clear rhinestones. 1.75in (4.5cm) long **D**

6. A pair of Jewels of India earrings. 1in (2.5cm) wide. 1in (2.5cm) long **B**

7. A 1950s mistletoe necklace, bracelet and earrings set, in silver-plate. 17in (40.5cm) long **C**

1930s

1950s

DOUBLE BOW PIN

Like many other designers, Trifari sometimes revisited successful designs, reinterpreting them to suit the latest styles. The 1930s faux emerald double-bow pin, with baguette and diamanté, rhodium-plated setting shown on the left was revived in the 1950s in fashionable gilt and set with faux rubies. The older pin is more collectible in today's market thanks to the period look of the diamanté and baguette stones used in the setting, and the additional work that was involved in making it. Both pins are 3in (7.5cm) long but the 1930s example is worth $180–220 (£100–150) while the 1950s piece is worth $80–120 (£50–80).

1. A 1960s abstract pin, in gilt metal, with large faux emerald. 2.5in (6.5cm) long **C**

2. A 1960s flower pendant necklace, with red marquise- and chaton-cut pastes, and aurora borealis. 15.75in (40cm) long **D**

3. A 1950s Forbidden Fruit pin, with gilt and clear diamanté. 2in (5cm) long **C**

4. A 1950s leaves and berries pin, in matte-finish gold-alloy, with elongated faux pearls. 4in (10cm) long **C**

5. An early 1950s floral spray pin and earrings set, in gold-plate with faux amethysts, peridots, emeralds, and jonquils, and aurora borealis stones. 1in (2.5cm) long **D**

6. A late 1950s Trifari flower necklace, in brushed gilt Trifanium, with bakelite flowers. 17in (40.5cm) long **D**

7. A 1950s tulip pin, in brushed gilt. 3.5in (9cm) long **C**

3

4

5

6

7

1. A 1960s necklace and bracelet set, with faux turquoise and pearls. Necklace 17in (43cm) long **C**

2. A 1960s necklace, hinged bracelet, and hoop earrings set, in gold-plate, with clusters of red rhinestones. Necklace 14.5in (37cm) **D**

3. A 1950s head pin and earrings set, with enamel, the seaweed-like hair set with diamantés. Pin 2in (5cm) long **F**

4. A 1960s pin, in brushed gold-tone metal, with clear rhinestones and moonstone-coloured glass cabochons. 2.25in (6cm) long **B**

5. A 1990s limited edition Safari flamingo pin, in gold-tone metal with pink rhinestones and enamel. 3.25in (8.25cm) long **C**

6. A pair of 1970s pendant earrings, in gold-tone metal with channel-set clear rhinestones and faux yellow and black onyx. 2.75in (7cm) long **B**

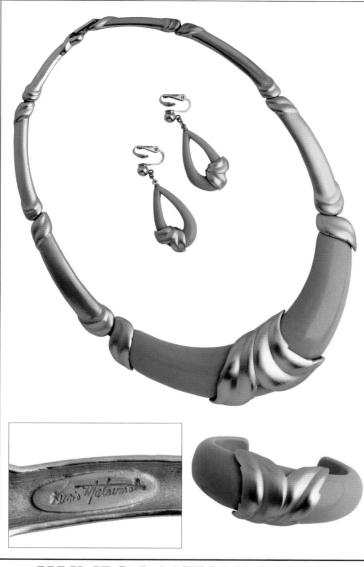

KUNIO MATSUMOTO

Japanese architect Kunio Matsumoto designed pieces for Trifari in the later 1970s. He generally designed parures and demi-parures using brushed gold-tone metal, diamanté, or rhinestones and plastic which resembled enameling or cabochon stones such as turquoise.While little is currently known about him, his pieces are rising in value and collectors are beginning to research his work which is likely to result in higher prices in the future. It is believed that all his pieces were marked with his name in script.

This Kunio Matsumoto parure consists of a necklace, bracelet and earrings, and features brushed gold-tone metal and chunky plastic faux turquoise. It is currently worth $150-200 (£100–120).

3

4

5

6

MIRIAM HASKELL

If Miriam Haskell's work were a person, it would be the glamorous 1930s screen icon Joan Crawford, who was a major fan. Haskell's bijoux fantaisie made costume jewelry more fashionable than fine jewelry and helped it become a valuable art form in its own right.

Miriam Haskell was born in Indiana, in 1899. She majored in education at the University of Chicago, but left before finals to earn a living. Although not a designer, Haskell was adept in design selection and at recognizing talent in others. In 1924, she opened a store in the McAlpin Hotel in New York City, selling costume jewelry by well-known designers such as Coco Chanel.

When she established the Miriam Haskell Company in 1926, she appointed Frank Hess as chief designer. Hess had been a window dresser at Macy's department store, and Haskell's trust in his ability was repaid. With asymmetry as his watchword, Hess designed innovative and stylish pieces for Miriam Haskell.

The 1930s saw Haskell open retail outlets in the Saks Fifth Avenue store in New York City and Harvey Nichols in London. This further elevated her profile and prestige, building on her already strong reputation. She had employed highly skilled artists from Europe in the 1920s and 1930s, and maintained exceptional standards of design, craftsmanship, and components.

From the 1940s through the 1950s, Frank Hess designed intricate, handmade designs featuring baroque and seed pearls, rhinestones, and iconic combinations of colored beading, woven tapestry-style

5

1. A 1950s flower pendant necklace, of faux black pearl disks, rose montées, faux black seed pearls, gilded brass, and gilded brass filigree backing. 14in (37cm) long **G**

2. A late 1920s necklace and earrings set, of glass beads and pumpkin pearls, linked by brass rings on a brass chain. 16in (40.5cm) long **F**

3. A probably 1940s half-moons choker, in gold-plate, with rhinestones and baroque pearl dangles. 15in (38cm) long **M**

4. A 1940s leaf necklace and earrings set, designed by Frank Hess, of seed pearl and rhinestone decoration. Necklace 15in (38cm) long **M**

5. A pair of 1930s drop earrings, in pink glass and diamanté. 2.25in (6cm) long **C**

6. A 1950s windy flowers pin, with central baroque pearl. 3in (7.5cm) long **D**

6

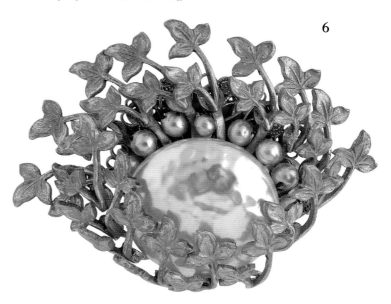

onto antiqued filigree backs that became known as the signature Haskell style. Nature was a strong inspiration, referenced through floral, foliate, and sometimes butterfly designs, as well as the use of pearls, shells, nuts, coral, and woven cords.

Miriam Haskell and Frank Hess frequently traveled abroad to source the best materials: there were glass beads from Murano, Italy; faceted crystals from Austria and Gablonz, Bohemia (present-day Czech Republic), including her signature flat-backed roses montées set in pierced metal cups; and Japanese faux pearls. These quality components were artfully woven together, and it was this attention to detail that made Haskell's work so compelling. During World War II, many restrictions were placed on manufacturing, and innovators such as Haskell turned to materials such as wood, plastics, and even feathers for feature components.

Miriam Haskell retired in 1951 because of her health, and her brother Joseph took over the company, which he later sold to Morris Kinsler in 1954. Frank Hess continued to work for the company until 1960. Fortunately the company continued to attract high-quality designers, who continued his fine work.

Robert F. Clark, who started working for Haskell in 1958 and became head designer after Hess, is best known for his bibs and festoon necklaces, chunky chokers, and a love of symmetry and repetition. His sophisticated designs frequently featured mother-of-pearl and pearlized metals. After a brief period working under Peter

Raines, Larry Vrba became Haskell's head designer in the 1970s. Vrba is known for his oversized, elaborate, and colorful designs, beloved of New York's transvestite community today. This work was the most fantastic produced by Haskell. Millie Petronzio, who took over as chief designer in 1980, was responsible for the "Retro Line" in 1992, which recreated old Haskell designs, sometimes with a new twist.

Usually no Haskell design ever emulated classic fine jewelry. The bold, unusual, and glamorous look she captured appealed to the world of show business: Haskell pieces were featured on stage, film, and television, including designs for the Ziegfeld Follies and *The Phantom of the Opera* on Broadway, *The Lucille Ball Show*, and many Hollywood stars, such as Joan Crawford.

Apart from a rare set of pre-1940 pieces marked with a horseshoe for a store in New England, Haskell did not begin trademarking jewelry until the 1940s, so identifying pieces before this period is a matter of experience. Referring to advertisements from the time may help: Larry Austin was one of the advertising artists at Haskell during the Frank Hess era, so his artwork can be used to identify Hess's unsigned pieces. After 1940, the signature "Miriam Haskell," set in an oval, was used.

Miriam Haskell died in 1981. Her company is still in operation today, and continues to produce vintage-Haskell-style jewelry.

1

2

JAPANESE PEARLS

Pearls maintain a timeless popularity and Haskell's faux-pearl jewelry is among the most varied and refined on the vintage market. Originally, fine-quality imitation pearls came from Gablonz, Bohemia. However, in the late 1930s Japan entered the market as an alternative and competitively priced supplier of faux pearls. After the end of World War II, it was to Japan that Haskell turned to source her pearls. The seed and baroque pearls were immersed several times in a blend called *essence d'orient*, a solution of cellulose, fish scales, and resins. These gave the pearls a deep luster that European rivals could not match, and they are highly prized by collectors today. Baroque pearls, with their crinkly surface and irregular shapes, were exclusively supplied to Haskell.

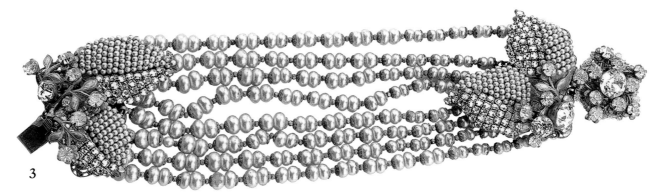

3

1. A 1950s three-strand bracelet, of faux pearls, with glass cluster clasp inspired by Rousselet. 7in (17.75cm) long **E**

2. A 1950s clamper bracelet, of baroque pearls, faux turquoise, and gilt metal. 7in (17.75cm) long **E**

3. A mid-1950s multi-strand bracelet, in pearl and gilded brass filigree, the tongue-and-box catch with seed pearls and roses montées". 7in (17.75cm) long **E**

4. A 1950s clamper bracelet, of faux pearl, diamanté, and gilt metal. 7in (17.75cm) circ **E**

5. A 1950s two-strand necklace, of nugget pearls, with jeweled clasp. 14in (35.5cm) long **E**

6. A 1950s floral and fruit motif pin and earrings set, with silvered faux black baroque and seed pearls, on a filigree gilt metal casting. Pin 2in (5cm) long. **D**

CLASP

The level of detail in Haskell's jewelry is always extremely high. Here, even a clasp, which would have been hidden, gets the full treatment, and is decorated to the high standard.

DISC PEARL

The disc pearl shows off the incredibly high quality pearlized coating to great effect. The texture of the surface is enhanced by the rose montée and gilt setting that surrounds it.

SETTING

This necklace is extremely complex, and would have taken a great deal of time and skill to produce.

MOTIF

Natural motifs, such as flowers, were commonly used by Haskell, and are popular today.

1

2

3

1. A 1950s flower pendant necklace, of simulated pearl disks, diamanté, gilded brass, and gilded brass filigree backing, with two strands of graduated faux pearls. 13.75in (35cm) long **F**

2. A pair of 1950s earrings, with green glass pumpkin-cut beads, amber beads and simulated pearls. 3cm (1.25in) long **C**

3. A 1950s three-strand clamper bracelet, of graduated faux pearls, with peridot glass flowers and diamanté. 7cm (2.75in) diam **E**

4. A 1950s floral clamper bracelet, in gilded brass, with leaves and filigree flowers set with simulated pearls and seed pearls. 6cm (2.5in) internal diam **D**

5. A floral pendant necklace, of pink, blue, and red glass beads, seed pearls, clear rose montées, and amethyst poured glass, with two strands of faux pearls. c1960 14in (35.5cm) long **M**

6. A 1950s festoon necklace, in gilded brass filigree, with clusters of faux seed pearls, and round-cut clear rhinestones. **M**

JOAN CRAWFORD

Many celebrities helped to popularize Miriam Haskell's designs. Florenz Ziegfeld used pieces for the Ziegfeld Follies and the Duchess of Winsor was known to be a fan. However, it is perhaps Joan Crawford who is best known for wearing Haskell designs and she was often photographed wearing them. Crawford regularly bought Haskell jewelry from the early 1930s to the late 1960s. When she died in 1978 her large collection of costume jewelry was sold by the Plaza Art Gallery in New York. Here, she can be seen in January 1933, with husband Douglas Fairbanks Jr.

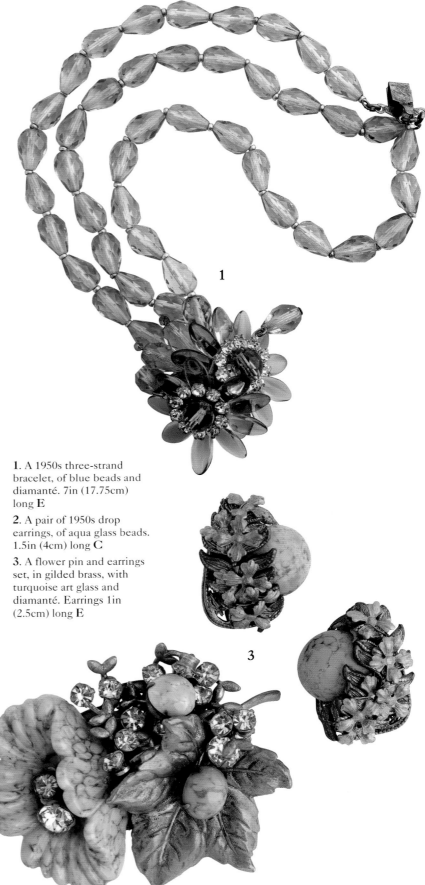

1. A 1950s three-strand bracelet, of blue beads and diamanté. 7in (17.75cm) long **E**

2. A pair of 1950s drop earrings, of aqua glass beads. 1.5in (4cm) long **C**

3. A flower pin and earrings set, in gilded brass, with turquoise art glass and diamanté. Earrings 1in (2.5cm) long **E**

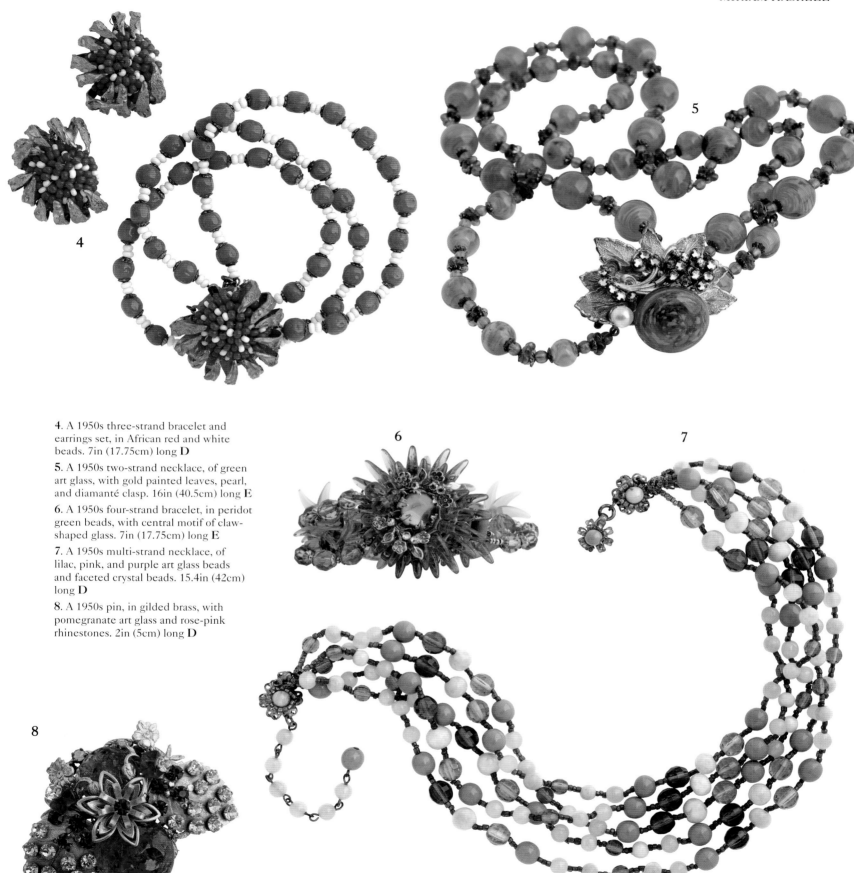

4. A 1950s three-strand bracelet and earrings set, in African red and white beads. 7in (17.75cm) long **D**

5. A 1950s two-strand necklace, of green art glass, with gold painted leaves, pearl, and diamanté clasp. 16in (40.5cm) long **E**

6. A 1950s four-strand bracelet, in peridot green beads, with central motif of claw-shaped glass. 7in (17.75cm) long **E**

7. A 1950s multi-strand necklace, of lilac, pink, and purple art glass beads and faceted crystal beads. 15.4in (42cm) long **D**

8. A 1950s pin, in gilded brass, with pomegranate art glass and rose-pink rhinestones. 2in (5cm) long **D**

1. A mid-1960s butterfly pin, probably designed by Robert Clark, in gilded brass, with blue glass, faux pearl and rhinestones. 2in (5cm) long **D**

2. A fruit and leaf pendant necklace, of faux pearls, seed pearls, and clear rose montées, with gilt metal chain. c1960 Pendant 3.75in (9.5cm) long. **L**

3. A 1960s tutti frutti necklace. 16in (41cm) long **D**

4 A pendant necklace, two pins, and earrings parure, of black resin beads and cabochons and square-cut clear rhinestones. c1960 Necklace 14.75in (38cm) long **M**

5. An early 1960s floral pin and earrings set, possibly designed by Robert Clark, in faux pearls, rhinestones, and gilded brass filigree. Earrings 1in (2.5cm) long **F**

6. A 1960s Chinese-style necklace, marked "MIRIAM HASKELL" on clasp and label. Pendant 6in (15cm) long **D**

4

5

6

STANLEY HAGLER

Stanley Hagler described his elaborate and vivid costume jewelry designs as "just plain pretty." Adorning the décolletage, wrists, or earlobes of the rich, famous, and beautiful, his work is so much more than "pretty."

Hagler was born in Denver, Colorado, in 1923. A veteran of World War II, he graduated from the University of Denver with a law degree in 1949. His design career began in the early 1950s on a dare, when he designed a bracelet "fit for a queen" for Wallace Simpson, the Duchess of Windsor (see page 66). He established the Stanley Hagler Jewelry Co. in New York's Greenwich Village 1953 with Edward Nakles. *Vogue* magazine followed his work with enthusiasm, and the *Denver Post* described it as "opulent and provocative" in 1956.

He had worked as a business advisor to Miriam Haskell in the late 1940s, and his jewelry was heavily influenced by Frank Hess's designs, with both designers favoring intricate floral motifs. Hagler also produced Oriental-inspired pieces and figural work, such as butterflies. However, he is perhaps best known for another Haskell theme—his faux baroque pearls, which displayed exceptional luminosity. Hand-blown beads were dipped up to 15 times in pearl resin, and individually strung to emphasize their quality.

Hagler's choice of other components was no less exacting: hand-blown "art glass" stones from Murano; Swarovski crystals in clear, vibrant pinks, coral, purples, and greens; rose montées; seed pearls and seed beads; and exceptional Russian gold-plated filigree all feature, as do more unusual materials such as carved-bone flowers. His work was hand-wired—"manipulated jewelry," as he described it to the Vintage Fashion and Costume Jewelry Club in 1995.

1

2

1. A 1960s acorn bib necklace and earrings set, with pastel glass beads and baroque pearls. Necklace 16in (40.5cm) long **G**

2. A 1960s oyster necklace and earrings set, in gilt bronze, with faux pearl and diamanté. Necklace 15in (38cm) long **F**

3. A 1960s orchid composite necklace and earrings set, of glass beads and rose montées, the necklace with three faux pearl strands. 16in (40.5cm) long **F**

4. A 1960s orchid pin, with faux coral composite petals, and amber and topaz rhinestones. 3in (7.5cm) long **D**

5. A 1960s flower basket pin, in gilt brass, with hand-wired blue and lilac glass and crystal. 7cm (2.75in) long **D**

6. A late 1950s/early 1960s leaves and flowers necklace and earrings set, with pink and green beads, hand-carved bone flowers, and pressed Murano glass. 16in (40.5cm) long **F**

Hagler's attention to detail made his designs exemplary. To this end, pieces were adaptable: accessories could be added to change the look of earrings; necklace clasps doubled as hair clips or pins; necklaces could be worn as bracelets; and pieces were designed to look as stunning from the back as the front. A design classic, his "wardrobe necklace" consisted of three necklaces made up of two strands of pearls, held together with a large, oval, gold vermeil pin. Each element could be worn separately or in a range of combinations.

Hagler also designed non-jewelry items, such as boudoir clocks, and gold filigree box bags, as part of his "boutique" collection, and created a collection of Obi sashes, bedecked with large pendants, for Japan's Seibu department stores.

Through the 1950s and 1960s, he designed collections for New York's biannual Press Week fashion shows, which he described as "Shocko" pieces, as opposed to the more feminine designs he favored normally. In 1968, Hagler won the Swarovski-sponsored "Great Designs in Jewelry" award for the first of 11 times. In the 1950s, many costume jewelry companies produced Christmas tree pins, of which Hagler's are considered exceptional. Also immensely popular was his range of jeweled crosses, as worn by Madonna.

In the 1970s, Hagler used found metal off-cuts from instruments to create a structural, modern range, called "Tomorrow." Although appreciated for its originality, it did not sell well.

Hagler later moved to Europe for a time, where he worked in precious stones, gold, and silver. However, he found that his clients still demanded his characteristic jeweled and beaded pieces and he returned to New York.

In 1989 Ian St Gielar (see page 70) joined the company as chief designer and in 1993 the business relcoated to Florida. After Stanley Hagler's death in 1996, the company was continued, with St Gielar at its head.

Marks include "Stanley Hagler" straight across an oval disk, from the 1950s until 1983; "Stanley Hagler N.Y.C." on the curve of the oval from 1983 until c1993; while "Stanley Hagler N.Y.C" was used from 1993 onward for designs by Ian St Gielar, who also used tags bearing his own name from this date. Reproductions made by former employees of Hagler's are also on the market, bearing Hagler marks.

1

1. A 1950s/1960s bib necklace and earrings set, of coral beads, diamanté, and gilded bronze leaves. Earrings 1in (2.5cm) diam **F**

2. A pair of 1980s flower earrings, in gray and rose-pink glass, with large pink glass drops. 3in (7.5cm) long **D**

3. A pair of drop earrings, of red glass. 3in (7.5cm) long **D**

4. A 1950s/1960s necklace and earrings set, of coral, coraline, faux pearl, and diamanté. Necklace 15in (38cm) long **F**

5. A 1960s floral necklace and earrings set, in cobalt blue glass with blue rhinestones. Earrings 1in (2.5cm) diam **F**

6. A 1960s floral pin, of green and coral molded glass and glass beads, with gilded bronze and faux coral flowers. 3in (7.5cm) wide **D**

7. A 1960s/1970s flowers and leaves pin, of lime-green molded glass, glass beads and green rhinestones. 3in (7.5cm) long **D**

CLASP

Apart from the vibrant colors, one of the main distinctions between Hagler and Haskell pieces is the relative simplicity of Hagler's clasps.

COLOR

Hagler s jewelry is known for its rich use of color. This deep coral is especially striking, and is enhanced by the warm Russian-gold plated leaves.

HAND WIRING

Every petal is encrusted with tiny glass beads, all hand-wired onto its filigree back. Level on level, it is built up, making it extremely three dimensional.

MOTIFS

Like Haskell, Hagler is known for his floral and foliate forms. Each of the gilded bronze leaves used in this necklace has been cast by hand.

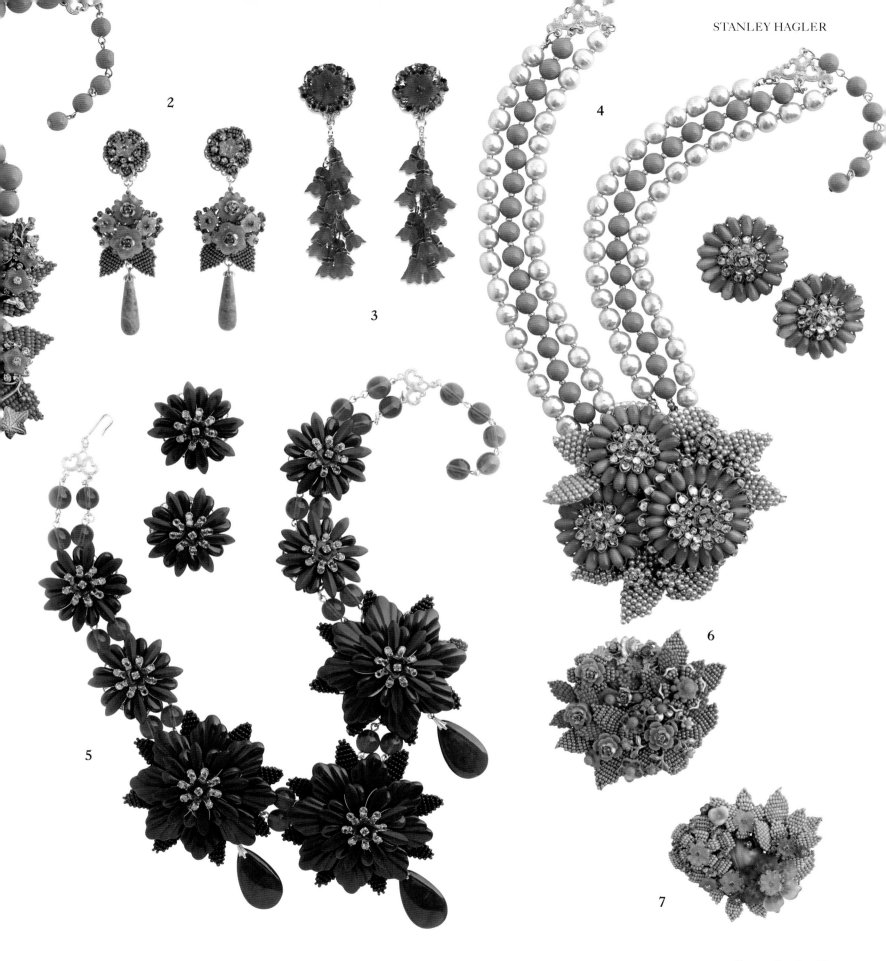

2

3

4

5

6

7

WALLACE SIMPSON

When Stanley Hagler was challenged to make a piece of costume jewelry in the early 1950s, he made a bangle that would be "fit for a queen" for Wallace Simpson, the Duchess of Windsor. The result was a gold-plated bangle decorated with seed pearls which the Duchess—who loved precious and costume jewelry—fell in love with. She became a huge fan, piquing the interest of the style-conscious when she wore Hagler's bracelet to the Bal de Masque at the Waldorf Astoria Hotel in New York City. At the insistence of the staff of *Vogue* magazine, Hagler went on to reproduce the design using a profusion of multi-colored glass beads and flowers.

1

2

1. A 1970s floral bangle, in gold-plate, with molded glass beads, colorless crystal rhinestones. 7.5in (19cm) circ **H**

2. A pair of 1980s drop earrings, of Venetian jet, pink glass, and diamanté, with black drops. 2.5in (6.5cm) long **C**

3. A 1960s floral pin, with turquoise and jade molded glass flowerheads and leaves, glass beads, and blue diamanté. 2in (5cm) wide **C**

4. A 1950s/1960s floral pin, with pink and white molded glass flowerheads, pink and clear diamanté, and glass beads, and gilded brass. 2.5in (6.5cm) wide **C**

5. A 1960s bracelet, of turquoise glass beads, the clasp with centerpiece of three jeweled flowers. 3in (8cm) diam **D**

6. A 1980s necklace and earrings set, of French jet and diamanté and gilded bronze, the necklace with three strands and two bows. Earrings 3in (7.5cm) long **F**

3

4

5

6

ART GLASS

The gold-colored flowers were created on the Venetian island of Murano, famous since the mid-15th century for its glassmaking prowess. These flowers have great clarity and color.

SEED PEARLS

Like Miriam Haskell, Hagler favored faux pearls and tiny seed pearls. Hagler's pearls are glass beads, dipped repeatedly in opalescent coating, before being used in the design.

IVORINE

The carved white beads are ivorine, a plastic developed by Alexander Parkes in the late 19th century, which resembld ivory in color and texture. Ivorine is often found in later Hagler pieces.

CLASP

Hagler's jewelry features gold plated clasps and backings. The length of this necklace can be adjusted by using the hook fastening, allowing it to be worn with different necklines.

1. A 1960s flower pendant necklace and earrings set, of citrine glass, gilded brass, and Ivorine. Necklace 17.75in (45cm) long **F**

2. A 1960s cameo and floral necklace and earrings set, of lilac beads, seed pearls, and faux pearls, the large necklace centerpiece hung with five lilac drops. Necklace 18in (46cm) long **F**

3. A 1960s floral clamper bracelet, of coral beads. 2.75in (7cm) diam **D**

4. A 1960s floral bracelet, of peridot and emerald glass, and emerald rhinestones, and gilded brass, signed "Stanley Hagler N.Y.C." 4.25in (11cm) long **D**

5. A pair of 1960s drop earrings, in gilded brass filigree and diamanté. 3.5in (9cm) long **C**

6. A probably 1950s pin and earrings set, in faux pearl, diamanté, and gilded brass. Pin 2.5in (6.5cm) wide **D**

IAN ST GIELAR

In 1989, a Polish-born admirer of Hagler's work, Ian St Gielar, joined the company as chief designer. He had worked for Hagler part-time since 1985 and studied his specialty techniques—collage and wiring components to filigree plate. His early projects included designing a "Retro" collection using vintage components, especially vintage baroque pearls, usually with an antique gold finish, for Domont, a Californian retailer.

St Gielar also worked with floral motifs, and his exuberant designs explore texture and dimension. In a letter in 1995, Hagler said of him: "Ian St Gielar is indeed a genius, and, without question, in time, all of his designs will rank equally with the masters of twentieth century costume jewelry." St. Gielar went on to own the company after Stanley Hagler's death in 1996, working under his own, and Hagler's, name. He used delicate filigree backings which were decorated with Murano glass beads, mother-of-pearl, Limoges porcelain, and antique ivory. Ian St. Gielar died in 2007 and his wife continues his work.

1. A 1990s flower pin, designed by Ian St. Gielar, with irridescent shell petals, and red glass and topaz rhinestones. 3.5in (9cm) diam **D**

2. A 1960s stylized camellia pin, with pearlized metal blue petals, pressed red glass, red faux seed pearls, and colorless rhinestones. 3.25in (8.25cm) diam **E**

3. A 1980s floral and foliate pin, of yellow and green pressed glass, and yellow, red, and green beads. 5in (12.75cm) long **E**

4. A 1980s flower pin, with brown plastic leaves, citrine glass beads, brown onyx cabochon, and gilt filigree backing, signed. 3.5in (9cm) diam **C**

5. A 1980s floral pin, with gray faux seed pearls, green poured glass, and jade glass beads. 3.75in (9.5cm) diam **E**

6. A 1960s camellia pin, in jet with rhinestone highlights. 3.5in (9cm) **D**

7. A 1960s necklace and earrings set, in faux turquoise and coral, the necklace with three strands of faux turquoise beads. Necklace 20.5in (52cm) long **E**

7

5

6

1

2

CORO & COROCRAFT

Coro covered all the bases: as both innovator and imitator, the company was attuned to the market and produced a vast range of quality jewelry that addressed every fashion and every pocket, from dime-store pieces to top-end treasures.

Coro was established in 1900 as Cohn & Rosenberger, a boutique selling outsourced designer jewelry. The company reached its zenith in the 1930s, after opening a factory in Providence, Rhode Island, to manufacture its products. It eventually employed around 3,500 staff.

The Coro brand was synonymous with well-made lower- and mid-priced pieces reflecting the latest fashions. By the mid-1930s, Coro had retail stores in many US cities, and factories in Britain and Canada as well as the United States: its diversity and volume of output made it the world's largest costume jewelry manufactory.

The company also had a range of upmarket brands, Corocraft being the best known. Corocraft products were high quality and featured expensive materials, such as sterling silver and crystal rhinestones from Europe. The Vendôme line, introduced in 1944, was its most exclusive label and was so successful the brand became a subsidiary of the firm in 1953. Coro's sets for Vendôme are in great demand. Pegasus was another Coro brand, but it is not as collectable as the "Duettes" or Vendôme pieces. Top-end Coro Pegasus rhinestone pieces compare with the very best from other companies.

3

5

1. A 1940s blowfish pin, with large blue stone, pink rhinestone eyes, and colorless rhinestones. 3.25in (8.5cm) wide **F**

2. A late 1930s ostrich pin, in rhodium-plate, with colorless rhinestones and hand-painted legs, beak, and eye. 3in (7.5cm) long **F**

3. A camellia bangle and earrings set, with large prong-set cabochons, pavé-set rhinestones, and enamel painting, marked "Corocraft" and "STERLING." c1939 7in (17.75cm) long **G**

4. A 1930s squirrel pin, enamel painted with cabochon stone for body, and diamanté. 1.5in (4cm) long **C**

5. A late 1930s ribbon and sunburst necklace, in sterling silver, with green and colorless rhinestones. 16.5in (42cm) long **D**

6. A late 1930s grape fur-clip, with pearl cabochons and diamanté. 3in (7.5cm) long **D**

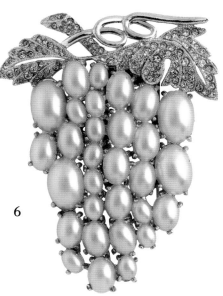

6

Coro's sales team, led by Royal Marcher, took the products across the United States, opened a factory in England in 1933, and contributed hugely towards the company's success. However, the success of Coro & Corocraft cannot be attributed solely to the company's market presence. It was also due to the talent of its designers: "François," Robert Geissman, Oscar Placco, Massa Raimond, Gene Verecchio, and Albert Weiss.

In 1924, the highly creative Adolph Katz joined as design director. His design style was delightfully whimsical, and his talent made a huge contribution to the company's success. He was responsible for the delicate *en tremblant* floral pins, featuring elements that "tremble" and move, and his "Jelly Bellies" and other animal pins are avidly collected. From the 1930s to the 1950s, "Jelly Belly" pins were all the rage: they featured a stone—often colored-glass cabochons or Lucite—in the center to represent the animal's belly. Lucite, a plastic, was developed by DuPont in 1937 and proved an effective substitute for a range of rock crystals, such as chalcedony and moonstone. Lucite was quickly adopted by many costume jewelers, and Coro mainly used it in its translucent white form for "Jelly Belly" pins.

The skills of jeweler's son Gene Verecchio ("Verri"), who joined the firm in the 1930s, swiftly took him to the position of chief designer, which he held for 33 years. His key pieces include the "Camellia Duette," the "Owl Duette," the "Twin Birds Duette," and the "Flower Duettes."

1. A Charlie McCarthy (ventriloquist's dummy) pin, in painted cast metal. 1in (3cm) long **C**

2. A 1940s love birds pin, with diamanté, glass, and faux pearls. 2.25in (5.5cm) wide **D**

3. A 1940s bow pin, in vermeil sterling silver with rhinestones, marked "Corocraft Sterling" to reverse. 2.5in (6.5cm) long **C**

4. A mid-1940s stylized floral pin, in vermeil sterling silver, with red glass cabochons and round-cut clear rhinestones. 3.25in (8.25cm) wide **D**

5. A hand pin, in vermeil sterling silver, with crystal "ring" and "bracelet", and enamel painted finger nails. 1944 2.5in (6.5cm) long **D**

6. A pair of "his and hers" penguin pins, in enameled pot metal, with pink cabochons and diamanté. Each 1.25in (3cm) long **D**

RHINESTONES

The deep red multi-faceted rhinestones and the colorless rhinestones (diamanté) are used as a dramatic and effective contrast to the vermeil sterling silver.

VERMEIL

Like many of the pieces in Coro's upmarket "Corocraft" line, this pin was made in either high-quality veimeil sterling silver. Other pieces are found in sterling silver.

SETTING

The faux rubies are held in place with large prongs, which have been used as a feature of the design.

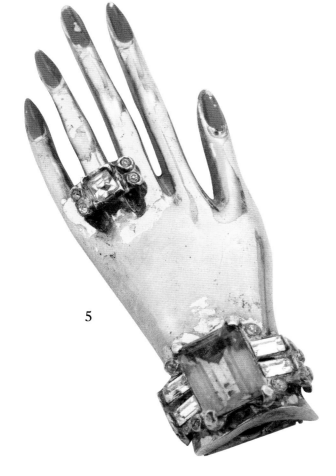

Coro's most collectible jewels were made during the 1930s and 1940s. After that they stopped making their more desirable silver pieces, and focused on necklace and earring sets in thermoset plastic, which are typically not as valuable.

Especially desirable pieces include "Jelly Bellies" (see pages 216-217), whimsical Adolph Katz designs, enameled tremblers, and the Mexican sterling silver pieces. During World War II, Coro also produced many patriotic pieces. The "Emblem of Americas" pin (featuring the US flag surrounded by the flags of the other countries in Latin America and South America) is rare, and highly sought-after by collectors.

The company ceased trading in the US in 1979, but Coro Inc. continued production in Canada until the mid-1990s.

"CR" was the earliest mark used by the company. The mark "François" was used on higher-end pieces created for top clients until World War II. Many pieces were signed "Vendôme" from 1944 onwards, with the full line launching in 1953. "Coro" (sometimes with the year of production) was used from 1919. In 1937 "Coro Craft" (later "Corocraft") was introduced for top-end pieces. "Pegasus" came into use after World War II; and "Coro Originals" was also used from that time.

1. An oriental-style Buddha pin, in vermeil sterling silver, with carved fruit salad stones and clear rhinestones. c1945. 1.5in (3.75cm) long **E**

2. A 1930s hobo pin, in gold-tone metal, with rhinestones. 1.25in (3.25cm) high **B**

3. A 1930s girl and lion pin, in gold-tone metal, with enamel, and rhinestones. 1.5in (4cm) wide **C**

4. A 1950s girl walking a dog chatelaine pin, in gold-tone metal, with turquoise, pink, and red crystals, signed "Coro." Girl 2in (5cm) high **D**

The faux coral beads and crystal rhinestones have been glued in place. This indicates that this pretty set is from a less expensive range.

The gold-tone metal leaves are highlighted with white enameling. Once chipped this is virtually impossible to repair.

6

7

5. A 1950s floral necklace and earrings set, in gold-tone metal with faux coral beads, colorless rhinestones and enamel. Necklace 16in (40.5cm) long **C**

6. A 1940s "Norseland" bird pin, in sterling silver. 2in (5cm) wide **C**

7. A 1950s floral bracelet, silver-tone metal, with jonquil-colored rhinestones. **B**

8. A pair of 1950s earrings, in white metal, with faux pearls and faux smoky-gray rhinestones. 1.25in (3cm) diam **A**

9. A 1960s pin and earrings set, in gilt filigree and topaz rhinestones. Pin 2.75in (7cm) long **B**

8

9

FRAME

1

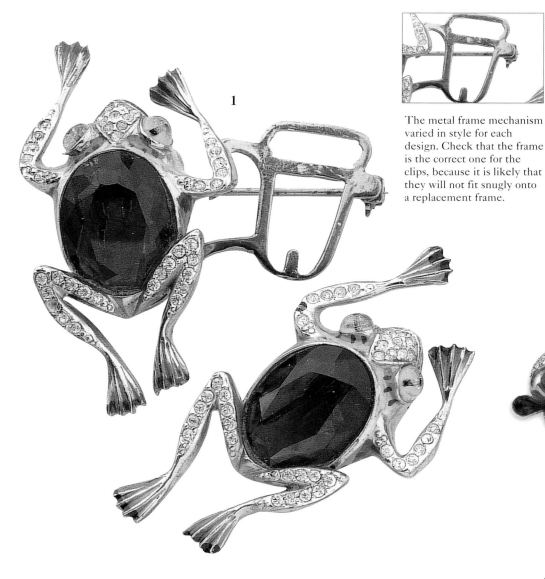

The metal frame mechanism varied in style for each design. Check that the frame is the correct one for the clips, because it is likely that they will not fit snugly onto a replacement frame.

2

3

4

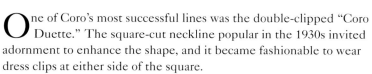

One of Coro's most successful lines was the double-clipped "Coro Duette." The square-cut neckline popular in the 1930s invited adornment to enhance the shape, and it became fashionable to wear dress clips at either side of the square.

Designer Adolph Katz patented the interlocking catch mechanism of the "Duette," similar to Trifari's "Clipmate," in 1931. The two clips, which could be worn individually or conjoined, were often figural designs based on flowers, animals, or cherubs, made of sterling silver and decorated with enamels and crystal rhinestones. They were sometimes sold as part of a pin and earrings set. Bright and charming, these clips where hugely popular, and similar pieces were produced by many other companies.

The similarity of Coro's "Duette" to Trifari's "Clipmate" was the subject of some legal wrangling, and just one example of parallels in the production of the two companies. Trifari began a long legal case against Coro, aiming to establish fashion jewelry as copyright works of art. Trifari won the case in 1954.

1. A frog Duette, possibly designed by Gene Verri, in sterling silver, with faux amethyst, diamanté, yellow cabochon eyes, and enamel details. 1944 22.5in (6cm) long **E**

2. A 1940s owl Duette, in sterling silver, with blue enamel, and pavé-set aquamarine and clear rhinestones. 1.5in (3.75cm) high **D**

3. A mid-1940s monkey Duette, in gold-plate, with red, green, and clear crystals. 2.25in (6cm) wide **E**

4. A 1940s parrot Duette, in yellow-metal, with enamel paint and pavé-set clear rhinestones. 2.5in (6.25cm) long **D**

5. A "Quivering Camellia" Duette, designed by Gene Verri, with enamel and rhinestones, the flowers gilded and lacquered. c1938 3in (7.5cm) long **E**

6. A 1940s floral Duette, in gilt white metal, with green crystal baguettes and clear rhinestones. 2.5in (6.5cm) long **D**

7. A 1930s/1940s heart and overmantel Duette, in white metal, with clear crystal rhinestones and ruby glass "fires." 3in (7.5cm) long **D**

8. A 1930s/1940 leaf Duette, in rhodium-plate, with round- and baguette-cut clear rhinestones. 2.5in (6.25cm) wide **D**

"My dream is to save women from nature."

Christian Dior

1

2

3

CHRISTIAN DIOR

Christian Dior was the most influential designer of the 1950s, storming the fashion world with his "New Look." From 1947 he accessorized his clothes with opulent jewelry, such as flower tremblers, assymmetrical crystal necklaces and animal pins, especially commissioned for each collection.

Christian Dior was born in Normandy, France, in 1905. He got his break in the fashion world when he sold sketches to Parisian couture houses, eventually earning an apprenticeship with Robert Piguet in 1938. After serving as an officer in World War II for a year, Dior found a position with couturier Lucien Lelong in 1941. It was a challenging and educational environment for Dior: Lelong was attempting to revitalize Paris's couture industry by dressing the wives of Nazi officers and French collaborators.

In 1946, a friend from Normandy gave Dior the opportunity to revive a struggling clothing company owned by textile manufacturer Marcel Boussac, the "King of Cotton." Boussac was impressed by

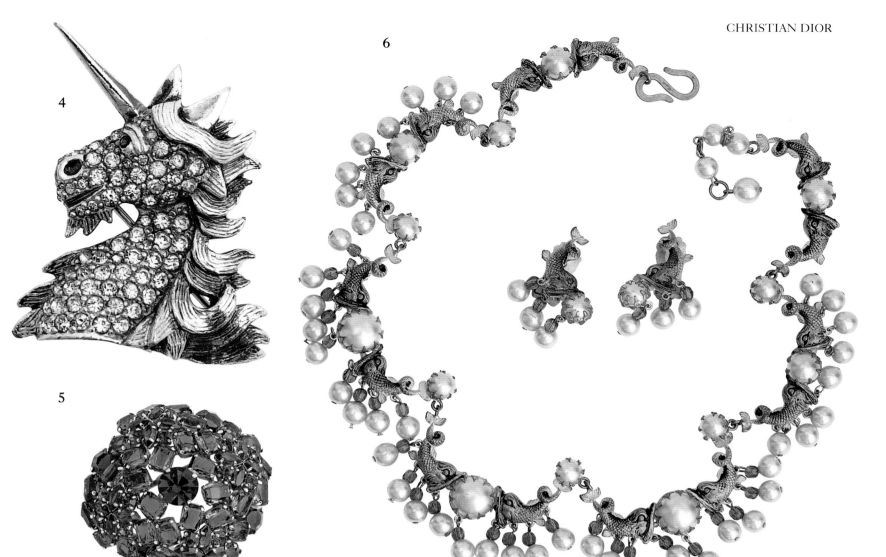

Dior's idea for a curvaceous new look with full, billowing skirts and agreed to fund his new couture house. The first Christian Dior couture show was held in February 1947, and the company was flooded with orders from the world's most beautiful women, including Rita Hayworth and Margot Fonteyn.

"Your dresses have such a new look," Carmel Snow, editor in chief of *Harper's Bazaar*, told Dior on seeing the new "Carolle" line's silhouette. But the New Look attracted both approval and disdain: a bewildered Coco Chanel wondered how women could function in "that thing," which flew in the face of her own practical style ethos.

However, post-war women, desperate to bring some glamor back into their lives, flocked to buy New Look pieces with their hourglass silhouettes. The opulent, curvaceous shapes were accessorized with crystal jewelry designed for the first Dior collection by the French manufacturer, Maison Gripoix, or with strings of faux pearls, creating a glamorous and feminine finish.

This "flower women" look, as Dior described it, fulfilled a political agenda, too: women were expected to return to the home as wives and mothers, leaving the factory and field jobs to demobbed soldiers. The New Look reinforced that traditional feminine role.

1. A pair of earrings, in silver-tone metal, prong-set with citrine and clear rhinestones, marked "Christian Dior 1958". 1958 1.5in (3.5cm) long **C**

2. A rare late 1940s lily of the valley pin, designed by Francis Winter, in white metal, with rhinestones. 4.25in (11cm) long **M**

3. A wreath pin and earrings set, in silver-tone metal, with gold-tone decoration, prong set with clear rhinestones, marked "ChrDior 1959". 1959 Pin 2.5in (6.5cm) long **E**

4. A mid-1950s unicorn pin, designed by Mitchell Maer, in rhodium-plate, pavé-set with clear rhinestones. 2.5in (6.25cm) high **C**

5. A circular pin, with olive green and smoky topaz rhinestones. 1958 2in (5cm) diam **D**

6. A rare mythical sea creatures necklace and earrings set, in gilded metal, with faux pearls and green glass, marked "Christian Dior 1959". 1959 Necklace 14.5in (37cm) long **K**

QUALITY

The large circular stone at the top of the pin has been given a complicated multi-faceted cut. This is a sign of the high quality of the piece.

SETTING

Rather than being hidden away, the gold-tone metal settings are very much a part of the design of this pin, and add to its dramatic apperance.

COLORS

As is typical of Dior, subtle coloring has been used for this pin: in this case, a graduation from colorless, to light gray to dark gray.

CUTS

As well as different shapes, variety of different cuts have been used on this piece. This is a sign of the high quality Dior is known for.

1

Dior designed pieces of jewelry as an integral part of his collections, using them to enhance his couture. Initially, he created jewelry for individual clients, such as Marilyn Monroe and Bette Davis, or for specific outfits. From 1948 onward, designs were made as part of each collection. Jewelry pieces were soon being produced under license for Dior and sold in exclusive stores, a practice which the House of Dior continued after the designer's death.

Dior was insistent that the quality of the costume jewelry designed for the House of Dior reflected the standard of the couture. Only the most talented designers and reputable companies were used, including Henry Schreiner and Kramer in the United States; Mitchell Maer in England; Henkel & Grosse in Germany from 1955 onward; and in France Josette Gripoix and Robert Goossens, who also worked for Chanel.

Dior's jewelry took its inspiration from historical styles, but the designs were given a modern flavor through the use of unusual pastes and stones, deliberately selected for their artificial colors and forms, which made the pieces visually challenging and stunning. In this vein, Dior developed the multi-colored "aurora borealis" line of rhinestones with Swarovski in 1955, which were used widely in his designs. Floral forms were another signature element in his work, reflecting his love of gardens and the countryside. Lily of the valley was a particular motif of Dior's and at least one model in every show

would wear a corsage of his favorite flower. Other jewelry forms, including circus animals, unicorns, and fish were made and are highly collectable today. Pieces are always signed and dated.

Dior dominated the fashion world of the 1950s, attracting the elite of Europe and North America, designing outfits and jewelry for the Duchess of Windsor and Hollywood goddesses, and employing the most talented designers, including Pierre Cardin. In 1957, Dior died of a heart attack and his financial backer, Marcel Boussac, promoted a talented 21-year-old apprentice, Yves Saint Laurent, to designer in chief. In 1960, Mark Bohan replaced Saint Laurent in the role, followed by Gianfranco Ferré in 1989 and John Galliano in 1996. The House of Dior remains a global brand today.

1. A pin, in gold-tone metal, with irregularly shaped glass stones. 1962 2.75in (7cm) long **D**

2. An abstract pin, made by Henkel & Grosse, with faux pearl and green, amber, and clear rhinestones. 1962 2.75in (7cm) long **E**

3. An early 1960s necklace, with prong-set red and clear crystals, and removable pin-pendant. 22in (56cm) long **K**

4. A 1960s *en tremblant* flower pin, made by Kramer, in rhodium-plate, with pavé-set rhinestones. 2.5in (6.5cm) long **C**

5. A 1960s heart-shaped pin and star earrings set, in silver-tone metal, with prong-set oval-, round-, and navette-cut aquamarine, chalcedony, pale green, and fuchsia pastes. Pin 3.5in (7cm) wide **E**

MITCHELL MAER

American Mitchell Maer moved to London in the 1930s and began designing jewelry for Dior's seasonal collections, under license, in 1952. Maer used designers in Paris and produced the pieces in London, marking them "Christian Dior by Mitchell Maer". This arrangement lasted for four years, until Maer went bankrupt.

Maer's work was original and distinctive, utilizing luxurious-looking rhinestones and faux pearls to underpin the classic opulence of Dior's designs. The most popular of his designs echoed Victorian and Georgian styles, and his "Byzantine" collection was also a huge success. He is known for his use of floral motifs and for his unicorn pins, which are avidly sought by collectors today.

6. A pair of 1950s earrings, in silver-tone metal, with black and clear rhinestones and faux baroque pearl drops, signed "Christian Dior by Mitchell Maer". 2in (5cm) long **D**

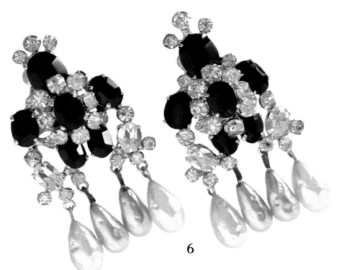

6

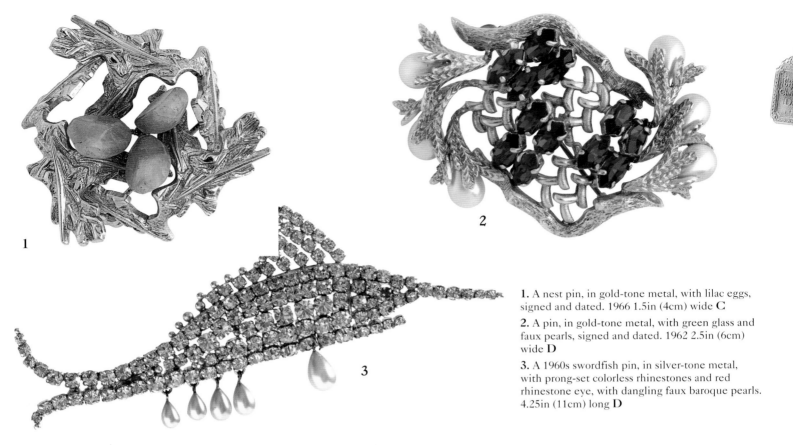

1. A nest pin, in gold-tone metal, with lilac eggs, signed and dated. 1966 1.5in (4cm) wide **C**

2. A pin, in gold-tone metal, with green glass and faux pearls, signed and dated. 1962 2.5in (6cm) wide **D**

3. A 1960s swordfish pin, in silver-tone metal, with prong-set colorless rhinestones and red rhinestone eye, with dangling faux baroque pearls. 4.25in (11cm) long **D**

AN EYE FOR FASHION

Whether it was inspiring the world with the 1947 "New Look," or employing cutting-edge designers such as John Galliano to continue to push the brand forwards, Christian Dior has always been at the forefront of fashion design. The pendant necklace (shown left) from the company's 1950 collection was designed to set off the strapless evening gowns that were fashionable at the time. More recently Galliano has been inspired by the label's past to create couture gowns and jewelry which recall its 1950s masterpieces . For example, the flower earrings shown above, which date from c2005, feature faux tortoiseshell petals, citrine bead drops, and clear rhinestone highlights. ($120–180/£80–120)

JEUNESSE de CHRISTIAN D'OR

4. A necklace and earrings set, made by Henkel & Grosse, in silver-tone metal, with faux pearls and rhinestones, marked "Dior", with original swing tag. 1968 **F**

5. A 1960s pin, with faux pearl and crystal flowers, signed, with original swing tag. **D**

6. A 1980s twisted rope double heart pin, in gold-tone metal. 2in (5cm) wide **C**

7. A mid-1970s Indian-style necklace, in gold-tone metal, with faux lapis lazuli and turquoise, marked "Dior". **E**

1

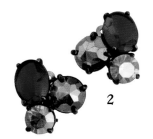

2

ELSA
SCHIAPARELLI

Flamboyant. Eccentric. Outrageous. Surreal. Elsa Schiaparelli commands some of the most colorful adjectives to describe both her work and her personality. In her day, she shocked and delighted in equal measure. Today, Schiaparelli is a design icon.

Elsa Schiaparelli was born in 1890 to a wealthy family in Rome, Italy. Rebellious from an early age, she once attended a ball simply wrapped in a length of fabric that, of course, unwound, bringing shame and scandal to her family. Her marriage to Franco-Swiss theosophist William de Wendt did not last, leaving her a single mother to the couple's daughter, Gogo. Determined to succeed independently and with a passion for the arts and fashion, she moved to Paris in the 1920s, where top designer Paul Poiret introduced her to the world of couture. In 1927, she established her first maison couture, in the Rue de la Paix. In this highly charged world of artistry, she became friends with Surrealist Salvador Dalí, and became the archrival of Coco Chanel.

Schiaparelli shared with Chanel the belief in costume jewelry as an art form—not dependent for its value on the materials used—and also as an integral part of fashion design, but there the similarities ended. Her work was constantly compared to Chanel's elegant designs, but

Schiaparelli's early creations drew on whimsical themes. She took inspiration from African iconography, sailors' tattoos, Paganism, butterflies, and musical instruments; featured circus or astrological motifs; took natural forms and stylized them; or selected exotic and unusual floral or faunal forms, such as a pea-pod pendant, the "Eye" pin, or a clear plastic necklace printed with insects.

Schiaparelli also showed great talent in drawing out the skills of her collaborators, among whom Lyda Coppola, Jean Schlumberger, Jean Clément, and Roger Jean-Pierre stand out. A painter with a chemistry degree, Clément was taken on as a designer by Schiaparelli in 1927. He was skilled at working in plastics, and married his own innate good taste with Schiaparelli's outrageous concepts to create sophisticated objects, many of which are museum pieces today.

Schiaparelli channeled the philosophies of Dadaism and Surrealism into her work, as evinced in her "Shocking Pink" collection of 1936, including her "Shocking" perfume and cosmetics. "I gave to a pink the nerve of a red," read her company's manifesto. The concept she developed centered on the Surrealist metaphor of splashing the "black cocktail dress" of society with vivid and outrageous color.

1. A pair of 1950s earrings, with blue aurora borealis stones and clear rhinestones, with button clip. 1.5in (4cm) long **D**

2. A pair of 1950s earrings, with prong-set red and aurora borealis stones. 1in (2.5cm) long **D**

3. A 1930s/1940s woven chain necklace, in gold-tone metal, with hand-cut crystal drops. 17in (43cm) long **H**

4. A 1950s pin and earrings set, with prong-set blue cabochons, and blue and green crystal rhinestones. Pin 2.5in (6cm) wide **E**

5. A 1930s antique-style pin, in gold-tone metal, with enamel and clear rhinestones, marked "SCHIAPARELLI". 3in (7.5cm) long **E**

6. A 1950s bracelet, pin, and earrings set, in gilt metal, with green stones, signed "Schiaparelli." Bracelet 7in (17.5cm) long **F**

7. A probably 1950s "ice crystal" bracelet, in pewter-tone metal, with aurora borealis rhinestones, marked "Schiapaelli." **E**

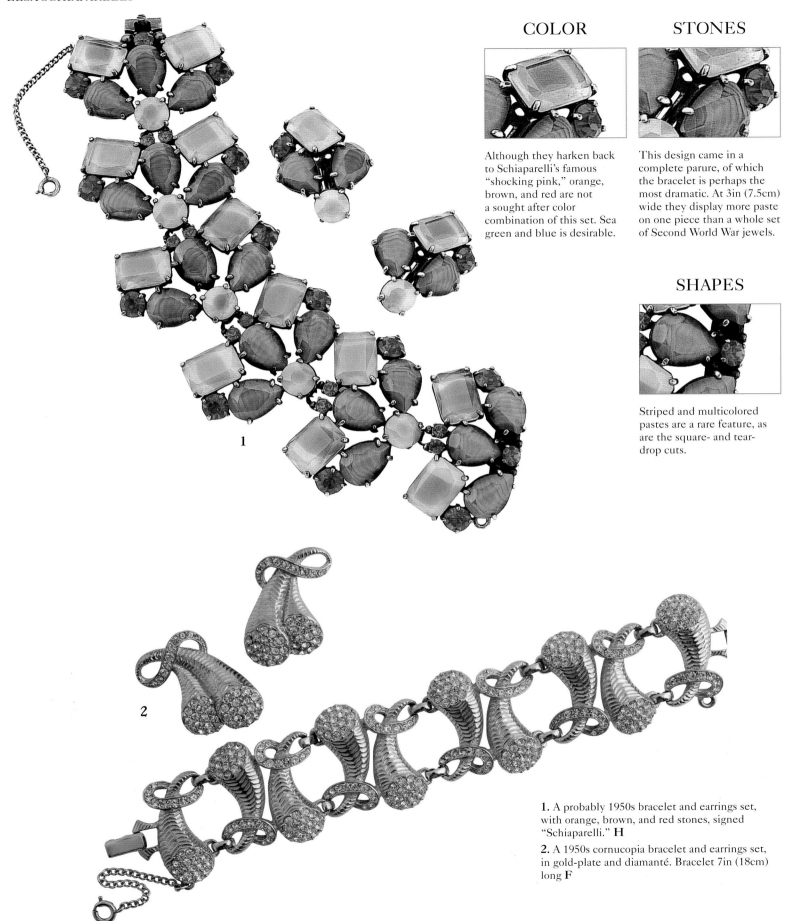

COLOR

Although they harken back to Schiaparelli's famous "shocking pink," orange, brown, and red are not a sought after color combination of this set. Sea green and blue is desirable.

STONES

This design came in a complete parure, of which the bracelet is perhaps the most dramatic. At 3in (7.5cm) wide they display more paste on one piece than a whole set of Second World War jewels.

SHAPES

Striped and multicolored pastes are a rare feature, as are the square- and tear-drop cuts.

1. A probably 1950s bracelet and earrings set, with orange, brown, and red stones, signed "Schiaparelli." **H**

2. A 1950s cornucopia bracelet and earrings set, in gold-plate and diamanté. Bracelet 7in (18cm) long **F**

Her jewelry used of bright, exotic stones in vibrant pink. From this point onward, shocking pink—"unreal pink"—became her signature color. Schiaparelli's approach won over many critics, as well as receiving acclaim from her Surrealist circle, including Dalí and Jean Cocteau, who designed jewelry for her, and from fashion illustrator Christian Bérard. It also revealed her continuing quest for presenting an alternative to contemporary fashion.

After fleeing to New York City during World War II, Schiaparelli returned to Paris in 1945, but found it changed. In 1949, she established a ready-to-wear outlet in New York and licensed DeRosa to make her jewelry, labeled "Designed in Paris—Created in America." She returned to the United States in 1954, closing her Parisian fashion house and leaving behind her assistants, Pierre Cardin and Hubert de Givenchy.

In 1950s New York, Schiaparelli turned her attention fully to costume jewelry, creating abstract, floral, or faunal designs using unusual and highly colorful iridescent "fantasy" paste stones and glass, in incredibly fake oranges and pinks, studded with rhinestones. Charm bracelets were all the rage at the time, thanks to Grace Kelly, and Schiaparelli made some of the best.

Elsa Schiaparelli's costume jewelry line ceased production in the late 1950s, and she died in 1973.

Examples of Schiaparelli's Parisian work from the 1930s are rare: many are museum-quality pieces, fetching record sums. Pieces from the 1940s and 1950s are most commonly found today. Collectors seek designs with frosted glass leaves, jagged "ice" glass, or strangely colored pearls set as grapes. Heavy enamel pins featuring her surreal motifs, such as bagpipes or clowns, are also sought after.

Most French Schiaparelli work is unsigned, although a few pieces are marked with "Schiaparelli" in block letters on a rectangular plate. Most of her later French work and all American pieces are signed "Schiaparelli" in script. This mark was in use from 1927, and patented in the US in 1933. Schiaparelli fakes abound, and the collector should also consider whether pieces are 1980s reproductions when valuing.

3. A 1950s organic leaf pin and earrings set, in gold-plate. Pin 3in (8cm) long **E**

4. A pair of 1950s shell earrings, with faux pearl and diamanté. 1in (2.5cm) long **C**

5. A probably 1950s leaves bracelet, in blue frosted glass. 7in (17.5cm) long **D**

6. A pair of 1950s earrings, with faux amethyst cabochons and gold-tone metal tassels. 1.5in (4cm) long **D**

GOOSSENS

It can often be difficult to attribute pieces of unsigned jewelry. The necklace shown above is a prime example, with some attributing the design to Elsa Schiaparelli, and others attributing it to Robert Goossens, who is best known for his work with Chanel. Chief jewelry designer from 1960 until 1971, he helped create many of the most iconic Chanel "jewels," such as her Byzantine crosses and three-hoop earrings. Goossens has also created other pieces inspired by ancient civilizations for several other famous couturiers, including Cristobal Balenciaga, Yves Saint Laurent and Christian Dior.

A 1940s sunburst-style leaf necklace, in gold-tone metal, with faux amber, rhinestones, and faux pearls. 14in (35.5cm) long I.

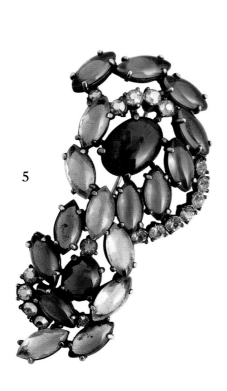

5

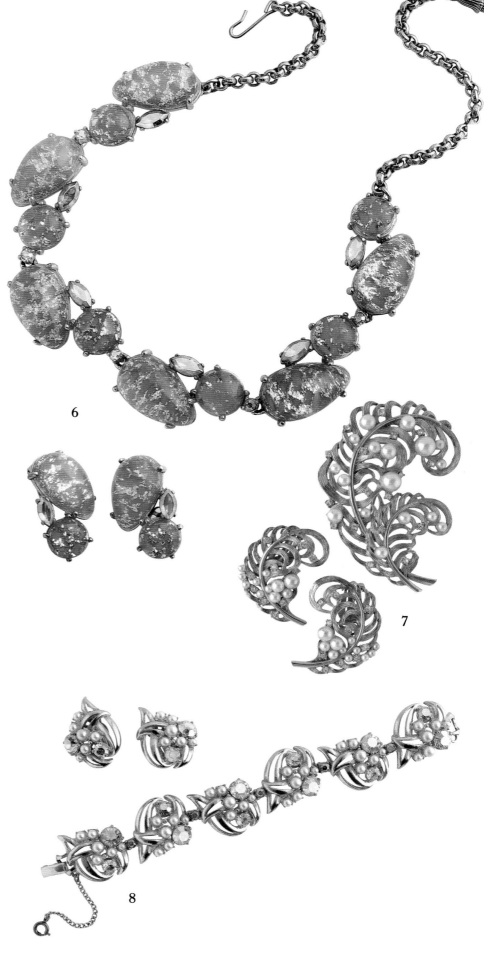

6

7

8

1. A pair of 1950s acorn and leaf earrings, in gold-tone metal, with aurora borealis stones. 1.5in (4cm) long **C**

2. A pair of 1950s earrings, with brown and green moonstones. 1.75in (4.5cm) long **C**

3. A pair of 1950s earrings, in gun-metal-plate, with carved rose stones, and red and clear aurora borealis stones. 1in (2.5cm) long **B**

4. A 1950s "peacock fan"-style pin, with green rhinestones and faux mother-of-pearl, stamped "SCHIAPARELLI." 2in (5cm) diam **D**

5. A 1950s pin, in gilt metal, with prong-set green and blue glass stones, and small aurora borealis rhinestones. 3.5in (9cm) long **F**

6. A 1950s necklace and earrings set, with bakelite cabochons and aurora borealis stones. Earrings 1.25in (3cm) long **E**

7. A 1950s feather pin and earrings set, in gold-tone metal, with simulated pearls and diamanté. Pin 3in (8cm) long **D**

8. A 1950s bracelet and earrings set, in gold-tone metal, with diamanté and faux pearl. Bracelet 7.5in (19cm) long **E**

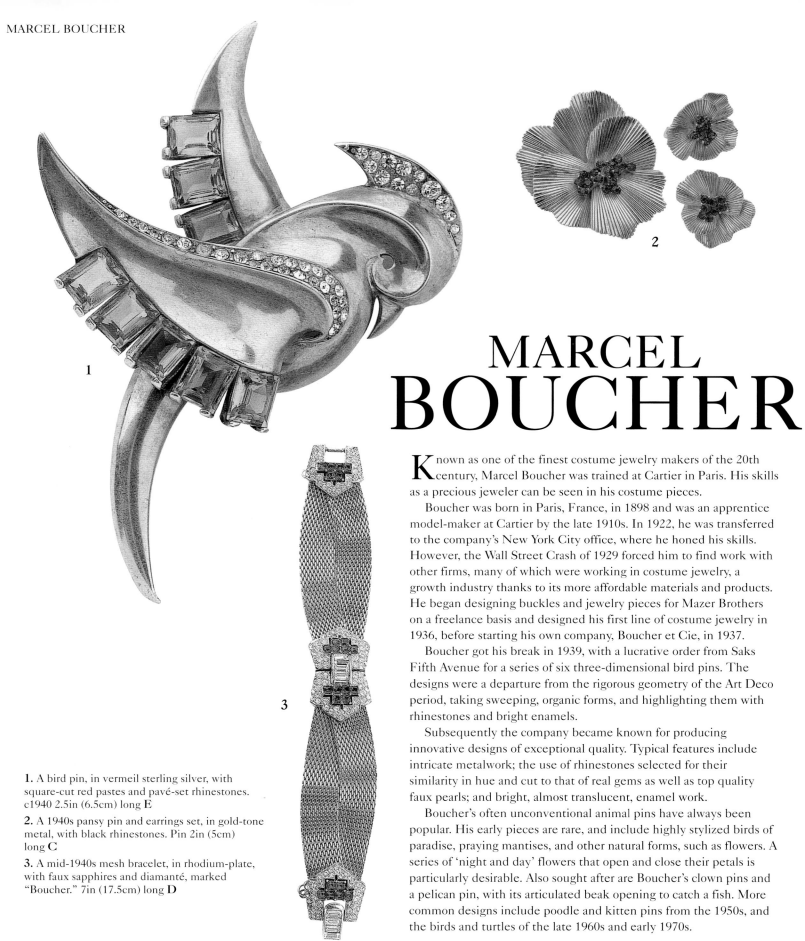

MARCEL BOUCHER

Known as one of the finest costume jewelry makers of the 20th century, Marcel Boucher was trained at Cartier in Paris. His skills as a precious jeweler can be seen in his costume pieces.

Boucher was born in Paris, France, in 1898 and was an apprentice model-maker at Cartier by the late 1910s. In 1922, he was transferred to the company's New York City office, where he honed his skills. However, the Wall Street Crash of 1929 forced him to find work with other firms, many of which were working in costume jewelry, a growth industry thanks to its more affordable materials and products. He began designing buckles and jewelry pieces for Mazer Brothers on a freelance basis and designed his first line of costume jewelry in 1936, before starting his own company, Boucher et Cie, in 1937.

Boucher got his break in 1939, with a lucrative order from Saks Fifth Avenue for a series of six three-dimensional bird pins. The designs were a departure from the rigorous geometry of the Art Deco period, taking sweeping, organic forms, and highlighting them with rhinestones and bright enamels.

Subsequently the company became known for producing innovative designs of exceptional quality. Typical features include intricate metalwork; the use of rhinestones selected for their similarity in hue and cut to that of real gems as well as top quality faux pearls; and bright, almost translucent, enamel work.

Boucher's often unconventional animal pins have always been popular. His early pieces are rare, and include highly stylized birds of paradise, praying mantises, and other natural forms, such as flowers. A series of 'night and day' flowers that open and close their petals is particularly desirable. Also sought after are Boucher's clown pins and a pelican pin, with its articulated beak opening to catch a fish. More common designs include poodle and kitten pins from the 1950s, and the birds and turtles of the late 1960s and early 1970s.

1. A bird pin, in vermeil sterling silver, with square-cut red pastes and pavé-set rhinestones. c1940 2.5in (6.5cm) long **E**

2. A 1940s pansy pin and earrings set, in gold-tone metal, with black rhinestones. Pin 2in (5cm) long **C**

3. A mid-1940s mesh bracelet, in rhodium-plate, with faux sapphires and diamanté, marked "Boucher." 7in (17.5cm) long **D**

4. A rare 1940s flower necklace, with poured glass flowers, diamanté, and faux pearls. Pendant 4.75in (12cm) wide **M**

5. A pair of 1950s earrings, in gold-plate, with faux citrin and topaz, with button clip. 1in (2.5cm) long **B**

6. A 1920s/1930s flower pin, in silver-tone metal, with enamel and diamanté. 4.25in (10.5cm) long **D**

7. A late 1940s sunburst pin and earrings set, in gilt metal, with faux jade cabochons and pavé-set sapphire and diamanté. Pin 1.5in (3.5cm) diam **D**

8. A late 1930s/early 1940s penguin pin, in silver-tone metal, with enamel and diamanté. 1.75in (4.5cm) long **E**

1

2

DIAMANTÉ

The classic combination of diamond and silver (here imitated by rhodium-plate) was the perfect accessory for the "little black dress," which had been championed by Coco Chanel the decade before.

1. A 1930s ear of wheat pin, in rhodium-plate, with diamanté, with Marcel Boucher logo. 4.5in (11.5cm) long **E**

DESIGN

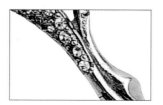

This design effectively portrays the movement of a sheaf of wheat in the breeze. This is a sign of quality.

ENAMEL

Examples of Boucher's ear of wheat pin have also been found with green enameled stems.

During World War II, when base metals were restricted for war use, Boucher moved the company to Mexico in order to exploit the country's silver supplies. After the war was over, the Mexican operation was sold and Boucher moved back to New York City.

In 1949, Boucher's business partner, Arthur Halberstadt decided to leave the company. Consequently Boucher invited French designer Sandra Semensohn to become his design assistant. Semensohn left to work for Tiffany & Co. from 1958 to 1961, before returning to Boucher. Later she became his second wife.

The company's work under Boucher and Semensohn in the 1950s followed the more sober trend for elegant, classic-looking pieces resembling fine jewelry. Boucher's standard—both for materials and design—remained high, so these items are also valuable.

Key pieces from this period include buckle motifs; leaf-forms decorated with rhinestones, especially in parures; and animal pins. Boucher also designed some plain gilt pieces that are likely to become highly collectible. His work with cabochon pastes during the 1950s and 1960s is especially fine: he used unusual lozenge-shaped pastes that suggested uncut precious stones, and set them in exquisite metalwork alongside myriad small, faceted rhinestones to create fabulously intricate pieces.

Early pieces were marked "MB"—topped with a Phrygian cap, the symbol of the French Revolution—from 1944 onward. This mark can be hard for the untrained eye to identify, as it was very small, so if in doubt contact a reputable dealer. A lesser-quality line was marked "Marboux." Later pieces were signed "Marcel Boucher" or "Boucher," with the copyright symbol. Additionally, almost all pieces produced from c1945 onwards were marked with a style-inventory number, which can help with dating, although consideration should also be given to later production runs.

When Boucher died in 1965, Semensohn took over the company, maintaining the quality of the work. In 1972, Boucher et Cie was sold to Dovorn Industries, an American watch manufactory. In 1976 Boucher et Cie. was sold again to the Canadian company D'Orlan, which was run by Maurice Bradden, who had trained under Boucher himself. Until 2006, when the company closed its doors, D'Orlan produced replicas of Marcel Boucher's designs using his original molds.

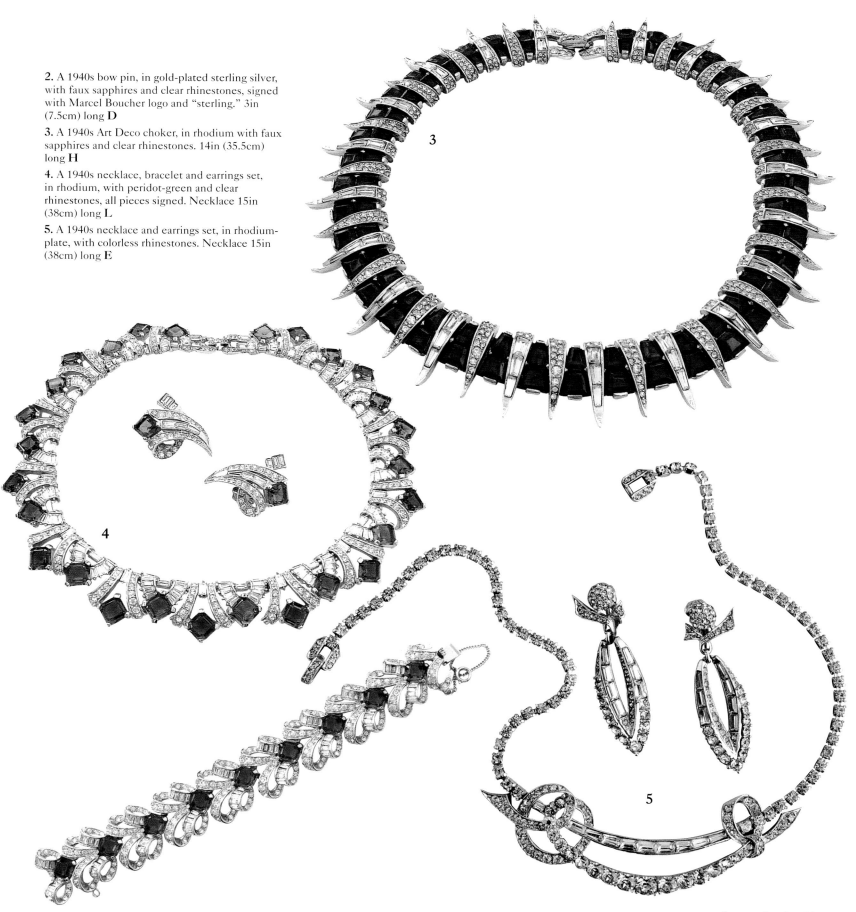

2. A 1940s bow pin, in gold-plated sterling silver, with faux sapphires and clear rhinestones, signed with Marcel Boucher logo and "sterling." 3in (7.5cm) long **D**

3. A 1940s Art Deco choker, in rhodium with faux sapphires and clear rhinestones. 14in (35.5cm) long **H**

4. A 1940s necklace, bracelet and earrings set, in rhodium, with peridot-green and clear rhinestones, all pieces signed. Necklace 15in (38cm) long **L**

5. A 1940s necklace and earrings set, in rhodium-plate, with colorless rhinestones. Necklace 15in (38cm) long **E**

LUCITE

The use of Lucite in this necklace marks it as obviously 1950s. This is currently a popular decade with collectors, and may add value to what is already an attractive piece.

COLOR

This color combination, with blue-green leaves and silver-plated metal, works well, producing a wintry effect. The bright blue is also very 1950s, which further adds to its desirability.

QUALITY

There is an extremely high level of detail on each of the leaves, which have not only large veins, but also smaller, subsidiary veins. This level of detail is a mark of quality.

1. A 1950s ivy necklace, in silver-plate, with turquoise Lucite leaves. 4in (35.5cm) long **D**

2. A 1950s piggy bank pin, in gilt white metal, with multicolored diamanté. 1950s 3.5cm (1.25in) wide **B**

3. A pair of holly wreath Christmas earrings, in gold-tone metal, with red and green beads. 1in (2.5cm) diam **A**

4. A 1950s leaf motif necklace, in silver-plate. 16.5in (42cm) long **C**

5. A necklace, in gold-tone metal, with bezel-set green cabochon pastes, and red and clear rhinestones. c1960 16in (40cm) long **D**

6. A 1950s flower pin, in gold-tone metal, with square-cut blue stones, and blue rhinestones. 2.25in (5.5cm) wide **C**

7. A pin, in gold-plate, with rhinestones and faux sapphires, signed "Boucher." 2in (5cm) long **C**

1

JOSEFF OF HOLLYWOOD

E ugene Joseff's bold designs were made for Hollywood, and Hollywood made him. He designed "the jewelry of the stars," taking inspiration from historical precedents and reinterpreting them, larger than life, to be clearly seen on the silver screen.

Born in Chicago in 1905, Eugene Joseff worked as a graphic artist in an advertising agency in the early 1920s, designing jewelry in his spare time. By 1927, he was training as a jewelry designer while working in Los Angeles to escape the Great Depression that was gripping the rest of the country.

It was during a discussion with Walter Plunkett, an established costume designer, that Joseff was challenged to start designing for the movie studios. When Joseff criticized *The Affairs of Cellini*, in which Constance Bennett's costume was accurately styled to the 16th century but her jewelry was 20th-century, Plunkett told him: "Well, if you're so smart, let's see what you can do."

Joseff's career took off in 1931 with the production of one-off, historically accurate pieces for Hollywood studios, made in his own workshops. Astutely, he rented these pieces to the studios, allowing for potential re-hire and amassing an archive of over three million pieces, which is still owned by the Joseff family today. In 1935, he opened a store, Sunset Jewelry, in Hollywood and founded a new company, Joseff of Hollywood. Joseff supplied historically accurate pieces for films including *A Star is Born* in 1936; *Marie Antoinette* in 1938; *The Wizard of Oz* and *Gone with the Wind* in 1939; and *Casablanca* in 1942.

Inspired by Hollywood goddesses such as Marlene Dietrich and Marilyn Monroe wearing the studio jewels off-screen, in 1937 Joseff began to produce replicas of the cinema originals for retail. Moviegoers could buy a little piece of film-star glamor, and Hollywood held such influence over the public that the replicas were a huge success. Sold through the finest stores in the United States at the time, these pieces are highly sought after by collectors today.

Through the 1940s, Joseff was the major costume jeweler to Hollywood, producing most of the pieces seen in historical films. In the February 1948 issue of *Movie Show* magazine, he gave his advice on styling and accessorizing: "Remember, gold can be worn with more things than silver and topaz is a good stone that looks smart with almost every type of costume." Joseff died in a plane crash in September that same year. The company continued under the aegis of his widow, Joan Castle Joseff (died 2010) and is still family run today.

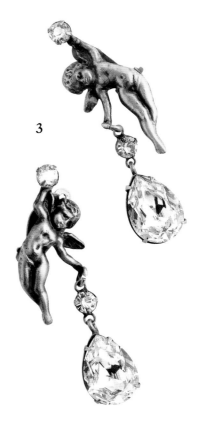

1. A very rare 1940s Moon God with ruff pin, in Russian-gold-plate, with clear rhinestone eye tremblers. 2.5in (6.25cm) diam **E**

2. A 1940s dolphin and shell-pendant necklace, in Russian-gold-plate, with faux pearl. Shell 1.25in (3cm) long **E**

3. A pair of cherub earrings, in Russian-gold-plate, with prong-set round, clear rhinestones, and clear teardrop rhinestone pendants. 1.5in (3.75cm) long **D**

4. A 1940s filigree tassel pin, in Russian-gold-plate, with facet-cut red stone. 5.25in (13.5cm) long **E**

5. A 1940s Ginger Rogers medallion pin, in Russian-gold-plate, with square rhinestone. 2.5in (6.5cm) long **D**

6. A 1940s chatelaine camel pin, in Russian-gold-plate, with faux ruby, emerald, citrine, jade, and aquamarine cabochons. 1.25in (3cm) wide **E**

SIGNS OF THE ZODIAC

In the 1930s and 40s, perhaps as a result of the uncertainties caused by the Great Depression, Americans became fascinated by astrology and the "secrets" it could reveal. Inspired by this, Joseff of Hollywood created a series of Signs of the Zodiac pins and earrings which have proved to be perennially popular. Of the twelves designs, the Leo examples have become the most valuable with collectors today because they are considered to be "cuter" than the others. The pin, which features a friendly lion, can fetch $450 (£300) —more than twice the value of those for other symbols.

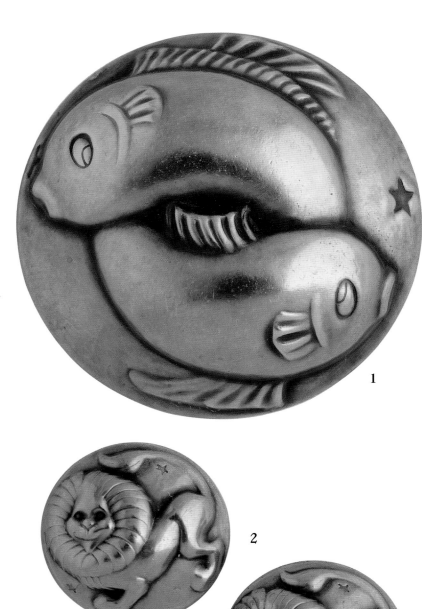

The key feature of Joseff's work is the semi-matte Russian gold-plating, a finish he developed specifically to overcome the problem of viewing highly reflective jewelry under strong studio lighting. This finish acquires a dark patina over time.

Joseff's work embraces a huge range of styles. He was inspired by history and drew on the spectrum of influences that had gone before, from Art Deco to Oriental styles, and he studied fine art to select motifs, such as the seashell inspired by Botticelli's *Birth of Venus*. The company's designs worn by Elizabeth Taylor in the 1963 film *Cleopatra* were based on pieces found at Tutankhamen's tomb in Egypt.

Typically, Joseff produced demi parures of a necklace or pin with earrings. His designs were unusual in costume jewelry at the time—plain metal pieces or pieces featuring neutrally colored pastes or faux pearls, used sparingly. Black, ivory, or Bakelite examples of his work also exist. However, like other designers of costume jewelry of the time, he maintained a deliberately "faux" impact. Forms were taken from nature: flowers, animals, and shells were favorite themes. A recurring form for necklaces was a decorative chain from which several large, repeating pendants were suspended, usually presented with matching earrings. Movement often featured in the form of stones on jump rings, or in undulating forms within the design.

Key pieces include the "Sun God" and "Moon God" pins, and the Elephant-head necklace and earrings parure, which is probably the most valuable of his designs.

According to family sources, Joseff's earliest pieces are marked "Joseff Hollywood" in block capitals. From 1950 onward, the mark gradually became "Joseff" in script, on an oval plate soldered to the back of the piece, but the overlap between marks was long, so this is not an accurate way of dating pieces. Joseff of Hollywood's work has been faked, and fakes may be identified by their more highly polished gold-plating. Stills of film stars wearing the original piece may contribute to the buyer's interest.

In the last decade or so, new pieces have been assembled from original Joseff components. As they use the limited stock of original material, they are not reproductions and are self-limiting, but prices have dropped slightly because of these pieces.

1. A 1940s "Pisces" zodiac pin, in Russian-gold-plate. 2in (5cm) diam **D**

2. A pair of 1940s "Leo" zodiac earrings, in Russian-gold-plate. 1in (2.5cm) diam **C**

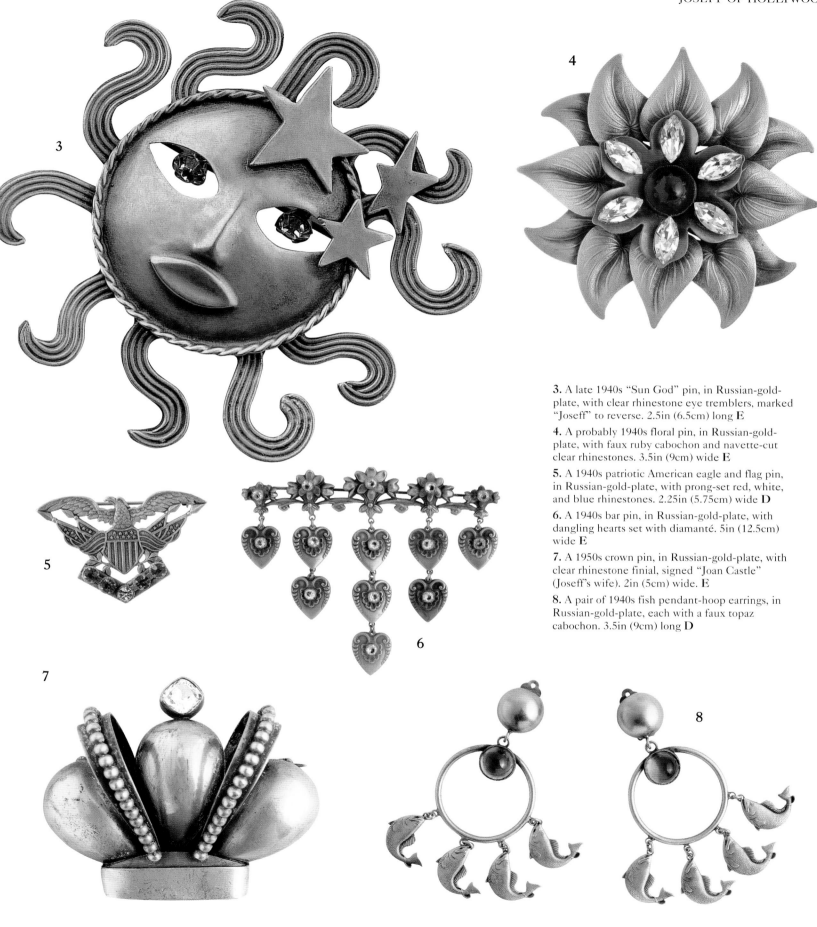

3. A late 1940s "Sun God" pin, in Russian-gold-plate, with clear rhinestone eye tremblers, marked "Joseff" to reverse. 2.5in (6.5cm) long **E**

4. A probably 1940s floral pin, in Russian-gold-plate, with faux ruby cabochon and navette-cut clear rhinestones. 3.5in (9cm) wide **E**

5. A 1940s patriotic American eagle and flag pin, in Russian-gold-plate, with prong-set red, white, and blue rhinestones. 2.25in (5.75cm) wide **D**

6. A 1940s bar pin, in Russian-gold-plate, with dangling hearts set with diamanté. 5in (12.5cm) wide **E**

7. A 1950s crown pin, in Russian-gold-plate, with clear rhinestone finial, signed "Joan Castle" (Joseff's wife). 2in (5cm) wide. **E**

8. A pair of 1940s fish pendant-hoop earrings, in Russian-gold-plate, each with a faux topaz cabochon. 3.5in (9cm) long **D**

1

HOLLYWOOD FAME

Joseff of Hollywood's historically accurate and camera-friendly jewelry was worn on- and off-screen by a host of celebrities which helped to market his designs to the public. Here, Jane Wyman—star of *You're In The Army Now* and *Johnny Belinda*—wears a necklace which is typical of Joseff's designs in that it features a series of repeated pendants. The pendants are set with faux amethysts and suspended from a Russian gold double chain set with flowers.

2

3

1. A rare 1940s leaf pin, in silver, with red bakelite. 4.75in(12cm) long **D**

2. A 1940s bee on flower pin and earrings set, in Russian-gold-plate, with central honey-colored glass cabochons. Pin 2.75in (7cm) diam **F**

3. A collection of 1940s bee pins, in Russian-gold-plate. Large 1.74in (4.5cm) wide **C**, medium: **C**, small: **B**

4. An early 1950s lizard necklace, in Russian-gold-plate, with faux turquoise cabochons, marked "Joseff". 16in (40.5cm) long **F**

5. A pair of probably 1940s star earrings, in Russian-gold-plate, with diamanté. 2.5in (6.5cm) long **B**

6. A pair of 1940s butterfly-wing/leaf earrings, in Russian-gold-plate, with faceted amethyst crystals. 2in (5cm) long **C**

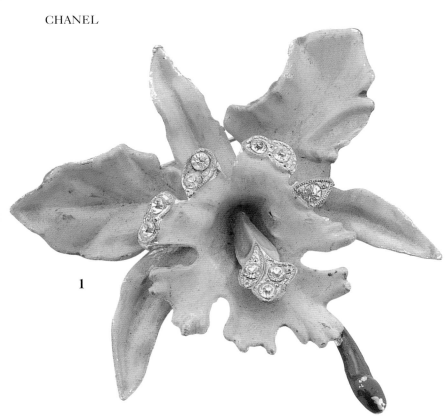

1

> *"A girl should be two things: classy and fabulous."*
> Gabrielle "Coco" Chanel

CHANEL

Coco Chanel was a pioneering designer: her concept of the "Total Look" proposed that individual pieces of clothing were not as important as the way in which they were accessorized and worn. She was the first fashion designer, along with Elsa Schiaparelli, to make costume jewelry essential to her style ethos, and is sometimes even credited with coining the term "costume jewelry."

Gabrielle Bonheur Chanel wove an intricately romantic version of her early history, claiming to have been born in France's rural Auvergne region in 1893 when she was in fact born in the Loire Valley town of Saumur ten years earlier. She trained as a seamstress and went to Paris to become a cabaret singer when she was 18, styling herself "Coco."

Chanel was shrewd and charismatic. She took wealthy lovers and, as her cabaret career faltered, developed her dressmaking skills and found the capital she needed to open her first Parisian boutique in 1912. Here, she promoted a chic new look for women that had simplicity and comfort at its core, doing away with the restrictive corsets of her forebears.

Chanel's unfussy designs provided a perfect canvas for accessories, and she began to produce jewelry decorated with inexpensive imitation stones and pearls so that her clients could afford to accessorize and personalize many outfits. These pieces were styled to emphasize their "faux" quality and worn to flout the convention of women using jewelry to define their status. Clients followed Chanel's lead in piling on strings of faux baroque pearls to create a glamorous, excessive look which was revolutionary.

By the 1920s, the fashion house was expanding and Chanel's jewelry lines extended to charm bracelets and jeweled belts, ropes, and gold-and-bead chains. Drawing on classical influences, her pieces featured clear and colored rhinestones and synthetic stones combined with real gems. They were designed to enhance her simple outfits, typified by the legendary "little black dress" of 1926—Chanel said she wanted to rid women of their frills. "Simplicity is the keynote of all true elegance," she told *Harper's Bazaar* magazine in 1923.

Throughout the 1920s and 1930s, Chanel was one of the leading names in Paris and worked with some of the great jewelers of the time. Notably, she collaborated with Maison Gripoix, whose designs featured "poured glass" stones. Gripoix specialized in *pâte-de-verre*, pouring glass into delicate brass frames to create rich Moghul- or Renaissance-style pieces. Chanel also worked with the Duke of Verdura, who had previously designed fabrics for her. Together, they produced some of the company's most desirable, classic pieces, including enameled and jeweled Maltese cross cuffs.

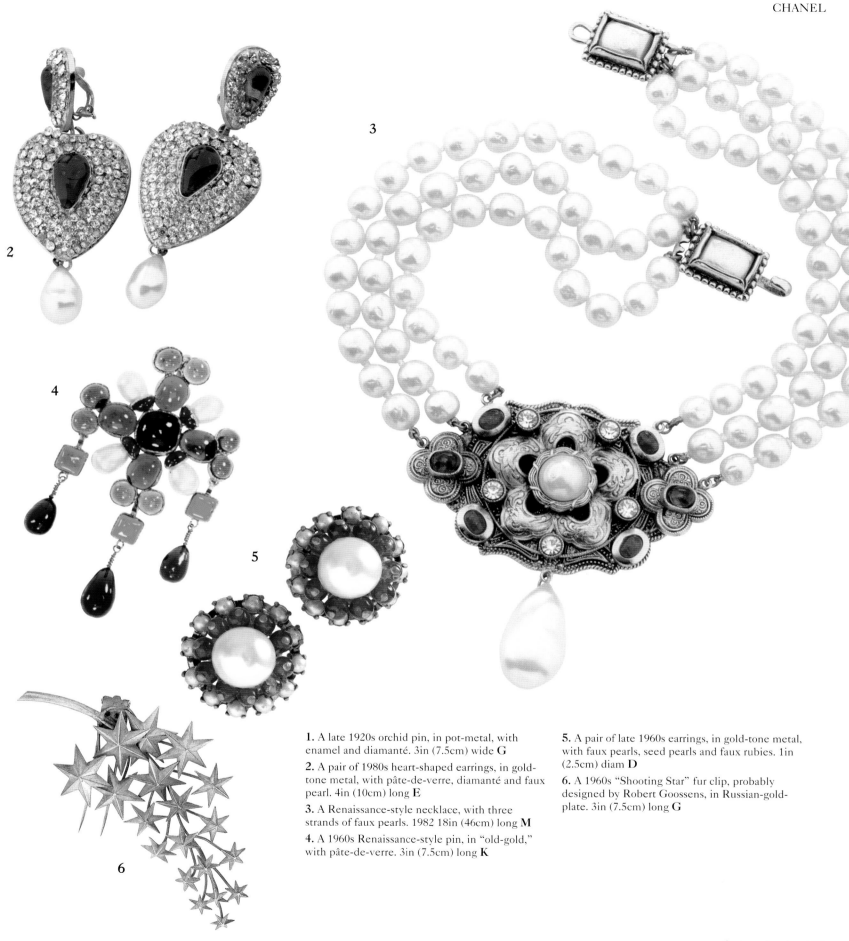

1. A late 1920s orchid pin, in pot-metal, with enamel and diamanté. 3in (7.5cm) wide **G**

2. A pair of 1980s heart-shaped earrings, in gold-tone metal, with pâte-de-verre, diamanté and faux pearl. 4in (10cm) long **E**

3. A Renaissance-style necklace, with three strands of faux pearls. 1982 18in (46cm) long **M**

4. A 1960s Renaissance-style pin, in "old-gold," with pâte-de-verre. 3in (7.5cm) long **K**

5. A pair of late 1960s earrings, in gold-tone metal, with faux pearls, seed pearls and faux rubies. 1in (2.5cm) diam **D**

6. A 1960s "Shooting Star" fur clip, probably designed by Robert Goossens, in Russian-gold-plate. 3in (7.5cm) long **G**

SETTING

Gold and pearl is a classic combination, and one that was popular during 1980s, when wealth was on display. Here the intricate metal design is emphasized by the simplicity of the faux pearl.

GILT CHAIN

Gilt chains were popular with Chanel from the 1920s onwards. She often wore several at a time. The cross pendant takes its shape from pre-Baroque pieces.

PEARL

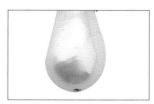

Chanel was the first to create costume jewelry that did not replicate precious jewelry, and by the 1980s this was common practice. The large size of this faux pearl drop makes it obviously false.

POURED GLASS

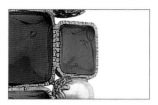

This piece can be distinguished from earlier Chanel by the "clunkiness" of the poured glass stones. Air bubbles can be easily seen. Like the pearl drop, these stones are proudly fake.

1

After her 15-year self-imposed exile in Switzerland during and after World War II, Chanel was ready to face the world again. Her Parisian comeback in 1954 saw her reinstated among the stars of haute couture, and she won back her admirers with the Chanel suit and pea jackets worn with bell bottoms.

In this new era, Chanel worked with gold- and silversmith Robert Goossens from 1955 onward, creating iconic designs such as Byzantine-style crosses on long chains of pearls and beads. Goossens was enchanted by artifacts from Parisian museums, drawing his influences from Maltese and Renaissance works, Byzantine mosaics, and stained-glass windows. He combined artificial gems with real stones collected on his travels. Rock crystal was his favorite material, lending delicacy to inexpensive pieces.

Most desirable to collectors are Maltese cross cuffs and pins by Verdura, floral-inspired necklace and earring sets by Maison Gripoix, and the rosary-style beaded pearl necklaces made by Goossens, which achieved iconic status in the 1960s.

Coco Chanel was still working when she died in 1971, at the age of 87. The company struggled under several creative directors until

2

"I don't understand how a woman can leave the house without fixing herself up a little—if only out of politeness. And then, you never know, maybe that's the day she has a date with Destiny. And it's best to be as pretty as possible for Destiny."

Coco Chanel

1. A 1980s Maltese cross necklace, in gold-tone metal, with poured glass and faux pearls. 20in (45cm) long **F**

2. A late 1980s/early 1990s cuff bracelet, in gold-tone-metal, with faux pearl and red and clear rhinestone. 6in (15cm) long **F**

3. A pair of 1980s "CC" earrings, in textured gold-tone metal. 2in (5cm) long **D**

4. A probably 1980s sautoir necklace, in gilded metal, with faux pearls, coins and "CC" motifs. 24in (61cm) long **D**

5. A 1990s Maltese cross pin, in gilt metal, with green, red, and pink poured glass cabochons. 2.5in (6.5cm) wide **C**

6. A pair of mid-1980s Chanel-style naively patterned sun earrings, in gilt metal, with faux baroque pearls. 2in (5cm) long **C**

1983, when Karl Lagerfeld became chief designer and started deconstructing the House of Chanel to modernize it. In a 1989 article for the *New Yorker*, fashion writer Holly Brubach accused Lagerfeld of desecrating the Chanel ethos—as symbolized by his brash overuse of the entwined "CC" logo—but his energetic reconstruction relaunched the brand. Under his leadership, the company produced costume jewelry echoing earlier designs, including long, gilt chains with pearls and glass beads, notably red and green, Coco's signature colors. Lagerfeld's first collection for Chanel was launched in 1983 and he maintains creative control of the house today. In 2005, Chanel acquired the company founded by Robert Goossens.

The 1980s saw branded luxury goods become the ultimate must-haves, and fakes abounded. Chanel's poured-glass pins from this time make good collecting as they were hard to fake, due to the difficult manufacturing process. Collectors also seek rare early Chanel jewelry in the original box. The box increases the value by at least 30 per cent.

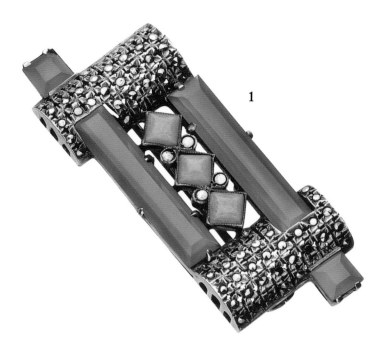

1

THEODOR FAHRNER

Fahrner is one of the most desirable names in European costume jewelry. The German company is known for its stunning Art Deco work, but it produced pieces in many other design styles.

Founded in 1855 in Pforzheim, southwest Germany, by Georg Seeger and Theodor Fahrner, the company originally made rings that reflected the contemporary interest in historicism. When Fahrner died in 1883, his son, also called Theodor, took over the company, expanding its output to cover all jewelry types and, more significantly, artistic styles.

Born in 1859, young Theodor Fahrner was a talented draftsman and designer who specialized in steel engraving at Pforzheim Art Academy. Innovative as well as highly creative, this pioneering industrialist joined the aesthetic reform movement known as Jugendstil, the German equivalent of Art Nouveau, and commissioned artists to create "modern" jewelry as the stock he had inherited from his father diminished. His intention was to raise the artistic quality of industrially or part-industrially made pieces to the level of art jewelry. Fahrner gave his designers great artistic freedom, as is revealed by the huge range of styles and techniques seen in the company's output. His ground-breaking use of the best artists to design mass-produced pieces was welcomed within the famed artists' community of Darmstadt, which provided many of the company's enthusiastic designers.

In 1900, the company won a silver medal at the Paris World's Fair for its *Künstlerschmuck* (artists' jewelry). This international recognition helped establish the company as the main manufacturer of Jugendstil artifacts in Germany. The "TF" trademark was introduced in 1901, and Fahrner began to export to England through Murrle, Bennet & Co., an Anglo-German agency with offices in both countries. Fahrner's work for Murrle, Bennet & Co. was often abstract, geometric, or organic, featuring elements such as stylized plants or birds. Pieces were marked with both companies' stamps.

In the early years of the 20th century, Fahrner was a leading figure in jewelry design, enabling, as he saw it, the "democratization of luxury." A selection of highly influential designers worked for the firm, including Georg Kleeman, Joseph Maria Olbrich, Franz Boeres, Rudolf Bosselt, Max Joseph Gradl, Hermann Haussler, Patriz Huber, Ferdinand Morawe, and others. Identifying the work of each specific designer can be problematic, however, because of the wide range of objects made and the broad selection of materials with which they worked. In addition, all archived information was lost when the Fahrner factory was bombed in 1945.

When Theodor Fahrner died in 1919, the company was sold to Gustav Braendle and renamed Gustav Braendle-Theodor Fahrner Nachfolger (German for "successors"), using the "Fahrner Schmuck" trademark.

In 1922, Braendle's new collections featured enamel and marcasite jewelry, combined with semi-precious stones. The enameling, done in-house and often with a matte finish, gave a distinctive edge to the work. The company's fabulous Art Deco pieces brought it much acclaim. The powerful geometric designs encapsulated the essence of the Jazz Age and the Art Deco movement, exemplified by the

2

3

4

geometric creations of designers such as Viennese painter Anton Kling. These pieces often employed more expensive materials, typically marcasite, semi-precious stones, coral, and pearls, which lead to the high prices Fahrner "art jewelry" commands today. Black enamel and green agate, combined with coral and onyx, became signature colors for Fahrner and for the Art Deco period.

Braendle developed and launched Fahrner's filigree jewelry range in 1932, which became a hallmark of the company.

Unfortunately, German politics had an impact on the company's design freedom. More sumptuous pieces were exported to England and the United States, while the home market was encouraged to seek plainer styles. In 1933, the sample design catalogues featured sketches for swastika designs. Wartime production was reduced and labor was transferred to technical products.

The company never regained its pre-war standing. Gustav Braendle died in 1952 and his son Hubert took over, leading the company through the 1950s, when it produced an enormous variety of designs and objects. The 1960s saw the introduction of modern silver pieces with semi-precious stones, as well as the "Antique Art" collection, featuring gold or silver pieces inspired by Egyptian and Roman designs. However, production ceased in 1979.

Fahrner's pieces are well marked, either "TF" or "TF Germany" or "TF ORIGINAL." There are unmarked pieces on the market; however, the lack of mark will reduce the value of a piece by as much as 75 per cent. Pieces made for Murrle, Bennet & Co have both "TF" and "MBC" marks.

5

1. A 1920s pin, in white metal, with blue glass stones, faux turquoise and marcasites. 2in (5cm) long **H**

2. A 1900s Arts and Crafts buckle, in silver, with stained agate cabochons and enamel. 3.25in (8.5cm) wide **M**

3. An octagonal flower pin, designed by Hermann Haussler, in silver, with enamel. 1910 14 1.5in (3.5cm) long **F**

4. A rare 1930s pineapples bracelet, in silver, with marcasites and aquamarine baguettes. 7in (18cm) long **M**

5. A dress pin, in silver, with lapis lazuli. 3in (7.5cm) long **F**

WEISS

Weiss designed some of the most beautiful, if underrated, rhinestone jewelry of the post-World War II period, skilfully presenting its Austrian crystal rhinestones of exceptional clarity and colour in handcrafted designs.

Albert Weiss learned to design and make costume jewelry at Coro, the largest costume jewelry manufactory in the United States, before going on to found the Weiss Company in New York City in 1942. The company flourished in the 1950s and 1960s, becoming recognized for its well-crafted, rhinestone-encrusted costume jewelry. The company was so successful that it commissioned Hollycraft to produce some of its work, in order to meet demand.

Weiss was noted for its use of components of exceptional quality, especially its Austrian crystal rhinestones that were usually prong-set to maximize their clarity and color. The rhinestones were set in fairly traditional forms, including floral, fruit, foliate, and figural jewelry

pieces, as well as a range of Art-Deco-style geometric designs. The figural pieces from the 1950s, particularly forms such as butterflies, insects, and single flower pins studded with rhinestones, are keenly collected. Settings were of high-quality gold- and silver-plated metals, and alloys were also used, sometimes enameled, while japanning became a widely employed design feature in the 1960s. Another desirable form from the 1950s was the Christmas tree pin, heavily studded in Weiss's characteristic rhinestones. Many of Weiss's Christmas tree designs were emulated by other costume jewelers.

The fashionable "aurora borealis" rhinestone was favored by Weiss and his team in the mid-1950s. "All the colors of a rainbow, captured in a new imported Austrian stone," ran the advertisement for Weiss's "aurora borealis" jewelry. Weiss's presentation was innovative—stones were sometimes inverted to reveal the more intensely iridescent effect of the underside. In the mid-1950s, Weiss also

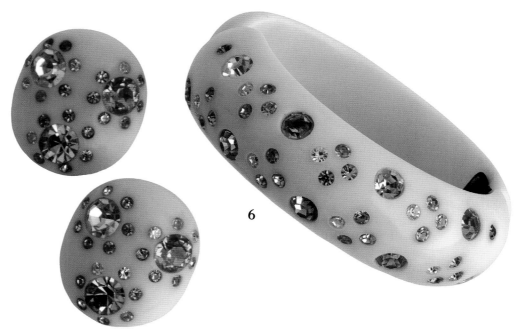

1. A 1950s parure, comprising a necklace, bracelet, pin, and earrings, with blue and green foiled Easter egg and poured art glass cabochon stones. Necklace 14.5in (37cm) long **E**

2. A pair of earrings, in gold-tone metal, with prong-set green, citrine, and clear aurora borealis rhinestones, marked "Weiss." 1.5in (3.5cm) long **B**

3. A pair of earrings, with rough-cut pink stone and lilac, green, and pink baguettes. 1.25in (3cm) long **B**

4. An *en tremblant* flower and butterfly pin, in gold-plate, with enamel and multi-colored rhinestones. 2.75in (7cm) high **B**

5. A 1950s flower pin, with white milk-glass navette petals, blue rhinestone chaton centre and green milk-glass navette leaf. 3.75in (9.5cm) long **C**

6. A 1950s clamper bracelet and earrings set, in cream celluloid, with multi-colored pastel rhinestone chatons. Bracelet 3in (7.5cm) diam **D**

1

2

3

4

1. A leaf pin and earrings set, in gold-tone metal, with prong-set light blue and turquoise rhinestones. Pin 2.75in (7cm) wide **B**

2. A pair of earrings, with faux aquamarine and emerald. 1in (2.5cm) long **B**

3. A 1950s pin, with green Austrian rhinestones. 2.25in (6cm) wide **D**

4. A pair of earrings, with prong set aurora borealis rhinestones, marked "Weiss." 1.5in (3.5cm) long **B**

developed a simulation of German smoky quartz, called "black diamonds." Set in typical Weiss designs, the "black diamonds" were highly realistic and very beautiful, and are keenly collected today. The copy for an advertisement in *Vogue* magazine in 1959 read: "Especially created for the smart new smoky-toned fashions. Distinctive gray Austrian rhinestones accented with tiny shimmering crystals designed by the pace-setter of fine jewelry, Albert Weiss."

When Albert Weiss retired in the 1960s, his son Michael took over the running of the company. As demand for costume jewelry declined in the late 1960s, the company failed. It ceased operations in 1971.

The Weiss Company's designs are comparable to those of Eisenberg and Bogoff but have been under-rated and under-priced by collectors, although prices are rising in today's market. Buyers should beware, however, as there are many Weiss fakes on the market. Collectors should be suspicious of poor color and clarity or stones that have been glued instead of prong-set. Weiss also manufactured unmarked pieces to sell wholesale through department stores. An experienced and reputable dealer can help collectors distinguish unsigned Weiss from fake.

From 1943, pieces were marked "Weiss" in script or block capitals, or "Albert Weiss" or "AW Co.," where the "W" is larger and in the shape of a crown. Tags may also bear this mark.

DESIGN

The Weiss look is based on more paste than metalwork, much like that of Kramer. This piece is especially desirable because it features Weiss's signature black diamonds.

STONES

The multi-faceted black stones glow and reflect many colors as the wearer moves, creating a pleasing effect. They contrast well with the diamanté and the silver-tone metal.

SHAPE

While the pin is asymmetrical, almost leaf-shaped, the earrings are much more symmetrical. Despite this they are clearly a set, due to their shared design elements.

CLASP

The relatively simple clasp is nevertheless part of the overall design. It is attractively curved, like the lighter details of the bracelet, and decorated with diamanté.

5

6

7

5. A 1950s bracelet, pin, and earrings set, in silver-tone metal, with black diamonds and diamanté. Pin 2.5in (6.5cm) wide **D**

6. A mid-1950s articulated bracelet, designed by Albert Weiss, in rhodium-plate, with prong-set baguette clear crystals, marked "Weiss." 7in (17.5cm) long **E**

7. A 1960s pin and earrings set, in silver-tone metal, with aurora borealis chatons and white opaque art glass cabochons. Pin 2.25in (6cm) long **C**

2

1

KRAMER

Louis Kramer created glistening, exuberant designs to suit all pockets. Such was the calibre of his work that he was invited to manufacture costume jewelry for Christian Dior in the early 1950s.

Kramer established his company, Kramer Jewelry Creations, in New York City in 1943, working with his brothers across a huge range of costume jewelry, in every price range. Like his contemporary Albert Weiss, Kramer favored a design style rich in stones. This extravagant look was especially suited to the well-dressed, luxury-loving glamor of the 1950s. Extensive diamanté and pavé rhinestone work, using the best Swarovski crystals, lent an exquisite sparkle to his beautiful, high-end pieces. Kramer's generous use of paste extended to crystal beads, textured glass, and faux colored pearls, as well as simulated lapis, jade, ruby, and sapphire. The "Golden Look" in the 1950s used gold-plate settings for his gorgeous gems, followed by the "Diamond Look" in the 1960s, which used silver plate to achieve an icy effect. Other key designs include rhinestones overlaid with black net.

Kramer preferred abstract patterns and his geometric designs found favor in the 1950s, but figural pieces are also known, including animals, birds, flowers, insects, and crowns. Along with many other costume jewelry designers, Kramer also made Christmas-themed pins that were especially popular during the Korean War, when they were worn and sent by mothers and wives to their menfolk abroad.

It was also during the early 1950s that Kramer began to manufacture pieces for Christian Dior in the United States. The House of Dior was insistent that costume jewelry sold under its name must reflect the design quality of the company's couture, and only the most reputable jewelers were commissioned to produce pieces. Dior recognized Kramer's skill and artistry. "Dior by Kramer" or "Kramer for Christian Dior" pieces are highly desirable to collectors and prices are rising. Christian Dior favored movement in his jewelry and may have

3

1. A late 1950s pin, with clear rhinestones, and sapphire crystal beads on jump rings, marked "Kramer." 2.5in (6.5cm) long **C**

2. A pair of earrings, with red, colourless, and purple rhinestones, and faux pearls, marked "KRAMER." 1in (2.5cm) high **A**

3. A late 1950s floral necklace, with faux sapphire and turquoise, marked "Kramer of New York." 16in (40.5cm) long **D**

4. A 1950s necklace, with pear-cut and chaton-cut diamanté. 15.75in (40cm) long **C**

5. A 1950s bracelet and earrings set, with facet-cut netted stones and black diamonds. Bracelet 7in (18cm) long **D**

6. A 1950s necklace and earrings set, with navette-cut faux sapphire and diamanté necklace. Necklace 17.5in (44.5cm) long **D**

4

5

6

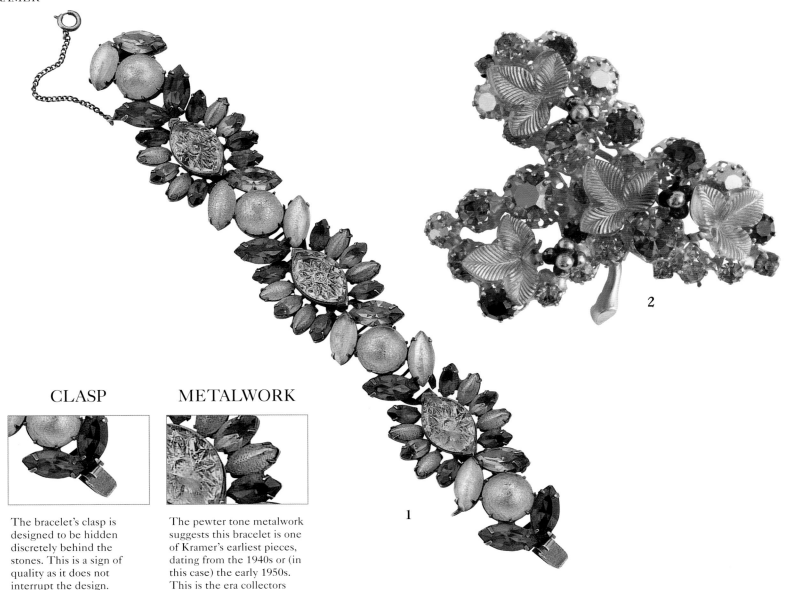

CLASP

The bracelet's clasp is designed to be hidden discretely behind the stones. This is a sign of quality as it does not interrupt the design.

METALWORK

The pewter tone metalwork suggests this bracelet is one of Kramer's earliest pieces, dating from the 1940s or (in this case) the early 1950s. This is the era collectors consider to be Kramer's best

DEPTH

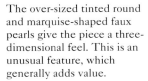

The over-sized tinted round and marquise-shaped faux pearls give the piece a three-dimensional feel. This is an unusual feature, which generally adds value.

STONES

These large and unusual textured stones are reminiscent of post-war Schiaparelli, and are desirable. Sadly, they would be impossible to replace.

inspired Kramer's use of crystal drops attached to jump rings, which catch the light as the wearer moves.

Astutely, Kramer's products were pitched at all price points: the higher-end pieces were marked "Kramer" or "Kramer of New York," while the lower-end items were simply tagged. "Kramer NY" and a pewter-toned metal setting dates a piece to the 1940s and 1950s, considered Kramer's best period. From the late 1950s onward, pieces were marked "Kramer" in an oval or triangular plaque. Other marks to look out for include "Amourelle," a line established by former Haskell designer Frank Hess when he went to work for Kramer in 1963, which is extremely rare; and "Kramer Sterling," which date from World War II, when sterling silver was used because other metals were restricted for war use. The company ceased production in the late 1970s.

Collectors look for wide bracelets with subtle color palettes, large rhinestone bibs, bows, and waterfall necklaces. Full parures, with the company's mark, are valuable. Along with its contemporary Weiss, Kramer is more highly regarded today than it was at the time, and prices are rising.

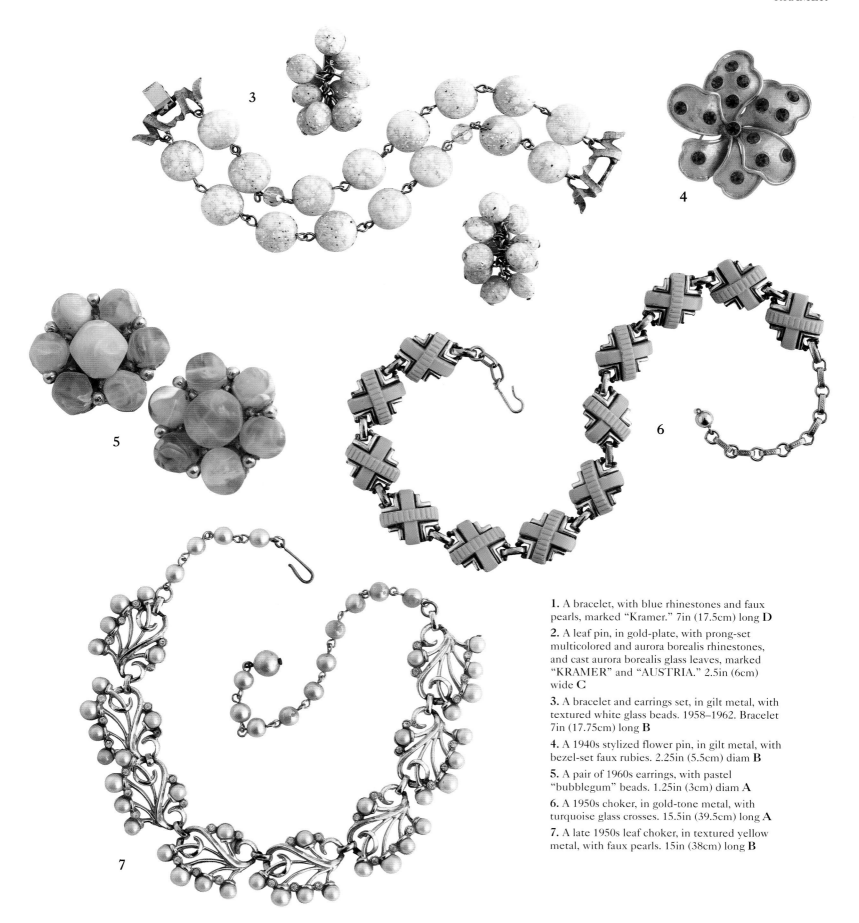

1. A bracelet, with blue rhinestones and faux pearls, marked "Kramer." 7in (17.5cm) long **D**

2. A leaf pin, in gold-plate, with prong-set multicolored and aurora borealis rhinestones, and cast aurora borealis glass leaves, marked "KRAMER" and "AUSTRIA." 2.5in (6cm) wide **C**

3. A bracelet and earrings set, in gilt metal, with textured white glass beads. 1958–1962. Bracelet 7in (17.75cm) long **B**

4. A 1940s stylized flower pin, in gilt metal, with bezel-set faux rubies. 2.25in (5.5cm) diam **B**

5. A pair of 1960s earrings, with pastel "bubblegum" beads. 1.25in (3cm) diam **A**

6. A 1950s choker, in gold-tone metal, with turquoise glass crosses. 15.5in (39.5cm) long **A**

7. A late 1950s leaf choker, in textured yellow metal, with faux pearls. 15in (38cm) long **B**

1

VENDÔME

In the 1960s, Vendôme became the byword for elegance and style in costume jewelry. Created by one of America's leading costume jewelry manufacturers, Coro, the brand brought the essence of Parisian chic to a rich and aspirational US market.

Coro first used the Vendôme mark on its charm bracelets, faux pearl necklaces, and other premium range jewelry items in 1944. By 1953, a complete Vendôme line was established which was designed to replace Corocraft, Coro's most expensive line. At this time, Vendôme began to operate as a separate, semi-independent subsidiary company. Named for place Vendôme, a Parisian square known for its fashion houses, the line was marketed at the wealthy American elite seeking to emulate the panache of post-war Paris.

In keeping with its premium image, Vendôme used the best-quality rhinestones and highly faceted crystal beads, imported from Austria and Czechoslovakia. Lucite came in colorless and colored forms. Faux pearls and enameling were of the finest quality. These components were hand-soldered to carefully wrought bases of silver-or gold-plated metals or gold-toned metal. Designs often had a three-dimensional quality where stones and settings overlapped, creating an expensive, well-crafted finish.

Until the 1960s, Vendôme presented pieces in standard floral or occasionally in geometric forms, and sales were low. However, the appointment of Helen Marion as chief designer changed the company's fortunes and her innovative designs and artistic integrity revitalized sales. Notable work by Marion includes elaborate reinterpretations of ethnic jewelry and delicate pieces with moveable parts. Most famously, she created a series of six collage-style pins based on the work of Cubist artist Georges Braque, consisting of a marine abstract, a Picasso-style face, the dove of peace, flying birds, an owl, and a pair of swimming fish.

The Richton International Corporation bought both Coro and Vendôme in 1957. The company closed in 1979. Pieces are marked "Vendôme" and feature a copyright sign, although the company also used a swing tag with the "V" and fleur-de-lis design.

1. A mid-1960s necklace and earrings set, with pearlized lilac plastic beads. 16in (40.5cm) long **D**

2. A 1950s bracelet, in yellow metal set with faux citrine and topaz cabochons. 2.5in (6.5cm) internal diam **D**

3. A 1950s fly pin, in clear and green diamanté, signed. 2.5in (6.5cm) long **C**

4. A pair of 1950s earrings, in silver-tone metal, with faux turquoise, colorless beads, and rhinestones. 1.25in (3cm) long **B**

5. A 1950s clamper bracelet and earrings set, in gilt metal, with faux pearl and diamanté. 3in (7cm) diam **D**

6. A 1950s Etruscan pin, in gold-tone metal, with faux turquoise, faux pearls, and rhinestones. 2.5in (6.5cm) diam **C**

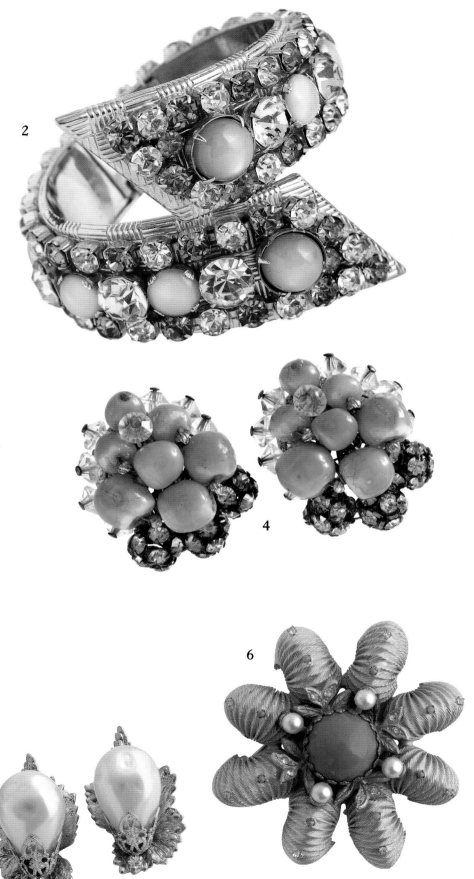

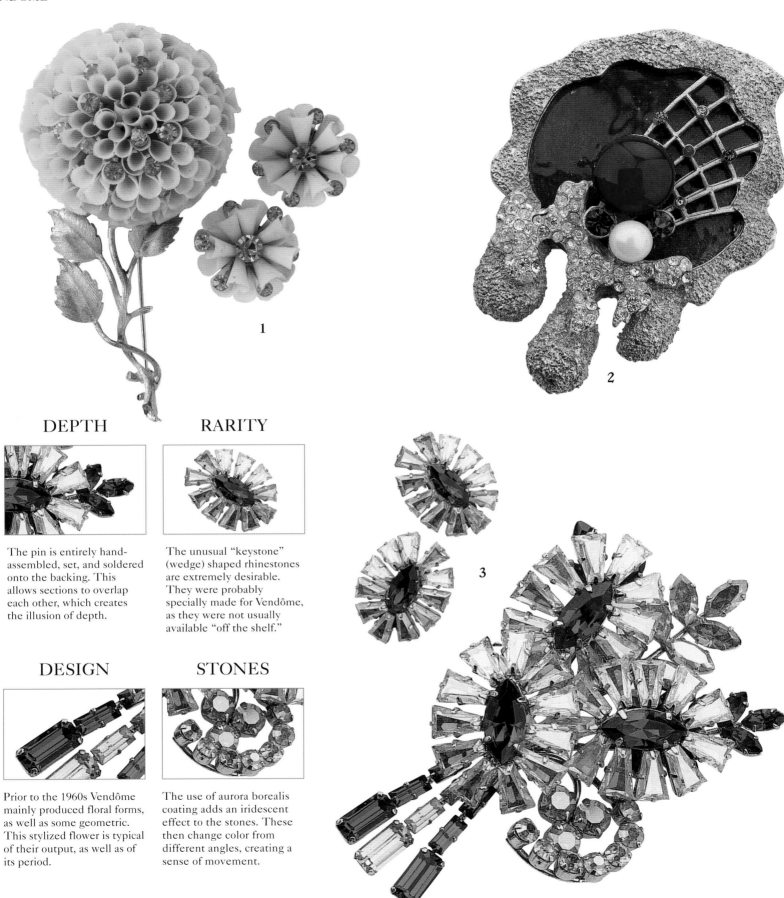

1

2

DEPTH

The pin is entirely hand-assembled, set, and soldered onto the backing. This allows sections to overlap each other, which creates the illusion of depth.

RARITY

The unusual "keystone" (wedge) shaped rhinestones are extremely desirable. They were probably specially made for Vendôme, as they were not usually available "off the shelf."

3

DESIGN

Prior to the 1960s Vendôme mainly produced floral forms, as well as some geometric. This stylized flower is typical of their output, as well as of its period.

STONES

The use of aurora borealis coating adds an iridescent effect to the stones. These then change color from different angles, creating a sense of movement.

1. A 1950s pompom flower pin and earrings set, in yellow metal, with yellow plastic petals and aurora borealis stones. Pin 4.5in (11.5cm) long **C**

2. A very rare mid-1960s George Braque-style pin, designed by Helen Marion, with a textured gilt frame around blue enamel. 2.25in (5.75cm) long **E**

3. A late 1950s bunch of flowers pin and earrings set, with green and clear aurora borealis stones. **D**

4. A 1950s necklace, sprung bracelet, and earrings set, of clear and blue glass. 2.5in (6.5cm) wide **D**

5. A 1950s feather pin, in white metal, with faux pearls and diamanté. 4.75in (12cm) long **C**

6. A mid-1950s bib necklace, in imitation hematite. 17in (43.5cm) long **D**

7. A mid-1950s floral pin and earrings set, in silver filigree, with green and blue crystal rhinestones and faux pearls. Pin 2in (5cm) long **C**

1

LISNER

Until recently, Lisner's clean, crisp, timeless style has been neglected by collectors on the lookout for bigger names. Now, the company's skilful designs in Lucite and rhinestones, coupled with their relatively low prices, are winning over collectors.

D. Lisner & Company was established in New York City in 1904. The company made its own fine-quality, unmarked jewelry and distributed pieces for others. In the 1920s, it sold well-made jewelry marked "Lanvin's Violet." Before the outbreak of World War II, Lisner became the US agent for Elsa Schiaparelli, importing and selling the designer's French-made pieces. Additionally, it had a license to produce her jewelry and accessories in the United States.

After the "Lisner" mark was introduced in the 1930s, the company became better known in its own right. It used the many jewelry manufacturers based in Providence, Rhode Island, to produce its pieces, including Whiting & Davis, known for its metal-mesh purses.

Lisner had its heyday in the 1950s, with its colored plastic and Lucite jewelry targeted at the lower end and mid-point of the market. Developed by DuPont in 1937, Lucite was an acrylic plastic that could be colored and shaped or molded. Many costume jewelers adopted it, and Lisner used it extensively, with impressive results. Lisner's color combinations and attractive designs, popular in their day, are again drawing attention. President of the company at the time was Victor Ganz, a creative driving force with a feel for fashion. He was keen to develop the clean, unfussy style that keeps Lisner pieces looking fresh today. Ganz told his daughter, Kate Ganz Belin, that he "tried to get away from the Mamie Eisenhower thing."

Working with Lucite or plastic, Lisner designed jewelry around geometric or abstract organic shapes, such as flowers. On higher-end pieces these crisply molded shapes were combined with clear or colored rhinestones, most frequently the much-loved "aurora borealis" rhinestone, or with exotic lava stones. Designs were set on silver-plated or chromed bases, or, in the 1960s, on black japanned metal. Metalwork was also enameled to great effect. These pieces were popular then and are desirable today.

2

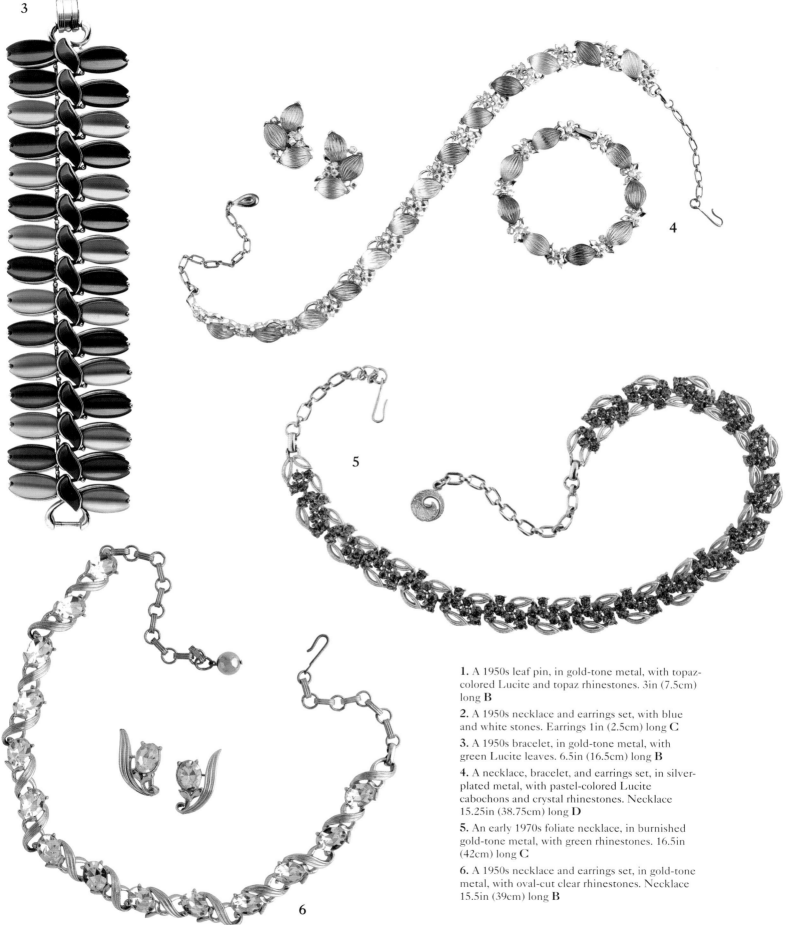

1. A 1950s leaf pin, in gold-tone metal, with topaz-colored Lucite and topaz rhinestones. 3in (7.5cm) long **B**

2. A 1950s necklace and earrings set, with blue and white stones. Earrings 1in (2.5cm) long **C**

3. A 1950s bracelet, in gold-tone metal, with green Lucite leaves. 6.5in (16.5cm) long **B**

4. A necklace, bracelet, and earrings set, in silver-plated metal, with pastel-colored Lucite cabochons and crystal rhinestones. Necklace 15.25in (38.75cm) long **D**

5. An early 1970s foliate necklace, in burnished gold-tone metal, with green rhinestones. 16.5in (42cm) long **C**

6. A 1950s necklace and earrings set, in gold-tone metal, with oval-cut clear rhinestones. Necklace 15.5in (39cm) long **B**

1

1. A 1950s leaf necklace, bracelet, and earrings set, in gilt-metal, with orange plastic and rhinestones. Necklace 16.5in (42cm) long **D**

2. A 1950s floral bracelet, in gold-tone metal, with white Lucite petals and clear crystal rhinestone. 6.75in (17cm) long **A**

3. A 1950s parure, comprising necklace, bracelet, pin, and earrings, in silver-plate, with pink, mauve, and white Lucite hearts and clear rhinestones. Necklace 16.5in (42cm) long **C**

4. A 1940s umbrella pin, in gilt metal, with yellow enamel and clear, faceted glass bead drops. 2in (5cm) long **B**

5. A 1960s garland pin, in silver-tone metal, inset with diamanté and faux pearls. 1.75in (4.5cm) high **B**

6. A 1960s Maltese cross pin, with faceted diamanté. 2.5in (6cm) long **B**

Lisner's pieces were not all of the highest quality but they reflected the design trends exemplified by high-end brands. The 1950s rhinestone sets are an example of this: while not of the calibre of jewelry made by Weiss or Kramer, they are still better made than comparable modern pieces. Similarly, Lisner's "leaves" are not of Schiaparelli's standard, but they are attractive and affordable.

In the late 1950s and into the 1960s, Lisner introduced a range marked "Richelieu," which was of better quality and more expensive. Pieces are scarcer today and, if in good condition, command relatively high prices.

Prices for Lisner designs were very low in the late 20th century, but as the price of work by more prized designers rises, so lower-division pieces such as Lisner's become more in demand. Well-designed marked pieces are set to increase in value.

The company used the "Lisner" mark in block capitals on its own pieces for the first time in 1935. In 1938, the "Lisner" mark in script was introduced. From 1959, "Lisner" in block capitals, with an elongated "L," was used. However, buyers should be aware that molds and dies were reused later, so the mark is not always a reliable indicator of the date of a piece..

In 1978, the company became the Lisner-Richelieu Corporation. Production ended in 1979.

2

COLOR

These pale 1950s shades are desirable, because they are wearable colors for many people. Other Lisner pieces can be found in orange and yellow, which is a less sought-after combination.

APPEARANCE

This set is very pretty with its pink and purple hearts, and mirrors the trends of more expensive pieces. It is also in excellent condition. All these factors add value and desirability.

PARURE

Complete parures are especially desirable to collectors. Often the earrings are missing, so that they are present in this set makes it more sought after.

DESIGN

The silver-plated metal complements the cool tones of the Lucite hearts and clear, colorless rhinestones.

1

2

KENNETH JAY LANE

The bright, bold, often extravagant designs of Kenneth Jay Lane embody his love of glamor and the spirit of the 1960s and 1970s. He was born in Detroit, Michigan, in 1930, and started working in the fashion world in the mid-1950s, first in the art department at *Vogue*, then designing shoes for Christian Dior and shoes and jewelry for Arnold Scaasi, before establishing his own business in 1963.

Lane's design career blossomed under the patronage of Diana Vreeland, the legendary fashion editor of *Harper's Bazaar* who became editor in chief of *Vogue* magazine in 1963. His high-impact designs spoke to Vreeland and she featured them in Vogue, where they had similar appeal to the fashionable women of the time. Lane's bold and brilliant work attracted an elite clientele, including Elizabeth Taylor, the Duchess of Windsor, and Jackie Kennedy. Wealth was not necessarily an issue, however, as Lane's prices have always been accessible to most.

Taking inspiration from the Renaissance and Egypt as well as Roman, Oriental, Asian, and Medieval styles, Lane favored the bright, the bold, and the colorful. His work played on many of the trends of the time, especially the interest in Asian and Oriental mysticism and religion. Preferred figural motifs include gods and goddesses, snakes, dancers, and religious figures such as the Buddha.

Pieces were innovatively designed and well made using good quality materials. Gilt base-metal pieces with intricate ethnic designs were encrusted with faux cabochons emulating semi-precious stones. Maharajah-style earrings, pins, and pendants were huge and pendulous and all his designs spoke of Lane's interest in Asian imagery. However, Lane did not draw solely on ethnic sources for his designs: the "Big Cats" pins from the 1960s were inspired by the "Panther" pieces Cartier's Jeanne Toussaint had designed for the Duchess of Windsor a decade earlier.

1. A 1960s ram's head bangle, in gold-tone metal, with rhinestones, marked "K.J.L." 3in (7.5cm) diam **D**

2. A 1970s snake pin, in silver-tone metal, with blue and clear rhinestones, marked "K.J.L.". 4.25in (10.5cm) long **E**

3. A 1980s Buddha and snake pendant necklace, in gold-tone metal, with mother-of-pearl and emerald glass cabochons, and with stone and metal pendants. Pendant 5.5in (14cm) long **D**

4. A 1970s twin ram's head bangle, in gold-tone metal, with clear, red, and green rhinestones. 3in (7.5cm) long **C**

5. A pair of 1960s Indian-inspired earrings, with faux ruby and amethyst, and diamanté. 3.75in (9.5cm) long **E**

6. A 1960s bib necklace, in white metal, with turquoise glass and clear rhinestones. Bib 7in (18cm) long **M**

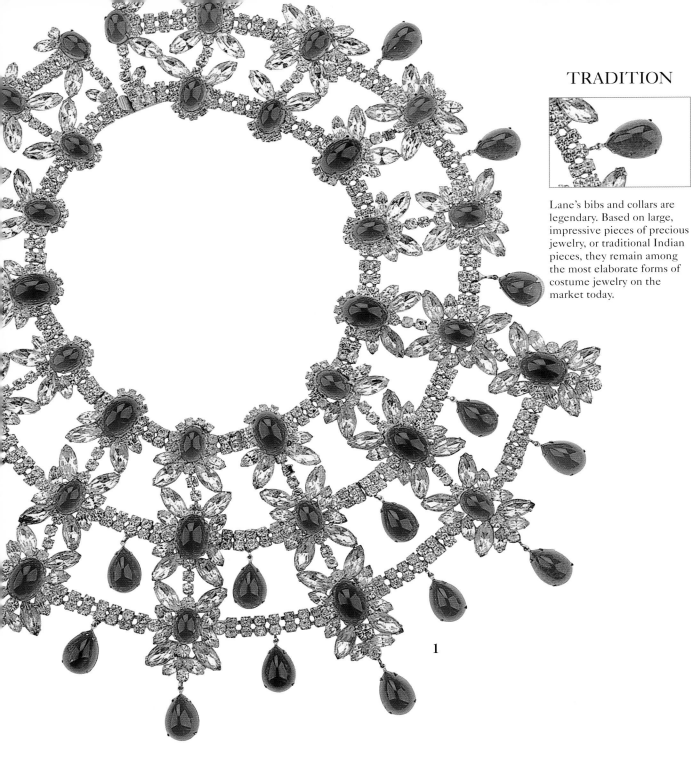

Lane's bibs and collars are legendary. Based on large, impressive pieces of precious jewelry, or traditional Indian pieces, they remain among the most elaborate forms of costume jewelry on the market today.

Each level is held to the one above with a "chain" of round, colorless rhinestones, with metal bands holding one to the next. These can sometimes snap, so it is important to check before purchasing.

STONES

The color of these large pieces is very important. Coral and turquoise are most sought after, and in these colors prices could be double what might be paid for this example, which is set with faux-carnelian.

1

Like the Cartier panther, Lane often created replicas of classic designs by the great jewelers such as Bulgari and Cartier. His creations are pieces of unbelievable opulence and magnificence, re-created in non-precious materials, yet they remain stunningly beautiful. These pieces were instrumental in persuading the jet set that costume jewelry was *en vogue*. Through the 1980s, when Lane started designing for Avon, and the 1990s, when he re-issued his "Jewels of India" line for sale via television shopping channel QVC, he continued to have a huge impact on the costume jewelry market.

His "Big Cats" pins are highly collectible today. Similarly sought after are other figural pieces, such as the ram's head, the walrus, the mermaid, and the chameleon. Enameled figural work is also especially desirable. Lane's classic pieces, which include chandelier earrings and opulent paste necklaces such as the one shown above, are also avidly collected.

Lane's designs dating from before the 1970s are marked "K.J.L." and are highly collectible. After the late 1970s, they are signed "Kenneth Jay Lane" or "Kenneth Lane."

1. A 1960s collar necklace, with prong-set carnelian-coloured stones and marquise rhinestones. 16in (40.5cm) long **F**

2. A 1970s catwalk pendant chain necklace, in gilt metal, with red and dark green glass beads. 29in (73cm) long **E**

3. A bracelet and earrings set, in gold-tone metal, with large green cabochons, blue beads, and diamanté. Earrings 1in (2.5cm) long **F**

4. A 1970s link bracelet, in gilt metal, with clear rhinestones. 1in (2.5cm) wide **C**

5. A 1980s coach pin, in gold-tone metal, with green, blue, and red rhinestones, faux amethyst drops, and faux sapphire cabochons. 3in (7.5cm) wide **C**

1

2

*"From the very beginning,
we never did subtle."*
Simon Wilson

BUTLER & WILSON

From humble beginnings selling vintage jewelry on a market stall in London, Butler & Wilson has become the name that puts the glitter into glitterati. Beloved of stars and favored by young royalty, the company brought vintage sparkle to the bling generation.

When their stall in the Antiquarius antiques market on London's King's Road proved successful, Nicky Butler and Simon Wilson opened a shop on the nearby Fulham Road in 1972. Unable to keep up with demand for their hand-picked vintage finds, they designed their first collection of costume jewelry, based on their period treasures. Able to call on their experience in handling antique Georgian, Victorian, Art Nouveau, and particularly Art Deco jewelry, the designers had a strong pedigree, and have re-interpreted vintage designs for the modern market for the last 40 years. Their influences are taken from vintage, Oriental, and Indian designs. The company's blend of traditional and modern styles consequently have exceptional global appeal.

1. An articulated lizard pin, in silver-tone metal, with clear rhinestones. 1985 7.75in (20cm) long **D**

2. A 1980s mask pin, in pewter-tone metal, with faux rubies, marked "B&W." 2.25in (6cm) high **B**

3. A 1980s tartan bow pin, in gold-plate, with red, blue, and green enamel. 2.5in (6.25cm) wide. **B**

4. A rare 1980s Amy Johnson pin, in plastic and chrome, signed "Butler & Wilson." 2.75in (7cm) wide **D**

5. A late 1980s Moorish prince pin, in gold-tone metal, with faux fire opal and red and green rhinestones, with faux baroque pearl drops, marked "B&W." 4in (10cm) long **C**

6. A late 1990s butterfly pin, in black enameled metal, with navette-cut pink and round black rhinestones. 2in (5cm) wide **A**

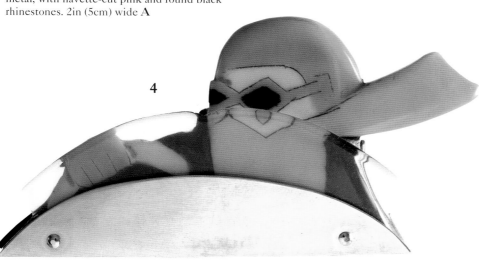

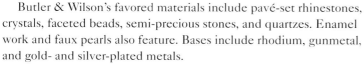

Butler & Wilson's favored materials include pavé-set rhinestones, crystals, faceted beads, semi-precious stones, and quartzes. Enamel work and faux pearls also feature. Bases include rhodium, gunmetal, and gold- and silver-plated metals.

Whimsy plays a strong part in Butler & Wilson's designs: teddy bears, champagne glasses, hands, spiders, bows, crowns, and monkeys all feature in the company's work. The striking black-and-white rhinestone-set dancing couple, with the lady wearing a fringed, swinging dress, and the articulated diamanté lizard that clambered up Princess Diana's lapel in Canada are both iconic pieces and much reproduced.

The articulated lizard pin is a fine example of Butler's & Wilson work, based on the silver, crystal-set lizard pins dating from Georgian and Victorian times. The beautiful pavé setting is a highly effective way of maximizing light through the rhinestones, as well as creating a lizard-skin effect. A skilful piece of design, the lizard's body and tail are not rigidly soldered, allowing the piece to "move."

The power-dressing couture of the 1980s demanded bold, showy jewelry and Butler & Wilson obliged with classics of the era such as huge jeweled bib necklaces and diamanté pins. Celebrities including Jerry Hall and Bianca Jagger modeled for the firm, snapped by photographers like David Bailey. Butler & Wilson's admirers include Madonna and Kylie Minogue.

The partnership broke up in the 1990s, with Simon Wilson retaining the name and taking the company to new heights during its 40th anniversary in 2009. Nicky Butler has continued to design jewelry under his own name.

Demand for Butler & Wilson's Christmas jewelry pieces, taking the form of a wide range of festive subjects, from Santa to reindeer, has gone from strength to strength. Featuring pavé-set rhinestones, their colors are bold and primary, and the figures are charming.

Early designs in particular have become highly collectable, notably the teddy bear, spider, and lizard pins. As 1980s fashion makes a resurgence, prices are likely to rise. Pieces may be signed "B&W."

MOVEMENT

The skirt is articulated, creating movement, which evokes the idea of dance. Although a 1980s piece, this pin has a very Art Deco feel, reminiscent of Clarice Cliff's "Age of Jazz" dancers, for example.

HUMOR

This pin has a lovely sense of humor about it, which is likely to make it appealing to collectors. The dancers' large multi-faceted stone heads are cut to reflect light and pick up color.

DESIGN

As a whole, this design is very well executed. The tightly-packed prong-set jet black stones contrast well with the large, single rhinestone heads of the couple.

1. A 1980s dancing couple pin, with prong-set clear paste heads, and black and clear rhinestones. 4.75in (12cm) long **B**

2. A 1980s charm bracelet, in gold-tone metal, with crown and fleur-de-lis pendants, and faux pearl drops. 7in (18cm) long **B**

3. A mid-1990s oriental dragon pin, in gold-plate, with blue and green metallic enamel and pavé-set clear crystal rhinestones and red cabochon eyes. 4.25in (11cm) long **D**

4. A 1980s snake necklace, with large black glass stones, and black, red, and colorless rhinestones. 21.5in (55cm) long **E**

3

4

1

HOBÉ

With "Jewels of Legendary Splendor" as its slogan, William Hobé's company made jewelry for film and theater, becoming a favorite of legendary director and producer Cecil B. DeMille.

Hobé was founded in Paris in the mid-19th century. Jacques Hobé was a master goldsmith and jeweler at the French court. However, with the advent of industrialization and mass production, Hobé began to produce costume jewelry with the same meticulous care he had previously devoted to making precious pieces.

In the mid-1920s, Hobé's grandson William emigrated to New York City. He began selling theatrical costumes and soon received a commission to make costumes and jewelry for the Ziegfeld Follies on Broadway, initiating the Hobé company's long association with the stage.

In 1927, William Hobé set up Hobé Cie in the United States, continuing the family firm's costume jewelry production. His antique-style jewelry became *en vogue* after *Gone with the Wind*, with its huge, romantic ballgowns, arrived on the silver screen in 1939.

Building on his ancestral interest in working with semi-precious and precious stones, William Hobé researched historical European jewelry. Consequently, from the mid-1920s until the 1950s, his designs and use of semi-precious materials set him apart from his contemporaries. Chrysoprase, lapis, garnet, amethyst, jade, and agate were combined with pearls and carved ivory panels, making his pieces, then as now, more expensive than typical costume jewelry. Vermeil silver pieces with hand-worked filigree created a romantic

feel popular in the 1930s and 1940s. Superb early pieces include carved cinnabar and ivory Oriental work and portrait miniatures, as well as highly prized reproductions of 16th- and 17th-century European precious jewelry.

Hobé is best known for floral pins designed as large bouquets, using a variety of semi-precious stones and quality pastes, and silver plate, vermeil, or platinum settings. His bouquet pins were popular in the 1930s and 1940s, selling in top-end stores, and are highly collectible today.

By the 1950s, Hobé rivaled Joseff of Hollywood as the jewelry supplier to the stars, including Bette Davis and Ava Gardner. His reputation with the public was consolidated by extravagant advertising campaigns using Hollywood's most beautiful actresses and top models.

Hobé succumbed to the more contemporary mood for glamor, and began using paste and base metals in glitzy designs in the vein of Kramer and Weiss. However, the designs were innovative and the pieces well made, so there is still high demand for this later work among collectors today, despite the cheaper materials. Additionally, Hobé maintained the quality of its craftsmanship and output by using only designs created by family members and designer Lou Vici, who worked for the company for 40 years from the 1930s onward.

The Hobé company remained in the family until the late 1990s, when it was sold. Today, it still produces signed pieces revisiting earlier designs.

1. A Hobé pin and earrings set, in gilt metal, with diamanté, pin marked "Hobé." Pin 2.5in (6cm) long **D**

2. A 1950s flower pendant necklace and earrings set, with gold faux pearls, peridot faceted crystal beads, and aurora borealis. Necklace 17.75in (45cm) long **D**

3. A 1940s bouquet bow pin, in sterling silver, with semi precious stones, marked "Hobé Design Pat." and "Sterling." 4in (10cm) long **E**

4. A late 1950s necklace and earrings set, with pale blue rhinestones and faux moonstones, marked "Hobé." 1in (2.5cm) long **D**

5. A 1950s heart pin and earrings set, in filigree gilt metal, with clear rhinestones and faceted faux sapphires. Pin 1.5in (4cm) long **D**

6. A 1950s necklace, bracelet, and earrings set, in gilt metal, with pink cabochons and aurora borealis diamanté. Necklace 13.5in (35cm) long **D**

1

SCHREINER

Henry Schreiner began his working life as a blacksmith in Bavaria, Germany. After immigrating to the United States in 1923, he used his metalwork skills to find employment in the thriving shoe buckle industry.

In 1939, Schreiner started making costume jewelry on a small scale, using high-quality colored crystal stones of unusual cuts. He established his own company in the early 1940s. His talent was spotted by Christian Dior, who gave him several commissions in the late 1940s and early 1950s. His work drew the attention of the fashion world and he went on to design pieces for American fashion designers Pauline Trigère and Normal Norell, making belts, buckles, and buttons in addition to his costume jewelry.

Schreiner became known for highly creative and elaborate designs, beloved of stars such as Marilyn Monroe and Bette Davis. Despite his growing reputation, Schreiner took the decision to keep the company small. Consequently, his exclusive designs were beautifully set and finished by hand. His work typically used paste, rhinestones, and top-quality diamanté and crystal in unconventional color combinations, to stunning effect. He commissioned the unusually shaped and colored crystals he preferred from manufacturers in Czechoslovakia and Germany.

Many designs were abstract, featuring unique paste stones in extraordinary settings. A characteristic of Schreiner's work was the inverted-set stone, where the pointed back of the stone was presented uppermost in the setting, with the flat front set face down.

The idea was to pick up the color of the garment being worn and to add sparkle. He also played with different cuts and subtle but unusual color combinations, favoring smoky grays, light browns, pale yellows, and soft greens. Stones were often unfoiled so that the wearer's clothes showed through, making pieces more versatile, with each creating a unique effect depending on the outfit being worn. Pewter-colored settings are typically Schreiner, and he used the less common hook-and-eye construction on necklaces.

Schreiner also made some figural pins. His "ruffle" flower pins present long, tapering, keystone-shaped stones at differing depths that lend each piece a three-dimensional, fluttering quality. Other figural subjects include a range of flowers such as daisies, geraniums, and sunflowers, as well as acorns, turtles, dragonflies, peas in a pod, pineapples, and carrots.

Schreiner's daughter Terry and her husband Ambrose Albert joined the firm in the early 1950s. Although Schreiner died in 1954, the company continued production until the mid-1970s, when the dramatic radicalization of fashion led to the decline of many established costume jewelers.

Pieces are marked "Schreiner New York," "Schreiner," or "Schreiner Jewelry" on an oval plate. Relatively few examples of Schreiner's work are on the market today, because of his exclusivity at the time, so pieces can fetch high prices. The beauty of his work is timeless, the quality of the stones superb, and the styles still appeal to collectors. Huge bib necklaces and parures fetch a premium.

1. A 1940s flower pin, in gold-tone metal, with green glass petals. 2.25in (6cm) wide **E**

2. A 1950s bib necklace and earrings set, marked "Schreiner New York." 14in (34cm) long **M**

3. A 1950s pin and earrings set, in faux gold filigree, with topaz, olive, and green crystal. Pin 3in (7.5cm) wide **D**

4. A pair of probably 1950s earrings, in clear paste, marked "Schreiner." 2in (5cm) long **D**

5. A pair of 1960s earrings, of faux aquamarine, with circular and teardrop-shaped rhinestones. 1.25in (3cm) long **C**

6. A 1950s pendant, marked "Schreiner New York" on a plaque to the reverse. Pendant 3in (7.5cm) long **H**

7. A 1950s necklace and earrings set, with faceted clear paste stones. Necklace 14in (34cm) long **K**

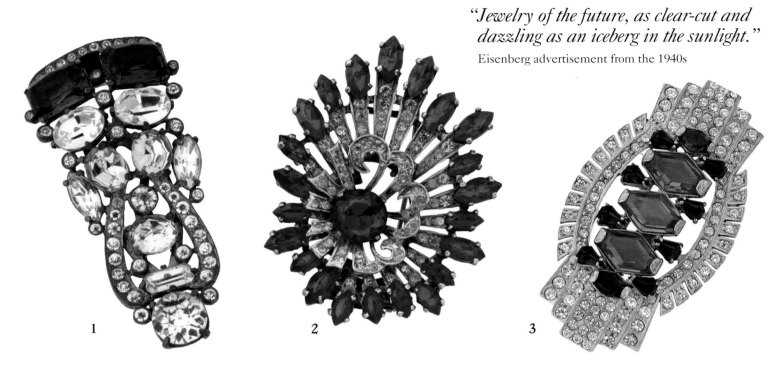

1 2 3

EISENBERG

Eisenberg was renowned as one of the finest costume jewelry companies of the 1930s and 1940s, as a result of its excellent workmanship and the stunning use of Swarovski crystals.

Eisenberg Original was an American clothing company, established in 1914 in Illinois by Jonas Eisenberg, an émigré from Austria. In the 1920s, the company began to accessorize its outfits with its own pin designs, pinning or sewing the pieces onto garments, which were sold only through the finest stores in the United States. The paste jewelry was so admired that when customers found out they could not buy it separately, they began to steal it. By 1930, Eisenberg began producing pins as a separate line, and soon the range was expanded to include necklaces, bracelets, and earrings.

Early Eisenberg Originals are large, free-flowing designs with asymmetrical bows and swirls, popularized at the time by Hollywood. In the 1940s, base metals were restricted for war use, so from 1943 to 1948 Eisenberg used sterling silver, and pieces became lighter and more detailed. Wartime rumors claimed that diamonds were being smuggled into America disguised as rhinestones in Eisenberg jewelry, but this has never been verified.

From 1940 to 1972, Ruth M. Kamke was head designer. She had started designing at Fallon & Kappel, who manufactured exclusively for Eisenberg. After her appointment she created almost all the pieces marked "Eisenberg Originals" and the "Eisenberg Ice" range.

The fashion in the 1950s, defined by Dior's "New Look," was for femininity. Emulating Kramer and Weiss, Eisenberg used richly colored rhinestones in dainty necklace and earring demi-parures, which replaced its large pins and clips. In "Eisenberg Ice" pieces, Swarovski rhinestones were now highly faceted.

Eisenberg is popular with collectors because of its craftsmanship and its bold, clean, and typically large designs featuring Swarovski rhinestones, the high lead content of which give exceptional sparkle. Simulated glass stones and faux pearls are also employed to great effect. The pieces use sterling silver, white base metal, or silver- and gold-plated metal. Typical forms include Art Deco-inspired, medallion-like pins or clips of aqua, ruby, and clear crystals, and organic, abstract pieces. Also popular are the pins featuring kings and queens, and those in the form of mermaids, ballerinas, and animals. Some represent children's characters or stories such as Puss in Boots. Early 1940s figures are avidly collected.

Also eye-catching are the citrine-set sterling silver pieces, branded "Topaz Quartz" by the company. In the 1970s, it also made simple, enameled floral pieces, and the more expensive "Artists" series, featuring hand-painted enamel on gold. Most rare of all is the 1994 Christmas tree pin featuring navette-cut "aurora borealis" rhinestones in two colorways—only 80 of each colorway were made.

From 1930 to 1945, pieces were marked "Eisenberg Original." From the mid-1940s onward, they bear the mark "Eisenberg Ice." Sterling silver pieces were marked "Eisenberg Sterling" from 1943 to 1948. From 1952 to 1970, many pieces were unmarked. From 1970 to the present, "Eisenberg Ice" is used. An initial or number on the back of "Eisenberg Originals" identifies which designer set the stones. The company is still in production today.

1. An early 1940s fur clip, in base metal, with Swarovski rhinestones and faux sapphires. 3in (8cm) long **E**

2. A 1940s starburst fur clip, in silver, with faux rubies and diamanté. 3in (8cm) long **F**

3. A 1920s pin, in silver-tone metal, with colorless, orange, and green rhinestones. 3in (8cm) long **D**

4. A 1970s "melons" necklace, bracelet, and earrings set, in silver-tone metal, with pavé-set diamanté. Necklace 17in (43cm) long **D**

5. A dress clip, with colorless rhinestones. c1935 4in (10cm) long **E**

6. An "Ice" bracelet, with colorless rhinestones. 1963 7in (17.5cm) long **D**

7. A mid-1930s flower pin, in silver, with prong-set cranberry-colored faceted stones and clear rhinestones. 4in (10cm) long **E**

8. A 1940s bow pin, in base metal, with colorless rhinestones. 3in (7.5cm) wide **F**

9. A 1940s pin, in sterling silver, with diamanté, stamped "STERLING." 3.25in (8.5cm) wide **E**

10. A pair of earrings, with colorless rhinestones. 2in (5cm) long **G**

1

MAZER & JOMAZ

"The precious look in fashion jewelry," ran an advertisement in *Harper's Bazaar* in November 1948. This sentiment epitomized the pieces produced by Mazer Brothers—and later by Jomaz—thanks to the company's close ties to traditional fine jewelry design.

A New York City firm founded in 1927 by the Russian émigré brothers Joseph and Louis Mazer, the company produced mid-range jewelry simulating precious pieces. It quickly gained a reputation for quality and affordability. In the early 1930s, Marcel Boucher began designing for Mazer Brothers, bringing his skills in fine jewelry design to the company and to the field of costume jewelry in general. Early work from Mazer consisted of classic floral or ribbon-and-bow motifs, featuring "Sea-Maze" faux pearls or rhinestones, often in highly worked settings.

Mazer's production from the 1930s and 1940s was made with the same care, precision, and quality for which the company had become known. Sterling silver or vermeil silver was predominant and pieces included lavish cocktail necklace parures and large, square-cut pastes. The 1930s surreal "Eye" bracelet and earrings set is avidly collected today. An opaque blue cabochon was used for the iris and baguette-cut rhinestones make up the eyelashes. The company also produced "Duette" pins and crown jewel pins, emulating those popularized by Trifari and Coro.

In 1946, Joseph Mazer went on to establish his own company, Joseph J. Mazer & Co. The name was soon shortened to Jomaz, although it was never registered as such with the U.S. Patent Office.

Production from the 1950s included pieces imitative of fine jewelry, including opulent paste jewels in lavish bib-necklace designs with pendant earrings. André Fleuridas produced many of the pieces from the early 1950s, and Adolfo designed some pieces for the company in the 1970s. Designs were innovative and unusual, many reflecting the influence of Marcel Boucher, especially where metals are combined to create a two-tone effect, with irregular outlines and texture. The company maintained a reputation for fine quality and was recognized for its exquisite stone cutting and setting.

Silver and rhodium-plated bases were used in Jomaz's early work, but gold-plating and gold-metal alloys became a design feature in the 1960s, often with innovative textured finishes and used as a setting for fine Swarovski crystals, pavé-set rhinestones, and brightly colored pastes. Production in the 1970s reflected the market's love of large and exuberantly colored costume jewelry.

Jomaz was run by Joseph Mazer's son in the 1960s, and by his widow for a short time after his death. Louis Mazer left Mazer Brothers in 1951 and the company ended production in 1977. The Jomaz company closed in 1981.

Mazer Brothers' large vermeil cuffs and vermeil chunky link bracelets are sought after, especially if they feature large pastes in aquamarine or amethyst. The heavy 1940s clips and pins still attract good prices for top-end pieces.

Early work is marked "Mazer Bros." Later work from Jomaz has the mark "Mazer," "Joseph Mazer," or "Jomaz."

1. A 1950s Jomaz sunburst pin, in silver-plate, with faux emerald and daimanté. 2in (5cm) diam **C**

2. A 1930s Mazer floral necklace and foliate earrings set, in white metal, with faux ruby and diamanté. Centerpiece 2in (5cm) diam **E**

3. A pair of 1950s Mazer earrings, in gold-plate, with pale blue crystals, clear rhinestones, and faux pearls. 1in (2.5cm) long **C**

4. A Mazer "King and Queen" crown pin, in sterling silver, with faux amethyst cabochons, and red, blue, green, and clear crystal rhinestones. 2.5in (6.5cm) high **E**

5. A pair of 1940s Jomaz earrings, in white metal, with baguette and paste stones, and faux pearls. 1.25in (3.5cm) long **C**

6. A Jomaz bracelet, pin, and earrings set, in gold-tone metal, with enamel and diamanté. Pin 1.5in (4cm) long **J**

7. A 1940s Mazer pin and earrings set, in vermeil sterling silver, with faux emeralds and rhinestones. 1.75in (4.5cm) long **E**

8. A late 1950s Jomaz necklace and earrings set, with blue cabochon crystals and clear rhinestones, marked "Jomaz." Necklace 15in (38cm) long **F**

1

HATTIE CARNEGIE

Legend has it that as the Kanengeiser family set sail from Europe for the promised land of America, their young daughter asked the name of the richest man in the country. Adopting industrialist Andrew Carnegie's name for herself, Hattie Carnegie went on to build a fashion empire and achieve spectacular commercial success.

Born Henrietta Kanengeiser in Vienna, Austria, in 1886, Hattie Carnegie emigrated to the United States with her family at the turn of the century. Initially, she worked as a milliner's assistant at Macy's department store in New York City, but in 1913, she opened the first of a series of dress and millinery shops with Rose Booth, who made the dresses while Carnegie designed the hats. The success of this enterprise led to her establishing Hattie Carnegie Inc. in 1918, and she started making jewelry to accessorize the company's outfits.

Carnegie was an innovative designer, eschewing the trend for copying fine jewelry in favor of creating her own—very expensive—designs. Early ideas were based on clips and pins in vermeil silver or base metal. She produced big, retro, abstract designs and enamel figurals in the form of animals and human faces, all commanding high prices today.

Hattie Carnegie Originals, her ready-to-wear line, was launched in 1928. By the 1930s, she was established as a top name in the fashion world. She was known for her palazzo pajamas and simple black dresses, which she accessorized with feminine designs, producing small quantities of jewels that are rare today. Joan Crawford was a big

fan, buying many of her pieces, as were other Hollywood goddesses, including Tallulah Bankhead, Joan Fontaine, and Norma Shearer.

She commisioned other designers, such as Norman Norell, Pauline Trigère, and Claire McCardel, to create her pieces. They incorporated many forms: floral and fruit motifs were used, alongside Oriental figures and stylized animal pins. But Carnegie is perhaps best known for "trembling" necklaces: the designs featured butterflies and flowers on springs that vibrated as the wearer moved. Materials included poured glass, faux pearls, plastic stones and beads, and rhinestones, with enameled, gold- or silver-plated bodies. The look was "frankly fake" and boldly chic.

Mass production of Carnegie jewelry by the late 1950s had mixed results, and some rather unexciting gilt flower pins and abstract paste designs were made. However, there were some flashes of brilliance: in the 1960s, the "Antelope" pin, inspired by primitive art, used bright plastic to emulate jade, coral, turquoise, and lapis, offset with shimmering pastes. The dramatic design was stylish and bold. Not as valuable but still collected are the elephants, fish, butterflies, and birds made in this style. Other desirable pieces include circus horses, clowns, and butterfly pins, as well as chandelier earrings.

In 1956, following Carnegie's death, the company was sold to Larry Joseph, then in 1976 it was bought by the Chromology American Corp. Marks include "HC" or "HAC" in a diamond shape, or "Carnegie" or "Hattie Carnegie."

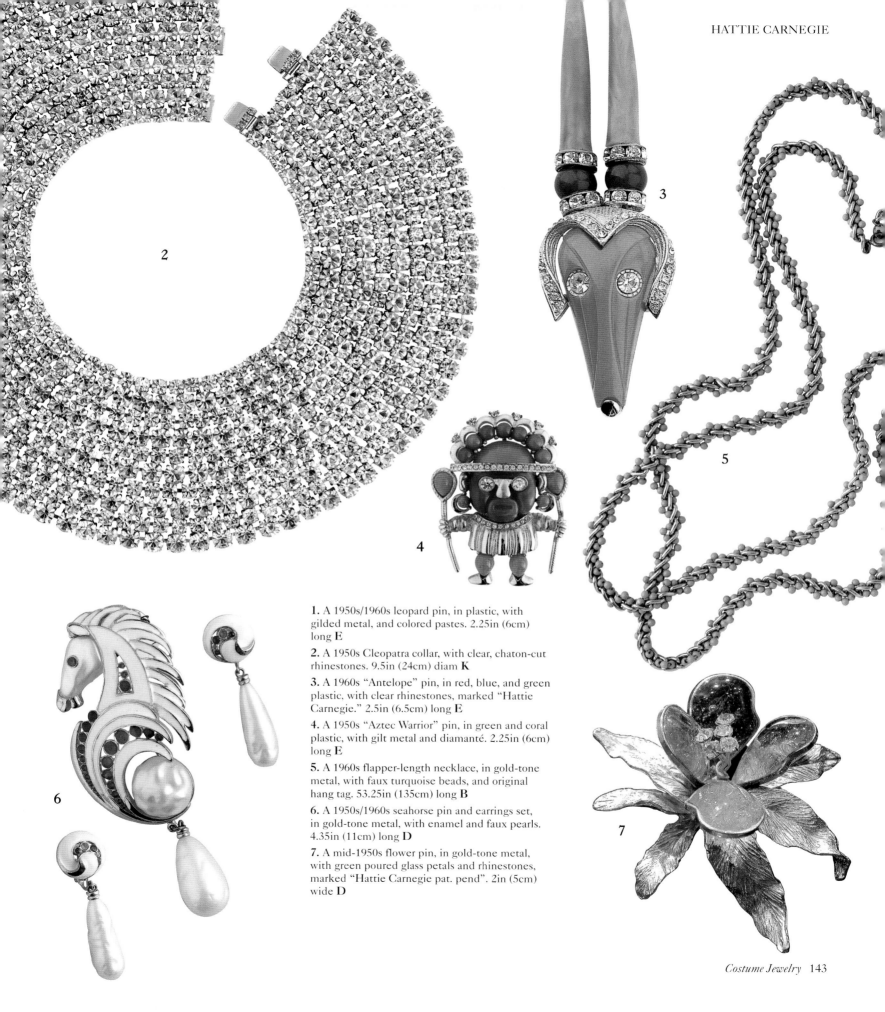

1. A 1950s/1960s leopard pin, in plastic, with gilded metal, and colored pastes. 2.25in (6cm) long **E**

2. A 1950s Cleopatra collar, with clear, chaton-cut rhinestones. 9.5in (24cm) diam **K**

3. A 1960s "Antelope" pin, in red, blue, and green plastic, with clear rhinestones, marked "Hattie Carnegie." 2.5in (6.5cm) long **E**

4. A 1950s "Aztec Warrior" pin, in green and coral plastic, with gilt metal and diamanté. 2.25in (6cm) long **E**

5. A 1960s flapper-length necklace, in gold-tone metal, with faux turquoise beads, and original hang tag. 53.25in (135cm) long **B**

6. A 1950s/1960s seahorse pin and earrings set, in gold-tone metal, with enamel and faux pearls. 4.35in (11cm) long **D**

7. A mid-1950s flower pin, in gold-tone metal, with green poured glass petals and rhinestones, marked "Hattie Carnegie pat. pend". 2in (5cm) wide **D**

1

2

HAR

Har was one of the manufacturers at the forefront of costume jewelry design in the 1950s. Yet the company's background is wreathed in mystery—as intangible as the fabulous, green-hued designs for which the firm is known.

The accepted belief was that Har was a Californian company, in production for a short period from 1955. However, jewelry historian Roberto Brunialti recently found information in the copyright files of the Library of Congress in Washington, DC, revealing that Har was owned by Hargo Creations of New York City. In fact, the company was founded in 1955 by a husband-and-wife team, Joseph Heibronner and Edith Levitt. Jewelry historian Susan Klein researched the pair, discovering that Heibronner was born in 1893 in Munich, Germany. He became a US citizen in 1948 and married Levitt in 1952. It is known that Heibronner died in 1968, and no further records of the company were found after 1967. Research has also shown that some of the most desirable Har pieces, such as the "Dragon" designs and the "Genie" set, can be dated to April 1959, according to U.S. copyright records.

At some point after 1955, the Har company was renamed "Art," presumably when it changed hands. Consequently, there are many designs by Har that have been found signed "Art," where existing designs were revisited by the new owners.

With its unusual and distinctive metalwork, the company's pieces, stamped "Har," often take fantastical and exotic forms—dragons, snakes, genies, and oriental and African figures, sometimes with a matte antique finish. As with much 1950s costume jewelry design, great use was made of the "aurora borealis" crystal produced by Swarovski. Its rainbow gleam gave a mystical air to Har's fabulous creations. The company also excelled at enameling, especially on figural pieces such as its "Monkey" pin.

Har jewelry is highly collectible. The small production runs and extraordinary, exotic designs, combined with the company's mysterious provenance, mean that Har pieces can fetch staggering prices today. Desirable pieces and parures, such as the "Dragon" design, with its gold-toned, green-enameled, sinuous form, set with iridescent stones to fantastical effect, are much sought after and

1. A "Dragon" necklace and earrings set, in yellow-metal, with enamel and aurora borealis. c1955 Earrings 1.5in (4cm) long **I**

2. A branch pin, in gold-plate, with faux turquoise, and red rhinestones. 2.5in (6.5cm) long **A**

3. A 1950s rabbit-on-a-carrot pin, in gold-tone metal, with enamel and clear rhinestones. 1.5in (3.75cm) long **C**

4. A "Dragon" pin, in gold-tone metal, with enamel and crystal, marked "Har". 1955 3in (7.5cm) long **B**

5. A pair of 1950s cobra head earrings, in gold-plate, with aurora borealis lava stones, enamel, and topaz rhinestones. 1.4in (3.5cm) long **D**

6. An oriental head pendant bracelet, in silver-plate, with Lucite head with faux jade cabochons and aurora borealis. 7in (18cm) long **D**

7. An early 1960s cart pin, in antiqued metal, with plastic fruit. 3in (7.5cm) long **C**

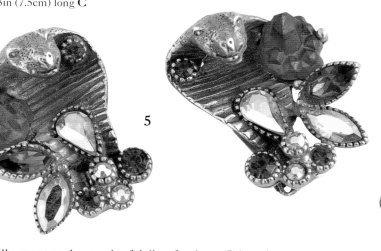

collectors will pay many thousands of dollars for them. Other pieces of Har jewelry, in good condition, also command high sums, including "Cobra" pieces; Oriental figures with faux ivory faces; and "Arabian Nights Genie" pieces.

Novelty pieces such as fruits, vegetables, leaves, flowers, and whimsical figures are gaining in popularity and are increasingly sought after by collectors. More traditional, classical jewelry designs with rhinestones and pearls, faux turquoise, and coral, are also desirable. Distinctive pieces also feature large, iridescent, irregularly shaped stones.

The metal Har used to make the bodies of its pieces is soft and can crack, so collectors should check items for damage and repairs. Similarly, the enameling can wear, affecting value.

LEA STEIN

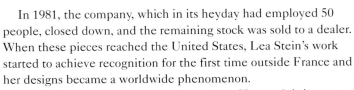

1

When the 1960s floated in on a cloud of flower-powered anti-establishment optimism, along with its vision for a new world that included futuristic materials in psychedelic colours, Lea Stein was poised and ready.

Stein was born in Paris in 1931 and trained as an artist. In 1957, she established her own textile design company and, from 1965, began to design and make buttons for the fashion industry. In 1967, she moved to a new process of button-making, which used laminated rhodoid. The process was developed by Stein's chemist husband, Fernand Steinberger, using a material—similar to Bakelite—which consisted of layers of colored cellulose acetate bake-bonded together. Stein adapted this process to the manufacture of costume jewelry in 1969, adding fabric, lace, metallic inclusions, or even straw between the layers to vary the color and texture of each piece. The composition was pressed, baked, stenciled, cut, and shaped, producing high-impact, polychrome "plastic" jewelry. As a result of the manufacturing process, each piece is unique.

The material was used to make pins, rings, bracelets, earrings, necklaces, and even jewelry boxes. Although Stein experimented with Art Deco-style geometric designs to great effect, figural pins dominated production. Favorite motifs included animals, birds, insects, children, cars, stars, hearts, rainbows, and eyes. The process even allowed for rare portrait pins, and pins of Joan Crawford and Elvis Presley were made. Possibly the most famous and highly sought-after is the "Scarlett O'Hara" ballerina pin, its voluptuous red skirt reminiscent of Vivien Leigh's sumptuous costumes in *Gone with the Wind*.

However, Stein's signature piece is the "Fox" pin. Due to a clever use of perspective, the fox, with its sweeping tail, appears to be jumping. Further detail is added using fabric or metallic inclusions in the laminate, the variation in texture and color enhancing the three-dimensional quality of each piece. A huge range of finishes is available, including glitter and snakeskin.

For collectors, the prize object is a pin from the "L'île aux Enfants" range. Based on characters from a French children's television series, the Casimir, Calimero, and Tiffins designs are charming and, since they were only produced in 1975, very rare. Early vintage pieces, such as the "Tennis Lady," Rolls-Royce, "French Sailor," and saxophone are also avidly collected.

In 1981, the company, which in its heyday had employed 50 people, closed down, and the remaining stock was sold to a dealer. When these pieces reached the United States, Lea Stein's work started to achieve recognition for the first time outside France and her designs became a worldwide phenomenon.

Lea Stein began designing again in 1988. Her work is in great demand by collectors, and the limited range of new designs she produces each year is eagerly anticipated.

Designs are marked "Lea Stein Paris." On pins this mark can be found on the distinctive V-shaped clasp. It is difficult to identify pieces to the first or second phase of production, so it is a good idea to contact a reputable dealer.

1. A mid-1990s "Fox" pin, in mottled orange celluloid, with inlaid eyes. 3.5in (9cm) long **B**

2. A late 1980s "Felix Brothers" cat pin, in red, black, gray, and blue laminated Rhodoid. 3.25in (8.5cm) high **C**

3. A late 1980s owl pin, in red, black, and gray laminated Rhodoid. 1.5in (3.5cm) high **B**

4. An early 1980s "half-Colorette" pin, in red, black, and grey laminated Rhodoid. 2in (5.5cm) diam **C**

5. A 1970s/1980s "Ballerina" (or "Scarlett O'Hara") pin, in red, white, and gray laminated Rhodoid. 2.5in (6.5cm) high **C**

6. A late 1980s "Ric the Dog" pin, in blue, gray, brown, and white laminated Rhodoid, with metallic inclusions. 3.5in (9cm) long **B**

7. An early 1980s "Indian Chief" pin, in blue, black, gray, and white laminated Rhodoid, with lace inclusions. 2in (5.5cm) high **C**

8. A tortoise pin, in red plastic, with glittering patterned shell. 3in (7.5cm) long **B**

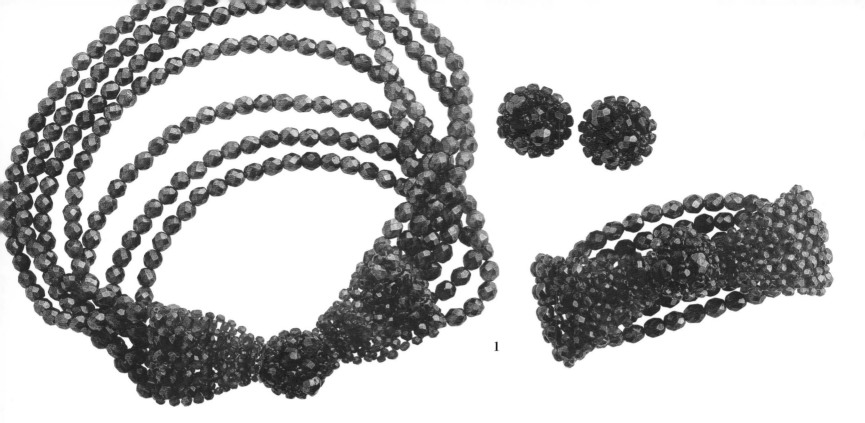

COPPOLA E TOPPO

The late 1950s and the 1960s saw ornate and voluptuous beaded jewelry become the height of fashion. The company at the forefront of this trend was Coppola e Toppo.

Jewelry designer Lyda Toppo established her costume jewelry company in Milan, Italy, in 1946. She worked with her brother, Bruno Coppola. The duo's early pieces, often multi-stranded strings of beads, were characterized by locally sourced beads of Murano glass and Austrian crystal, and by the exquisite use of graduated colored beads, which became a signature of the company. They also favored faceted glass rhinestones, plastic beads, faux pearls, and imitation seed pearls. These were set into gold-plated metal or tightly strung on brass wire. Coppola e Toppo's designs made the clasp integral to the overall look of the piece. Highly ornamental and often heart-shaped, clasps were worn asymmetrically or displayed in low-backed dresses. Famously, their designs adorned the whole neck, not just the front. The company's style was classical and tailored, creating a distinctive look that encapsulated the glamour of *la dolce vita*. Early pieces dating from the late 1940s and early 1950s were marked "Mikey," after their pet dog.

The company soon came to the attention of major fashion houses Balenciaga and Christian Dior, who commissioned pieces for fashion shows and retail—relationships which lasted through the 1950s. Elsa Schiaparelli also commissioned Coppola e Toppo to create a line called "Bijoux Voyages" using faux coral beads, which was hugely successful and catapulted the firm to center stage in the late 1950s. Coincidentally, the company's prominence was also fuelled by its hometown taking over from Paris as the world's fashion capital.

In the 1960s, beads enjoyed a resurgence in Western fashion unseen since Edwardian times. Design influences were drawn from India, Africa, and South America. Beads were "in" during the Swinging Sixties, diamanté and faux pearls were out. Notably, Coppola e Toppo's work for Emilio Pucci, the "Prince of Prints," often utilized in-vogue plastic beads. In 1962, the company also began making belts with crystal beads for Pucci's silk dresses. Extravagant and beautiful, Coppola e Toppo's 1960s beaded crystal bib necklaces are extremely valuable today. The quality of the work means that many pieces have survived.

Italian couturier Valentino, the "King of Fashion" who boasted such clients as Jackie Kennedy and Elizabeth Taylor, provided many lucrative commissions during the 1960s. This work enabled Coppola e Toppo to create more pieces under their own mark—"Made in Italy by Coppola e Toppo"—in the 1960s and 70s.

Key features to look out for in Coppola e Toppo's work include necklaces and bracelets with elaborate, multi-stranded designs featuring the exquisite use of beads, often Swarovski crystal, Murano glass, or plastic, and with the company's signature bead-encrusted heart-shaped clasp.

Look for the mark "Made in Italy by Coppola e Toppo" from the 1950s onward. Earrings were usually marked with a cut-out star on the clip. Coppola e Toppo pieces are highly sought after and very expensive: Doyle in New York sold a collar and two-bracelet demi-parure for $11,400 (£7,200) in 2006.

In 1972, the company was bought out by a larger Italian firm, and production continued until 1986.

1. A 1950s bow necklace, bracelet, and earrings set, of red Venetian glass beads, marked "Made in Italy by Coppolo e Toppo". Earrings 1.25in (3cm) diam **M**

2. An early 1960s foliate necklace, of dark blue, pale green, and turquoise glass beads. 28.5in (72.5cm) long **M**

3. A 1950s choker necklace, of blue, red, amber, and clear Bohemian crystal beads. 2in (5cm) wide **G**

4. A pendant necklace and earrings set, designed for Valentino, with faceted blue and clear Swarovski crystal stones, in gilt metal. 1970 Pendant 2.75in (7cm) diam **M**

5. A mid-1960s necklace, in white and blue crystal beads, with large beaded clasp. 14in (35.5cm) long **J**

MATISSE & RENOIR

Renoir, and later Matisse, specialized in hand-worked, solid copper jewellery, made in the spirit of the Arts and Crafts movement of the late 19th century and early 20th century, but in more modern geometric or abstract forms and patterns.

The company—Renoir of Hollywood—was founded in 1946 by Jerry Fels (born 1917), who had trained at the Art Students' League and at the National Academy of Design in New York, along with Curt Freiler and Nat Zausner. The company's name was changed in about 1948 to Renoir of California. Some time later, Renoir turned to mass production, but the high-quality copper finish, for which the company had become known, was never compromised. The most popular Renoir necklace is probably the graduated fringe design. A cuff bracelet, available in various designs using swirls, loops, and geometric shapes, is also extremely collectable. Designs are typically linear and geometric, some inspired by primitive art. Some pieces may be complemented with black enamel.

Matisse Ltd was established as a subsidiary company in 1952. The pieces produced under this name were also made from copper, but decorated with colourful enamels. Many pieces, particularly the pins, were created in more naturalistic forms, such as leaves and artists' palettes. Of these, the red, green, or white maple leaf pin is

one of the most famous and collectible. Other designs incorporated atomic or space themes, such as the Polaris pin. Renoir's pieces had largely been inexpensive (selling generally below the $10 [£5] mark), but Matisse jewellery was more costly, because of the enameling process. Many pieces are signed (some with both company names), and these are likely to be more desirable than unsigned pieces.

Gradually, the pieces produced by both companies became more abstract and streamlined, until production of both ceased in 1964. The early 1960s fashion for simple, A-line dresses, worn with elaborate jewelry, may have contributed to the decline in popularity for the firm's designs.

However, some of the Matisse ideals were continued in Curtis Jere, a company founded in the late 1950s by Fels and Frelier (the name being a contraction of their first names). At their California studio, Artisan House, they designed and hand-made wall sculptures and household accessories, many of which were in copper. Continuing the high standard of their art jewellery, Curtis Jere aimed to produce "gallery quality art for the masses." In 1972 they sold the company, which continues to produce sculptures.

Pieces were typically signed "Renoir" or "Matisse Renoir" and a copyright symbol was added after 1955.

1. A mid-1950s Matisse "Nefertiti" necklace and coordinating earrings, in copper, with pale blue enamel, the earrings marked "Matisse." Necklace 16in (40.5cm) long **D**

2. A pair of Renoir stylized corn sheaf earrings set, in embossed copper. 1.25in (3cm) high **A**

3. A 1960s Matisse artist's palette pin and earrings, in copper, with multi-colored enamel. Pin 4.25in (11cm) wide **D**

4. A mid-1950s Matisse maple leaf pin, in copper, with red enamel. 2in (5cm) long **C**

5. A pair of Renoir teardrop-shaped earrings, in embossed copper. 1.5in (3.5cm) high **A**

6. A mid-1950s Matisse necklace and earrings set, in gold-plated copper, with pastel pink enamel. Necklace 18in (46cm) long **D**

7. A 1950s Matisse swirl pin, in copper, with green enamel. 2.5in (6.5cm) wide **C**

8. A 1950s Renoir treble clef pin, in copper. 2in (5cm) wide **C**

9. A 1950s/1960s Renoir reticulated bracelet, in copper. 6.75in (17cm) long **C**

ACME
Alcozer
Art
Avon
Beaujewels
Jacob Bengel
Bogoff
Bond Boyd
Cadoro
Carolee
Castlecliff
Alice Caviness
Ciner
Sarah Coventry
Cristobal
DeLizza & Elster
Lily Daché
Danecraft
Robert De Mario
DeRosa
Eugene
Florenza
Givenchy
Gripoix
Grosse
Hollycraft
Harry Iskin
Christian Lacroix
Karl Lagerfeld
Lanvin
Judy Lee
Marvella
McClelland Barclay
Iradj Moini
Monet

Mimi di Niscemi
Napier
Panetta
Pennino Brothers
Rebajes
Regency
Réja
Robert
Nettie Rosenstein
Rousselet
Yves Saint Laurent
Sandor
Selro & Selini
Sherman
Adele Simpson
Hervé van der Straeten
Tortolani
Vogue
Larry Vrba
Warner
Vivienne Westwood
Whiting & Davies

Classic Designers

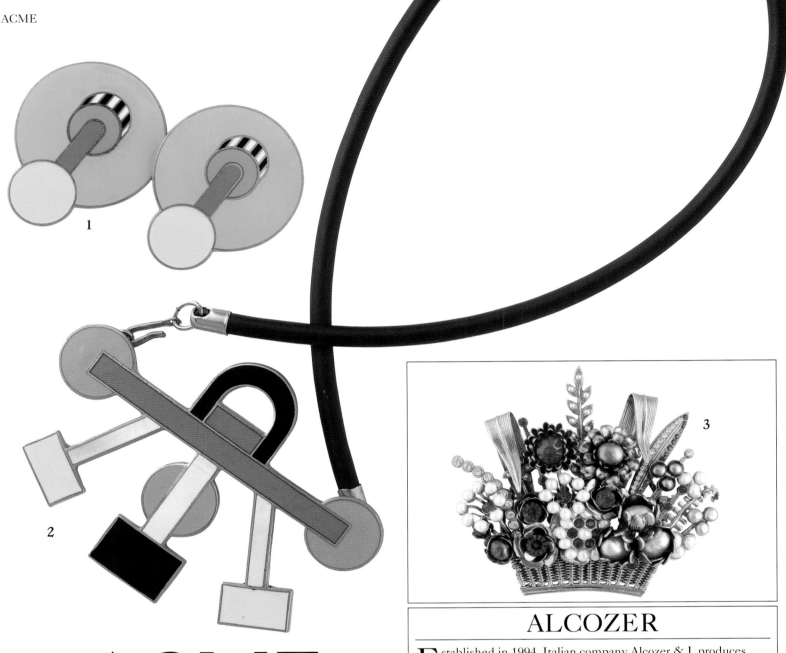

1

2

3

ACME

ACME Studios was founded in 1985 In Los Angeles by husband and wife team Adrian Olabuenaga and Lesley Bailey. It has since become known as the "Swatch of pens," but the company's debut collection was a range of Postmodern-style jewelry, designed by Peter Shire of the Memphis Group. With the help of writer Barbara Radice and designer Ettore Sottsass, this was followed in 1986 by a second, larger range: "MEMPHIS DESIGNERS for ACME." This collection featured over a 100 pieces, which were designed by 14 Memphis designers. Subsequent ACME ranges include "Alchimia for ACME" (directed by Alessandro Mendini). In 1988 the company relocated to Maui, Hawaii, and began making pens, watches and other accessories.

ALCOZER

Established in 1994, Italian company Alcozer & J. produces hand-made jewelry designed by Giampiero Alcozer. Collections include "Be-Baby," "Be-Baby Silver," "Classic," "Linea X," and a limited-production line, "UNIC." Of these, the best known is their speciality "Classic," which is created from hypoallergenic gold-tone metal, set with semi-precious stones, seed pearls and rhinestones.

1. A pair of 1980s Memphis for ACME earrings, designed by Michele De Lucchi, in enameled metal, marked "DE LUCCHI FOR ACME LOS ANGELES." 2in (5cm) high **D**

2. A 1980s Memphis for ACME necklace, designed by Ettore Sottsass, in enameled metal, marked "SOTTSASS FOR ACME STUDIOS." Pendant 3in (7.5cm) wide **D**

3. A 1990s Alcozer basket of flowers pin, in rose gold-plate, with semi-precious stones, cultured pearls, aurora borealis, and colorless and ruby rhinestones. 3.25in (8.5cm) wide **D**

ART

The New York company formerly known as Har (see pages 144–145) changed its name to Art (or ModeArt) around 1955, the new name presumably taken from that of its owner, Arthur Pepper. During the 1950s and 1960s (some have suggested into the 1970s), Art produced a huge variety of costume jewelry in a wide range of styles, including Renaissance-Revival, Victorian and Art Deco. Other pieces have Asian or figural motifs. It was mass-produced and sold at a reasonable price in department stores across America. As a result there tend to be plenty of examples on the market.

Characteristic Art materials include filigree metalwork and enamel, multi-colored plastics that were either carved or molded, and clusters of uniquely colored rhinestones. Flower, fruit, and leaf motifs are common, but so are figures, particularly those of animals. Art's pieces are similar to those of fellow New York company Florenza (see page 168), but are typically marked marked either "ART," "MODEART," "MODE-ART," or, from 1955 onwards, "ART ©."

1. A late 1950s Art apple pin and complementary strawberry earrings, with red aurora borealis, and green rhinestones. Pin 1.5in (4cm) long **D**

2. A 1950s Art Santa boot pin, in gold-tone metal, with enamel and faux pearls. 1.5in (4cm) high **B**

3. A mid-1950s Art wreath pin, in gold-tone metal, with pastel Lucite flowers and aurora borealis, marked "Art." 1.75in (4.5cm) diam **C**

This pin was a hostess gift, given as an inducement to hold Avon parties. It is therefore larger and more elaborate than other Avon jewelry, as well as being much rarer. These factors make it desirable.

In Babylonia and Persia, the peacock was seen as a guardian to royalty. It is also an ancient Christian symbol, representing the all-seeing church and the resurrection, as it sheds its feathers and grows new, brighter ones every year.

AVON

Avon was founded in the US in 1886 by a young door-to-door bookseller named David McConnell. He had previously given away samples of perfume to housewives who would listen to his bookselling pitch. Finding they were more interested in the perfume than the books, he switched careers. In 1920 the company released its first non-perfume products: a toothbrush, talcum powder, and a vanity set under the name Avon Products. In 1939 the company's name was officially changed to Avon.

Its first jewelry was released in 1971 and consisted of three pieces—an owl pin, a ring, and a pendant—that incorporated solid perfume in the designs. That year also saw the introduction of the "Precious Pretenders Collection," which featured intricate gold-toned filigree pieces set with faux diamonds. More collections followed, including several by well-known designers such as Kenneth Jay Lane. By 1975, Avon had become the largest manufacturer of jewelry in the world. Consequently its jewelry is widely available.

1. A 1970s Avon pendant cross necklace, in gold-tone metal, with a red glass cabochon. Cross 3in (7.5cm) long **B**

2. An Avon "Collectibles" peacock pin, in gun metal, with multi-colored pavé-set rhinestones, 2004. 7in (17.5cm) long **C**

3. A 1970s Avon mouse pin, in gilt metal, with yellow rhinestone eyes and articulated spectacles. 3.25in (8cm) wide **A**

1. A 1950s Beaujewels snowflake pin and earrings set, in white metal, with blue and aurora borealis rhinestones. Pin 2.75in (7cm) long **B**

2. A pair of 1950s Beaujewels earrings, in gilt brass filigree, with gold-tone and topaz marquise- cut rhinestones. 1.5in (3.5cm) long **A**

3. A 1950s Beaujewels snowflake pin and earrings set, in gold-tone metal, with red, pink, and aurora borealis rhinestones. Pin 2.5in (6.5cm) long **B**

BEAUJEWELS

Little is known about Beaujewels (or Beau Jewels). The most likely explanation is that these pieces (produced from the late 1940s to the early 1970s) were made by a U.S. company called Bowman & Foster, and were nothing to do with the company Beaucraft which was active at the same time. Beaujewels pieces are typified by floral or leaf motifs, and are usually decorated with faux pearls, richly colored rhinestones and textured-glass beads. Beaujewels pins are invariably unsigned, but the matching earrings should be signed "BEAU JEWELS" on the clip back.

JAKOB BENGEL

J akob Bengel founded a company in 1873 in Idar-Oberstein, Germany, and produced brass, tombac (a brass alloy), silver, and "Doublé Americaine" (a nickel alloy) watch chains.

In the late 1920s the company, now successful, began to make Art Deco costume jewelry. Some pieces were decorated with crystal or rhinestones, or were designed to be worn with silk or velvet cords, which were fashionable at the time.

Most of Bengel's output, however, comprised striking pieces in chrome and geometric shapes of colored Galalith. These were often hung on "brickwork" chains that heightened the machine aesthetic of the jewelry. Such pieces were created by top designers, such as Willhelm Wagenfeld, a graduate of the Bauhaus.

This unusual jewelry was extremely popular both in Germany and abroad—indeed by the mid-1930s most of the pieces were exported all over the world. Although Bengel did have its own manufacturer's mark—an oval depicting a cannon and pyramided cannon balls—this is rarely seen on exported pieces. The country of origin was similarly omitted because of poor relations between Germany and the rest of Europe at this time.

With the arrival of World War II the use of Galalith for non-essentials was prohibited and Jakob Bengel's jewelry production consequently ceased.

The factory has now been re-opened as a museum and from 2003 has produced limited-edition reproductions of its Art Deco jewelry. These new pieces are made from the old pattern books with the original tools and using the same production methods.

1. A 1930s chain-link bracelet, in chrome and enamel. 7in (17.5cm) long **F**

2. A 1930s necklace, in chrome and enamel. 16in (40.5cm) long **H**

3. A 1930s pin, in chrome and green and black Galalith. 3in (7.5cm) long **E**

1. A Bond Boyd stylized flower pin, in textured gold, with jade cabochons and cultured pearls, marked "14KT." 2.5in (6.5cm) long **E**

2. A 1950s Bogoff necklace and bracelet set, in gilt metal with topaz and diamanté, with original box. Necklace 16.5in (42cm) long **D**

3. A Bond Boyd pin, in vermeil sterling silver, with faceted colorless and light blue rhinestones, marked "Sterling." 2.5in (6.5cm) long **D**

4. A Bond Boyd flower and leaves pin, in silver-plate, with purple rhinestones. 2.5in (6.5cm) long **C**

BOGOFF

From around 1946 to the early 1970s, the Bogoff Spear Novelty Company in Chicago, Illinois, produced delicate, feminine costume jewelry, designed by Henry Bogoff. These elegant pieces were made of good-quality materials, typically small rhinestones, molded glass stones, and faux pearls, hand-set in silver-tone metal. Some examples are unsigned, but many are marked either "Jewels of BOGOFF" or "BOGOFF."

BOND BOYD

Bond-Boyd was founded in 1940 in Ontario, Canada, and has remained a family-owned and -operated business ever since. During the 1940s and 1950s, the company specialized in small pieces of dainty jewelry, many set with round-cut semi-precious stones or rhinestones in bezel- or prong-settings. Such pieces were often made in sterling silver, with some examples in vermeil and gold-plated silver.

The modern company produces quality custom-made corporate jewelry, including a variety of badges, insignia products, medals, lapel pins, and rings, as well as Canadian souvenir pieces in gold and silver.

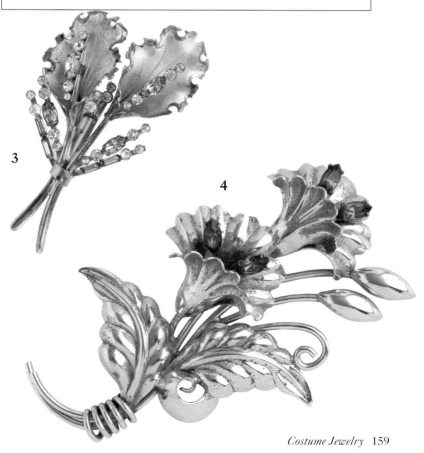

CADORO

Founded in New York by Steve Brody and Dan Staneskieu, Cadoro Inc. produced custom-designed, hand-crafted jewelry from 1945 until 1970. Its output included three-dimensional fish and animals, and Russian-inspired pieces, all of which were made in brushed-gold and silver-toned metal prong-set with rhinestones, glass crystals, and seed pearls.

CAROLEE

Carolee Designs was founded by architect Carolee Friedlander in 1973 from her home in Greenwich, Connecticut. It later moved to premises in Stamford, in the same state. Known for high-quality pieces and affordable prices, Carolee uses sterling silver, faux- and cultured pearls and rhinestones. The 1987 "Duchess of Windsor" range, based on Wallis Simpson's jewelry, was a great success. In 2001 the company was sold to Retail Brand Alliance.

1. A 1960s Cadoro teardrop pin, in gilt metal, with cabochons of faux pearls, emeralds, rubies, and turquoise. 2.5in (6cm) long **B**

2. A 1970s/1980s Carolee bracelet, in white metal, with colorless rhinestones. 7in (17.75cm) circ. **D**

3. A 1960s Alice Caviness necklace and matching bracelet, in japanned metal, with olivine and ruby glass cabochons, and aurora borealis, blue, and green rhinestones. Necklace 16in (40.5cm) long **E**

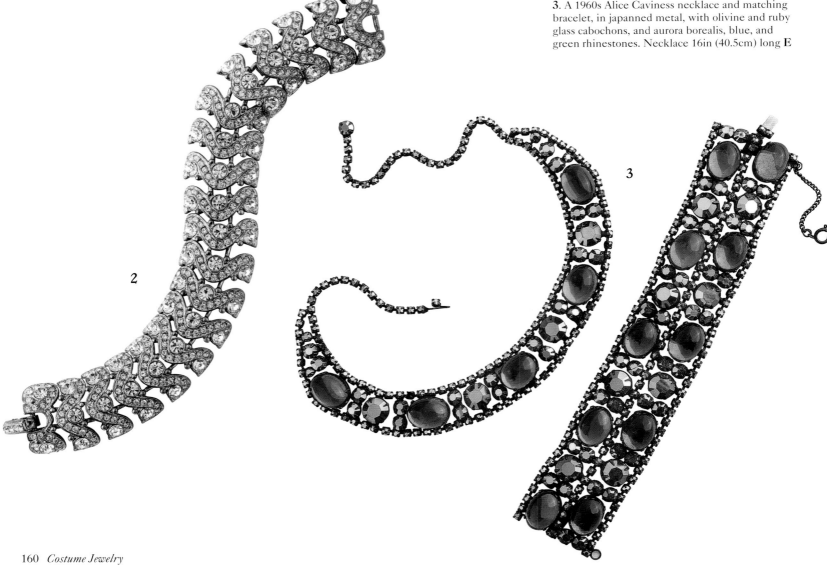

4. A mid-1970s Castlecliff Aztec cross necklace, designed by Larry Vbra, in Russian-gold-tone metal, with glass stones and enamel. Pendant 4in (10.5cm) **C**

4

STONES

The glass "stones" were made by a bead company originally called "Jewelry of Four Seasons," which Castlecliff owned. The beads were melted, forming the "stones" seen here.

DESIGN

Larry Vrba, who designed this piece, is well known for his historical motifs. He worked for Castlecliff from c1970–72. This Aztec-style line was one of their most popular ranges.

CASTLECLIFF

A New York company, Castlecliff was founded by Clifford Furst and Joseph Bobley and produced the vast majority of its output from the 1940s to the early 1970s. Under chief designer William Markle, the company created bold jewelry in a range of styles, including Art Deco, Gothic, and Native American. Larry Vrba designed for the company from 1970 to 1972.

ALICE CAVINESS

Former fashion model Alice Caviness began designing jewelry in the mid-to-late 1940s. In the mid-1950s she was joined at her factory in Long Island, New York, by talented designer Millie Petronzio, who worked for Caviness until 1982 when she left to become head designer at Miriam Haskell Jewelry. Together Alice and Millie designed highly imaginative pieces in sterling and gold-on-sterling cloisonné enamels and filigrees. These pieces were sold only in exclusive specialty shops and boutiques and can consequently be difficult to find today.

Alice Caviness died in 1983 and her business partner, Lois Steever, continued production until 2000.

5

5. A 1960s Alice Caviness raspberry and raspberry leaf pin, in textured gold-tone metal, with pavé-set faux ruby cabochons. 2.75in (7cm) long **B**

CINER

Emanuel Ciner founded a precious jewelry company in New York City in 1892. Around 1930, he began to make high-quality costume jewelry, and eventually dropped the fine jewelry completely.

Ciner's costume jewelry is designed to look like precious pieces, typically using gold-tone metal set with Swarovski rhinestones in natural colors. Rich enamels were also used, as were faux pearls, which were made especially for Ciner by Japanese artists. Ciner pieces continue to be produced today and the company is run by Emanuel's granddaughter Pat Hill. It is said that Elizabeth Taylor once bought $20,000 of Ciner jewels in one day.

SARAH COVENTRY

Sarah Coventry and its sister company, Emmons Jewelers, were founded in 1949 by Charles H. Stuart. All the costume jewelry sold by Sarah Coventry was made by other Rhode Island companies, but crucially it was sold through house parties hosted by female "Fashion Directors." These were extremely popular until the 1970s.

1. A 1950s Ciner floral bracelet, in gold-plate, with turquoise, aquamarine, ruby, emerald, and black crystal cabochons. 7.5in (19cm) long **E**

2. A 1970s Sarah Coventry "springtime" Celtic shield pin, in white metal, with chaton-cut blue, green, pink, and marquise-cut purple rhinestones. 3.75in (5.5cm) diam **B**

3. A Sarah Coventry Midnight Magic pin and earrings set, in japanned metal, with faux smoky quartz and pink crystals. Produced from 1957 to the 1970s. Pin 2.5in (6cm) long **C**

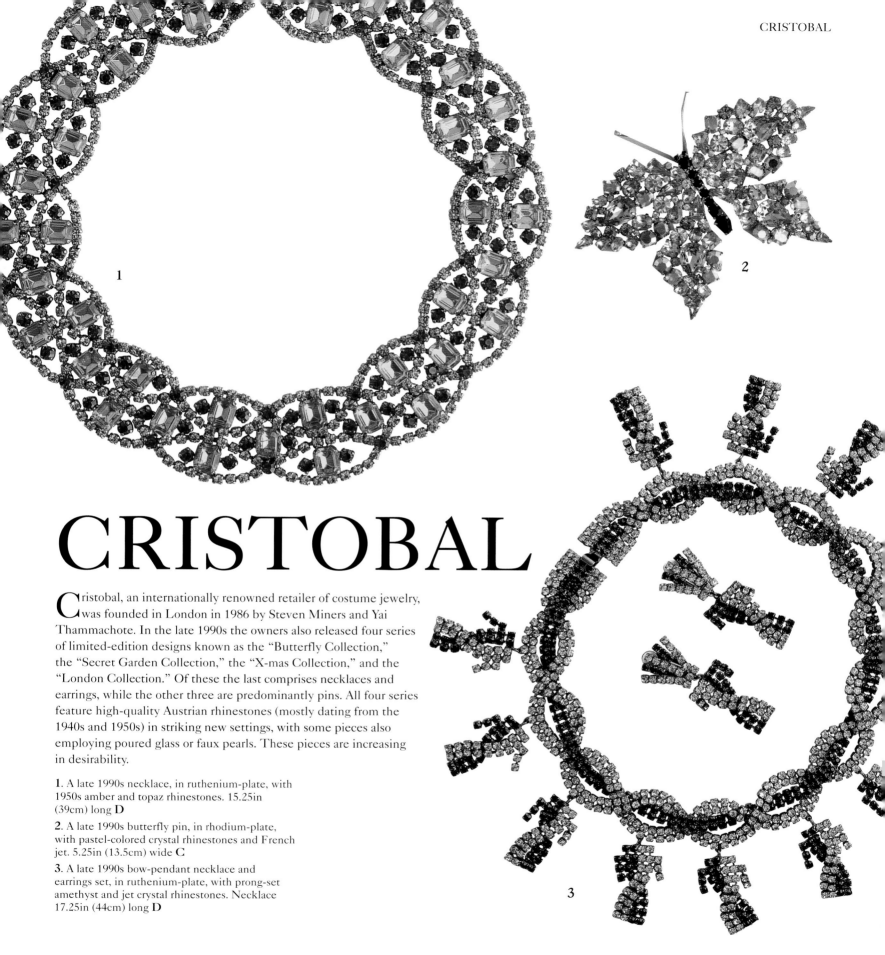

CRISTOBAL

Cristobal, an internationally renowned retailer of costume jewelry, was founded in London in 1986 by Steven Miners and Yai Thammachote. In the late 1990s the owners also released four series of limited-edition designs known as the "Butterfly Collection," the "Secret Garden Collection," the "X-mas Collection," and the "London Collection." Of these the last comprises necklaces and earrings, while the other three are predominantly pins. All four series feature high-quality Austrian rhinestones (mostly dating from the 1940s and 1950s) in striking new settings, with some pieces also employing poured glass or faux pearls. These pieces are increasing in desirability.

1. A late 1990s necklace, in ruthenium-plate, with 1950s amber and topaz rhinestones. 15.25in (39cm) long **D**

2. A late 1990s butterfly pin, in rhodium-plate, with pastel-colored crystal rhinestones and French jet. 5.25in (13.5cm) wide **C**

3. A late 1990s bow-pendant necklace and earrings set, in ruthenium-plate, with prong-set amethyst and jet crystal rhinestones. Necklace 17.25in (44cm) long **D**

1

2

DELIZZA & ELSTER

DeLizza & Elster produced pieces for many of the big names of 20th-century costume jewelry, but it is becoming increasingly well-known for the "Juliana" range it created for just two years.

The company was founded by Harold Elster and Guillermo (William) deLizza in New York City in 1947. A year later Guillermo's sons Frank and Anthony joined the company, working in the sales and production departments respectively.

The company became renowned for its use of high-quality art glass stones, three-dimensional designs and quality settings. Its pieces were unmarked and can be difficult to identify unless they have their original hangtags, which are typically marked "Juliana," or "Tara" or "Gloria," which were DeLizza & Elster's two other main jewelry lines. However, a number of online identification sites have been set up by enthusiastic collectors, and these offer tips on how to spot DeLizza & Elster pieces. Frank DeLizza contributes to these sites and is said to verify up to 100 pieces a week.

The company, which had a showroom on Fifth Avenue in New York City, made thousands of different designs. It also produced pieces for a number of companies including Alice Caviness, Coro (c1950), Kramer, Weiss, Hattie Carnegie, Joan Rivers, and Kenneth Jay Lane.

Guillermo was the main designer; later Frank's daughter Judy worked as designer too.

In the early years the company produced buckles, buttons, and jewelry hand-set with rhinestones and simulated pearls. After 1953 styles became increasingly complex and colorful and typically used different shapes and types of high-quality art glass stones in each piece.

The Juliana line—which was only produced in 1967 and 1968—was named after Frank and Anthony's mother Julia, and Anthony's mother-in-law Anna. Its creators were shrouded in secrecy until 2003 when *Vintage Fashion and Costume Jewelry* magazine revealed their true names.

DeLizza & Elster jewelry features gold-tone, silver-tone, or japanned backings with prong-set or glue-set stones. Typically open-backed—though foiled and closed-backed examples are also known—these stones include a mixture of rhinestones, aurora borealis, and distinctive center stones made from art glass. Elongated navette-cut rhinestones are typical.

The company ceased production in 1990 but Frank DeLizza is currently releasing new versions of original designs through a firm in Brooklyn, New York City.

1. A 1950s bracelet, in gold-tone metal, with faceted blue diamanté. 6.75in (17cm) long **B**

2. A pair of 1960s earrings, with large central Rivoli-cut pink stones and pink and purple rhinestone. 0.75in (2cm) square **B**

3. A 1960s pin, with green pear-cut and marquise-cut rhinestones, and pavé-set aurora borealis chatons. 3.25in (8cm) long **B**

4. A late 1950s necklace and earrings set, in green, colorless, and aurora borealis rhinestones. Earrings 1.25in (3cm) long **D**

5. A 1960s pin and earrings set, with prong-set, large, oval, green stone, and green, pear-, navette-, and chaton-cut rhinestones. Pin 2.5in (6cm) long **C**

6. A 1960s pin, in gilt brass filigree, with black, oval-, navette-, and chaton-cut glass and gilt filigree balls. 2in (5cm) wide **C**

7. A 1960s open-backed floral pin, with central Rivoli-cut margarita stone, and jonquil and topaz navette-cut rhinestones. 2.25in (5.5cm) wide **B**

LILLY DACHÉ

Lilly Daché (1898–1989) was a famous French-born American milliner and designer, who produced work for several film stars including Marlene Dietrich, Caroline Lombard, and Loretta Young. She is known to have said, "I like splashy jewelry that clinks when I walk, and I like my earrings big," and the jewelry she created reflects this. Her mark was first used on costume jewelry in 1923, and was apparently used sparingly thereafter. She retired in 1968. Her jewelry is now rare, and generally valuable.

1. A rare 1940s Lilly Daché flower pin, in silver-tone metal, with colorless and green rhinestones. 5in (13cm) long **F**

2. A 1980s Danecraft umbrella pin, in white metal and selected gilding, with iridescent blue enamel and green rhinestones. 1.75in (4.5cm) long **B**

3. A 1940s Danecraft medallions bracelet, in vermeil sterling silver, with large, faceted purple pastes. 7in (17.75cm) long **C**

DANECRAFT

Danecraft, the company now known as the Felch-Wehr Company, was founded in 1934 by Italian immigrant Victor Primavera in Providence, Rhode Island. It specializes in sterling silver and vermeil jewelry in forms often inspired by nature. Thanks to its high quality and an aggressive advertising campaign, Danecraft jewelry was extremely popular in the 1950s, and is still desirable today.

ROBERT DEMARIO

One of the members of the "School of Haskell," Robert DeMario founded his company in 1945 in New York City and continued making jewelry there until 1965. His beautiful designs often incorporate hand-sewn brass strung threads, faceted Austrian beads, rhinestones, and faux pearls. DeMario's jewelry is relatively rare and can command high prices today.

1. A Robert DeMario flower and leaf pin, in gilt metal, with faux anthracite and pearls, marked "DeMario N.Y." 2.5in (6.5cm) wide **B**

2. A late 1930s DeRosa boquet pin, in gold-plate, with enamel and rhinestones, signed "Derosa." 5in (12.5cm) long **M**

3. A 1940s DeRosa pin, in sterling silver, with rhinestones and faux sapphires. 1.75in (4.5cm) long **C**

4. A DeRosa fur clip, in vermeil sterling silver, with red and colorless rhinestones. 3in (7.5cm) long **D**

DEROSA

Founded by Ralph DeRosa in New York City in 1933 and later run by Elvira, Virginia, and Theresa DeRosa, DeRosa made jewelry until 1955. Striking floral and figural designs are common, as are retro motifs such as exaggerated bows, and designs inspired by precious jewelry, and typical pieces feature gold-plated metal castings set with richly colored stones and translucent enamelwork. Many DeRosa pieces are unmarked, but those that are signed are extremely collectible.

1

CRAFT

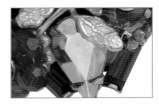

All Eugene pieces were hand-wired and hand-set (here with secure prong settings). This means they are typically of the highest quality and consequently very desirable.

INFLUENCE

The elaborate mix of stones (including red, black, and aurora borealis rhinestones) set in flower forms and the gilt-metal settings are very reminiscent of the work of Frank Hess.

STONES

These earrings employ numerous methods of catching and reflecting light, chief among them the pear-cut aurora borealis stones. The berry-shaped drop has numerous facets, which sparkle with movement.

EUGENE

Eugene (Gene) Schultz may have designed some of Miriam Haskell's early jewelry. Whatever the truth is regarding his employment at Haskell, Schultz was certainly inspired by the work of her chief designer, Frank Hess. He started his company, Eugene Jewelry in 1952, and opened a showroom on Madison Avenue, New York City. All Eugene's pieces were designed by the owner and hand-made by an in-house team that at its height comprised 15 craftsmen. The company failed in 1962, and Schultz himself died two years later.

2

3

4

1. A pair of 1950s Eugene floral earrings, in gilt metal, with baguette- and pear-cut red faceted crystals. 1.5in (3.5cm) long **B**

2. A pair of 1950s Eugene shell earrings, with faux pearl and rhinestones. 1.25in (3cm) wide **C**

3. A 1960s Florenza Victorian revival bar pin, in gilt metal, with faux turquoise and aquamarine rhinestones. 2.25in (5.5cm) long **B**

4. A late 1970s Florenza stylized floral pendant necklace, in gold-tone metal, with turquoise and amethyst glass cabochons. Pendant 3in (7.5cm) long **A**

FLORENZA

Daniel Kosoff started his New York company in the late 1930s, and began producing Florenza jewelry (named after his wife, Florence) in the late 1940s. The pieces produced under this trade-name were antique in style, evoking the Renaissance and Victorian ages with gold-tone metal, cameos, enameling, and frosted and aurora borealis rhinestones. Picture frames, ring boxes, pin-cushions, and lipstick holders were also made in this style, often for other companies. Most of these pieces were marked "Florenza" in script. The company closed in 1981.

1. A late 1980s/1990s chain-link necklace, in gilt metal, with colorless faceted paste, signed "Givenchy." 14in (35.5cm) long **D**

2. A pair of 1960s earrings, in silver metal, with blue glass. 1in (2.5cm) high **A**

3. A pair of earrings, in gilt metal. 0.75in (1.75cm) diam **A**

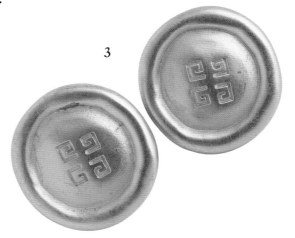

GIVENCHY

The House of Givenchy opened in Paris in 1952 under the directorship of designer Hubert de Givenchy. The fashion house soon became extremely influential and its modern, elegant pieces were seen worn by famously glamorous women, such as Audrey Hepburn and Lauren Bacall. Givenchy jewelry is typically made from heavy gold- and silver-plated metals, often adorned with rhinestones, glass, Lucite, plastic beads, and faux pearls. Such pieces are usually signed. Givenchy retired in 1995 and the design was taken over by John Galliano, passing through several famous hands before Riccardo Tisci became head designer in 2005.

1

GRIPOIX

Known for the costume jewelry it produced for Chanel (see pages 104–7), Dior (see pages 80–5), and other leading fashion houses, Maison Gripoix (est. c1870) has also made many pieces in its own name. Above all, it is known for *pâte-de-verre* pieces, which can be found in pale and vibrant colors, extremely translucent or opaque.

The company has always been family-run. From the mid-1920s it was run by Suzanne Gripoix (known as "Madame Gripoix" in the jewelry world), before passing to her daughter Josette in 1969, and then to Josette's son, Thierry, in the early 1990s.

Under Thierry Caluwaerts, Gripoix design was dominated by floral, foliate, and fruit imagery and a new brand name was introduced: "Histoire de Verre." As the name suggests, these pieces were still primarily made with *pâte-de-verre*, although faux pearls and rhinestones also feature in many designs.

GROSSE

Henkel & Grosse was founded by Florentin Grosse and Heinrich Henkel in Pforzheim, Germany, in 1907. The company, which initially produced only gold settings, began making costume jewelry from c1920, initially for the European market, and from the late 1920s for the U.S. Its designs received a certificate of honor at the 1937 Paris Exposition. The company became known as "Grosse" from World War II onwards. In 1955, it became the principal manufacturer for Dior, for which it created four annual collections. Grosse's jewelry was made with gold- and rhodium-plated base metals, prong-set with clear and colored rhinestones, faux pearls, lapis, turquoise, and ruby stones. From 1958 onwards, the company signed and dated all of its jewelry, whether from the Grosse or the Dior collections.

1. A 1990s Histoire de Verre flower pin, in gold-colored metal, with poured orange and green glass. 3.5in (8.5cm) wide **D**

2. A Grosse stylized flower pin, in gold metal, with inset turquoise nugget, marked "GROSSE 1961." 2.5in (6cm) diam **B**

3. A Grosse flower basket pin, in gilt metal, with faux sapphires and turquoise, marked "Made in Germany" and "Grosse" and dated 1963. 2in (5cm) long **C**

2

3

HOLLYCRAFT

The Hollywood Jewelry Manufacturing Company was founded in 1936 by Joseph Chorbajian, who was later joined by his cousins Jack Hazard and "Archie" Chorbajian. In 1948, the company's name was changed to "Hollycraft" (to avoid confusion with Joseff of Hollywood), under which it continued to operate until it closed in the mid-1970s.

Most Hollycraft pieces were made from Victorian-style gold-tone metal, set with pastel-colored rhinestones. The Christmas tree line is especially collectible. Unusually, Hollycraft jewelry is always signed. Many pieces from the 1950s onwards are also dated.

1. A Hollycraft necklace, in antiqued-metal, with pastel-colored rhinestones, 1956. 16in (40.5cm) long **D**

2. A pair of Hollycraft earrings, in antiqued-metal, with pastel-colored rhinestones, marked "Hollycraft Corp. 1957." 1.5in (4cm) long **C**

3. A 1940s Harry Iskin floral pin and earrings set, in vermeil sterling silver, with blue glass stones. Pin 2.75in (7cm) long **B**

HARRY ISKIN

British-born Harry Iskin (1886-1968) emigrated to America in 1908 and became a U.S. citizen. He began making jewelry in Philadelphia as early as 1917 and continued to do so until he was declared bankrupt in 1953.

Most Iskin pieces on the market today are floral forms in sterling silver or vermeil, sometimes highlighted with rose gold. These are sparingly set with glass stones in a variety of colors, and faux pearls. Designs range from simple to ornate. He also made rhinestone pins and hinged bangles.

CHRISTIAN LACROIX

A history of art student accidentally turned fashion designer, Christian Lacroix (born 1951) opened his fashion house in 1987 at the height of the consumer boom. From 1989, he produced lines of haute couture and ready-to-wear costume jewelry to accessorize his clothing. The latter was signature Lacroix, being bold gold pieces in arresting shapes, adorned with vibrantly colored faux stones. Typical pieces were gem-encrusted crosses and heavy, ornate charm bracelets. In 2009 the fashion house was put into administration.

1. A 1980s Rococo heart pin, in gold-tone metal, with shocking pink glass and entwined "CL" logo, marked "CL Paris Christian Lacroix." 2.75in (7cm) wide **B**

2. A mid-1980s charm bracelet, in gold-tone metal, with faux pearls. 7in (17.5cm) long **C**

KARL LAGERFELD

K arl Lagerfeld was born in Germany in 1933 and moved to Paris in 1953. There he worked for several fashion houses, before joining Chanel as head designer and creative director in 1983. Lagerfeld took Chanel's already famous motifs—coins, pearls, and the double C—and made them larger and more prominent to suit the consumer-driven 1980s. Bright yellow gilding was also essential. His own fashion house, formed shortly after he joined Chanel, produced similar pieces. Most are collectible today.

1. A pair of 1980s Karl Lagerfeld dangling hoop earrings, in gilt metal, with faux pearls. 3.25in (8cm) long **D**

2. A pair of 1980s/1990s Karl Lagerfeld stylized plant earrings, in gold-washed metal, with faux pearls. 1in (2.5cm) long **B**

3. A mid-1960s Lanvin pendant, in chrome and black plastic, with "fox-tail" chain. 16in (40.5cm) long **B**

LANVIN

J eanne Lanvin (1867–1946) started as a milliner and joined Paris's Syndicat de la Couture—a school which trained aspiring designers—in 1909. She went on to become one of the most influential designers of the 1920s and 1930s.

Today, Lanvin's best-known costume jewelry is a range of plastic and metal pendants, produced during the 1960s and 1970s, which were based around geometric forms that evoked the space age. Of these, an interchangeable pendant necklace frequently worn in the early 21st century by British actress Keira Knightly is one of the most sought-after by collectors.

1

JUDY LEE

Judy Lee is a trademark of the Blanch-Ette Company, founded by Blanche and Aldo Viano in Chicago in 1949. Like Sarah Coventry and Emmons, the jewelry was sold at parties in people's homes from the 1950s to the 1970s. Floral, Victorian-style pieces in rhinestone and faux pearls were common in the 1950s, with later pieces employing antiqued metalware and glass beads. After 1958 most pieces were marked "Judy-Lee," others "Judy-Lee Jewels."

2

3

MARVELLA

Marvella began as the trade name of Weinrich Bros. Co. which was founded in Philadelphia in 1911. In around 1950 the company name became Marvella Pearls Inc. and in 1965 it changed again to Marvella Inc. Typical pieces include faceted crystal beads and faux pearls combined with rhinestones. Such pieces are usually signed, but may be found with a variety of trademarks. In 1982 the company was bought by Trifari.

6

4

5

STONES

The faux sapphires are foiled to give them extra sparkle and enhance the beautiful, deep color. For extra security they are prong-set as well as glue-set, which is a mark of quality.

DESIGN

This high-quality Art Deco-style casting is bolted onto the base. This layering (and the variation in stone size) creates an attractive three-dimensional effect.

DIAMANTÉ

The small diamanté stones are only glue-set, which may lead to losses, as seen here. Others have blackened with age, but value is not greatly affected, as they can easily be replaced.

8

7

McCLELLAND BARCLAY

McClelland Barclay designed jewelry from the 1930s until his death in World War II. He designed many simple, stamped sterling silver and vermeil pieces depicting animals or flowers, as well as other metal pieces in an eclectic range of forms. However, Barclay is best known for his gold- or silver-plated geometric structures, which bridge that gap between Art Deco and what is known as 1940s Retro. Few comparable designs by other makers exist, and these pieces are extremely desirable as a consequence. Many of his pieces are signed, sometimes with "STERLING SILVER" as well as his name.

1. A 1960s Judy Lee double-strand "melon ball" necklace and earrings set, of plastic and faceted crystal beads. Necklace 20in (51cm) long **B**

2. A 1970s/1980s Judy Lee bracelet, in antiqued silver-tone metal, with aurora borealis rhinestones. 7in (17.75cm) long **B**

3. A 1960s/1970s Judy Lee pin and earrings set, in gold-tone filigree, with colorless, topaz, ruby, and gray-green rhinestones. Pin 2.75in (7cm) diam **B**

4. A pair of 1960s Marvella flower earrings, in gilt metal, with faux pearls. 1.25in (3cm) diam **A**

5. A 1960s Marvella fruit pin and earrings set, in gold-tone metal, with faux pearls. Pin 2in (5cm) long **B**

6. A 1960s Marvella pin and earrings set, with yellow faceted rhinestones. Pin 2.5in (6cm) wide **D**

7. A 1930s/1940s McClelland Barclay pin, in sterling silver, with faux sapphires and diamanté. 2.5in (5.5cm) diam **D**

8. A 1940s McClelland Barclay pin, in gold-plate, with pavé rhinestones and faux rubies. 2.25in (5.5cm) diam **E**

DESIGN

The cricket is very naturalistically and sensitively modeled. This is particularly true of the head, which is set with multi-faceted diamanté and purple rhinestone eyes.

SETTING

The pin is in very good condition. Although it was made recently, its many delicate brass protrubances and green stone-set cage body are susceptible to damage.

INSPIRATION

This cricket pin is one of a series inspired by the Pixar animation *A Bug's Life* (1998). The film is about an ant who mistakenly hires a group of circus bugs to help him repel a swarm of grasshoppers.

1

IRADJ MOINI

Iranian-born designer Iradj Moini trained as an architect and began designing jewelry in New York City in the late 1980s, creating pieces for Oscar de la Renta's catwalk shows. He started to create jewellery under his own name in 1989, and has made pieces for Bill Blass, Carolina Herrera, and Arnold Scaasi among others.

All Moini's pieces are handmade by a small group of craftspeople, and are typically large and three-dimensional; the most intricate often feature detachable settings. Each piece typically takes two weeks to complete. Moini employs unusual combinations of materials, such as brass, bone, wood, and brightly colored Austrian and Czech crystal and semi-precious stones, and no two pieces are ever exactly the same.

His work is sold through numerous up-market boutiques in New York City and Beverly Hills. It has been featured in numerous high fashion publications, including *Vogue* and *Elle*, and has been seen worn by stars such as Sarah Jessica Parker, Drew Barrymore, and Oprah Winfrey. As well as being purely fashionable, Moini's jewelry has also been acknowledged as works of art, with pieces exhibited at the Metropolitan Museum of Art in New York City and at the Louvre in Paris where three of his pieces are in the permanent collection.

2

1. A 1990s Iradj Moini frog pin, in brass, with jade-green baroque pastes, green and colorless rhinestones, and red glass cabochon eyes. 3.75in (9.5cm) long **G**

2. A 1990s Iradj Moini orange blossom pin. 4.25in (10.5cm) long **F**

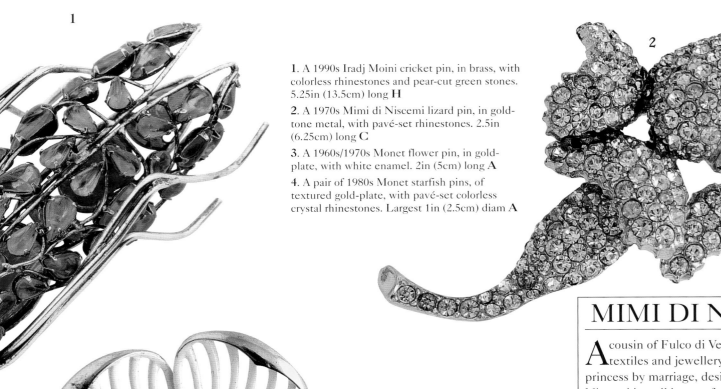

1. A 1990s Iradj Moini cricket pin, in brass, with colorless rhinestones and pear-cut green stones. 5.25in (13.5cm) long **H**

2. A 1970s Mimi di Niscemi lizard pin, in gold-tone metal, with pavé-set rhinestones. 2.5in (6.25cm) long **C**

3. A 1960s/1970s Monet flower pin, in gold-plate, with white enamel. 2in (5cm) long **A**

4. A pair of 1980s Monet starfish pins, of textured gold-plate, with pavé-set colorless crystal rhinestones. Largest 1in (2.5cm) diam **A**

MIMI DI NISCEMI

A cousin of Fulco di Verdura, who designed textiles and jewellery for Chanel, and a princess by marriage, designer Mimi di Niscemi is well known for her fantasy jewelry and large belt buckles. Born in Palermo, Sicily, she studied silversmithing and jewelry at Philadelphia Museum School. While at art school, she worked for a company producing Elsa Schiaparelli's jewelry, and later teamed up with designer Arnold Scaasi, Robert DeMario, and the bead house Brania. Her own jewelry company opened in 1962 in New York City. In 1968 she won a Great Design in Costume Jewelry Award. Her pieces, which typically use glass cabochons and Byzantine-influenced settings, are marked "Mimi di N." Niscemi has officially retired, but pieces cast from her original designs are being sold today.

MONET

Monocraft, now known as Monet, was founded by brothers Jay and Michael Chernow in 1929 in Providence, Rhode Island. The company began by making Art Deco-style purse adornments and started making costume jewelry in 1937, producing simple gold- and silver-tone designs. It developed a friction ear clip which made its earrings more comfortable to wear as the clip can be adjusted by the wearer. From 1981, Monet produced jewelry for Yves Saint Laurent. It has continually adapted to changing fashions and remains successful today.

1

NAPIER

Napier was founded in 1875 as Whitney & Rice in North Attleboro, Massachusetts, and originally made silverware, such as watch chains. The company moved to Meriden, Connecticut, in 1882 and opened a New York City office in 1883. After World War I, and with a change of management, it began to produce modern designs and, in 1922, gained its current name. The company is celebrated as a pioneer of fashion jewelry and in 1994 was the largest privately owned manufacturer of fashion jewelry in the U.S.

From the 1920s until it was sold to Victoria & Co. in the 1980s, Napier produced a prodigious amount of jewelry. In 1964, for example, there were 1,200 different design lines, and each season at least 50 per cent of products were new. Pieces were created in a variety of styles featuring faux pearls and beading, enamel, coins, antique seals, milk glass beads, and art glass charms. Napier's chunky gilt metal charm bracelets are particularly collectible.

All pieces were stamped "NAPIER" until 1980, when the trademark was changed to "Napier" in script letters. This mark was used until Napier closed in 1999.

2

3

1. A 1950s seashells bracelet and earrings set, in gold-plate, the shells comprising oysters, mussels, and clams. 7.5in (19cm) long **D**

2. An early 1950s chinoiserie charm bracelet, in gilt-metal, the catch-bar with Napier signature. 7.5in (19cm) long **E**

3. A 1960s stylized leaf pin, in high-gloss textured gold-tone. 3.5in (9cm) long **B**

4. A mid-1970s Eygptian-inspired necklace, in gold-plate. 14in (35.5cm) long **C**

5. A pair of drop earrings, in gold-tone metal. 2.5in (6.5cm) long **B**

6. A 1950s tutti frutti charm bracelet, in gold-plate, with faceted glass. 7.5in (19cm) long **D**

7. A 1950s chinoiserie charm bracelet, in silver-tone metal, with missing charms and links, and replacement catch. 7in (18cm) long **C**

4

5

6

7

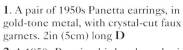

PANETTA

Italian-born Benedetto Panetta emigrated to America in 1901. He had owned his own fine jewelry shop in Naples, and brought his skills to work on costume jewelry pieces for both Trifari and Pennino before opening his own company in New York City in 1945 with his sons Amadeo and Armand. Panetta jewelry was designed to look "real" and was rejected by Panetta if it failed to convince. Art Deco-style platinum- or gold-tone metals, often set with high-quality rhinestones, simulated stones, and pearls, are typical. Successful styles could be made for 30 years. The company was sold to a Japanese buyer in the late 1980s and closed in 1995.

1. A pair of 1950s Panetta earrings, in gold-tone metal, with crystal-cut faux garnets. 2in (5cm) long **D**

2. A 1950s Pennino bird on branch pin, gold- and rhodium-plate, with diamanté, with articulated catkins. 3.25in (8.5cm) long **D**

3. A 1940s Pennino floral pin, in vermeil sterling silver, with purple, red, and colorless rhinestones. 3.5in (9cm) long **G**

MODELING

Prized for its romantic associates with freedom, the bird has been a popular motif for centuries. Many collectors focus on birds, and this naturalistically modeled example is likely to appeal.

DESIGN

Although a common feature in jewelry of this period, birds were not often found on Pennino pieces. Flowers and bows are more typical, making this piece rare, and potentially desirable.

STONES

The articulated catkins add interest to the pin—that they are covered with colorless rhinestones in different sizes is a nice touch, as these will sparkle as the catkins move.

PLATING

The leaves were cast with an effective veined texture. They were then plated with a warm gold, creating an attractive contrast to the cool rhodium-plate and colorless rhinestones.

PENNINO BROTHERS

Frank A.J. Pennino founded a jewelry company in New York City in 1926 with Otto, Frank, and Jack Pennino, as designer, master craftsman, and salesman respectively. It became Pennino Brothers in 1932 under the management of Oreste Pennino, and closed in 1966. Much of the jewelry was made by fellow Italian immigrants, such as Adrian Scannavino and Benedetto Panetta. Typical pieces were intricate and made from Austrian rhinestones and vermeil sterling silver in the shape of flowers, bows, scrolls, drapery, and abstract designs. Almost all were marked, and most are very collectible today.

REBAJES

Francisco Rebajes (1906–90) was born to Spanish parents in the Dominican Republic and stowed away on a ship to New York City in 1922. There, he struggled to find work and led a nomadic existence. He married in 1932 and his wife Pauline encouraged him to make art objects from tin cans to sell. In 1934, he opened a shop selling jewelry and *objets d'art*. Further success followed in 1937 with a medal of honor at the Paris Exposition Universelle and in 1939 he designed six murals for the US Pavilion at the New York World's Fair. By 1942 Rebajes owned a factory employing 40 workers and shops throughout New York, including a flagship store on Fifth Avenue. He moved to Spain in 1967, settling in Torremolinos, and continued to make jewelry there until his death.

Pieces made before the 1940s were almost exclusively in silver, and are now very collectible. Rebajes also used aluminium, nickel, tin, or a mixture of two or more metals, but he is best known for his copper work. These die-cut and embossed pieces display influences as wide-ranging as Picasso, Frank Lloyd Wright, Surrealism, and exotic cultures. Many pieces included three-dimensional elements. All Rebajes pieces are marked with his name.

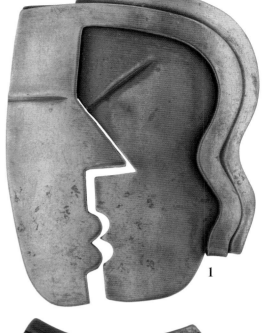

1

2

3

1. A "Kissing" pin, in copper. 2.5in (6cm) long **E**

2. An articulated "dancer" bracelet, in coper. 7.5in (19cm) long **D**

3. A "Chinese dragon" head pin, in copper, stamped "Rebajes." 1.75in (4.5cm) long **B**

4. A late 1940s stylized "African head" pin, in copper, with copper wire necklace and earrings. 3in (8cm) high. **E**

5. A late 1950s cuff bracelet and earrings set, in copper, the bracelet with articulated abstract forms. Bracelet 3in (7.5cm) diam **C**

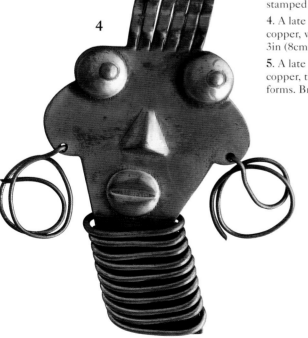

4

5

REGENCY

Unfortunately little information about Regency costume jewelry has survived today, but this has not diminished the interest of collectors. What is known is that the jewelry was made by the Regina Novelty Company, which was based in New York City and owned by the Polowitz family. The jewelry, which was sold directly to department stores in large cities, seems to have been introduced in the 1950s and was removed from production in the 1970s.

Regency's jewelry is characterized by excellent design, superior workmanship and good-quality materials, particularly high-quality rhinestones, which were usually prong-set. Some pieces are more collectable than others because of their use of differently shaped and textured stones—color is also important, with some pieces designed in complementary shades and others in contrasting ones.

As well as floral and foliate motifs, Regency produced a range of butterfly pins in various colorways and forms, which are regarded as signature pieces. Most pieces were marked "Regency," although many pin and earrings sets only have the pin signed.

1

2

3

4

1. A 1950s necklace, in pearlized gun metal, with prong-set blue and brown aurora borealis stones. 16in (40.5cm) long **C**

2. A 1950s pin, with facet-cut rose-pink glass and aurora borealis stones. 2in (5cm) long **C**

3. A mid-1950s pin and earrings set, in dark-coated metal, with lilac and amethyst rhinestones. Pin 3in (7.5cm) long **C**

4. A 1950s flower pin and earrings set, in gold-plate, with topaz and aurora borealis rhinestones, marked "Regency." Pin 3in (7.5cm) diam **C**

5. A 1960s leaf-shape necklace and bracelet set, with faceted blue and colorless diamanté. 7.5in (19cm) long **D**

6. A mid-1950s necklace and earrings set, with black/chocolate pearls and rhinestones. 16in (40.5cm) long **D**

7. A 1950s parure, comprising bracelet, pin, and earrings, in japanned metal, with marquise- and chaton-cut aurora borealis and peridot rhinestones. Bracelet 7in (18cm) long **E**

SETTING

The rhinestones have been prong-set into the setting. This attention to detail is a sign of quality—less prestigious manufacturers often glued stones in place.

STONES

The designer has used several different types of stone, including peridot and aurora borealis rhinestones.

MOTIFS

The bracelet features repeated motifs which, thanks to the hidden clasp, form an never-ending circle of jeweled flowers.

CUT

Most of the stones are marquise cut—an oval, faceted style that reflects light and provides plenty of sparkle.

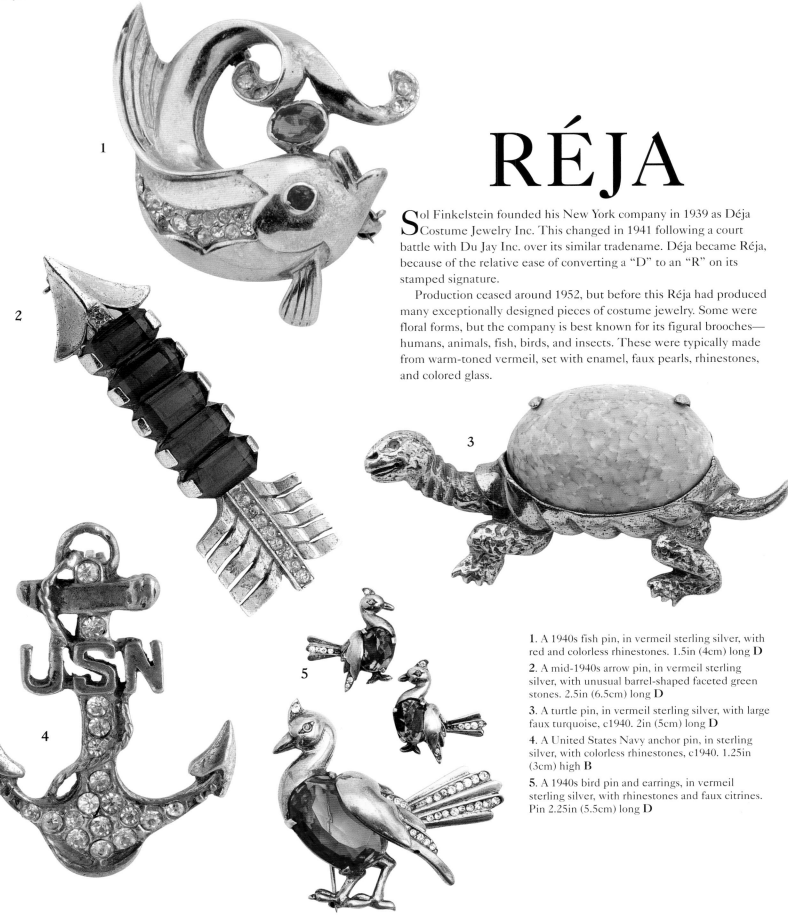

RÉJA

Sol Finkelstein founded his New York company in 1939 as Déja Costume Jewelry Inc. This changed in 1941 following a court battle with Du Jay Inc. over its similar tradename. Déja became Réja, because of the relative ease of converting a "D" to an "R" on its stamped signature.

Production ceased around 1952, but before this Réja had produced many exceptionally designed pieces of costume jewelry. Some were floral forms, but the company is best known for its figural brooches—humans, animals, fish, birds, and insects. These were typically made from warm-toned vermeil, set with enamel, faux pearls, rhinestones, and colored glass.

1. A 1940s fish pin, in vermeil sterling silver, with red and colorless rhinestones. 1.5in (4cm) long **D**

2. A mid-1940s arrow pin, in vermeil sterling silver, with unusual barrel-shaped faceted green stones. 2.5in (6.5cm) long **D**

3. A turtle pin, in vermeil sterling silver, with large faux turquoise, c1940. 2in (5cm) long **D**

4. A United States Navy anchor pin, in sterling silver, with colorless rhinestones, c1940. 1.25in (3cm) high **B**

5. A 1940s bird pin and earrings, in vermeil sterling silver, with rhinestones and faux citrines. Pin 2.25in (5.5cm) long **D**

ROBERT

In 1942 Robert Levy, David Jaffe, and Irving Landsman founded the Fashioncraft Jewelry Company in New York City. The company, which had been trading as Robert for some time, officially changed its name to Robert Originals in 1960.

Robert is perhaps best known for its Haskell-inspired pieces, which feature faux pearls, colored glass, and crystal rhinestones in gilded filigree metalwork. It also produced a wide range of cold-enamel pieces and these are rare and collectible today.

Most pieces are signed, though with varying trademarks. "Original by Robert" was used from 1942 to 1979, when Jaffe's daughter Ellen took over the company, changing the company name to Ellen Designs.

1. A 1950s flower brooch, in enameled metal. 3in (7.5cm) long **B**

2. A 1940s/1950s necklace and earrings set, in faux baroque pearl and pink crystals, the necklace with two strands of faux pearls, marked "Robert." 16in (40.5cm) long **D**

3. An early 1950s flower brooch, in enameled metal, marked "Original by Robert." 4in (10cm) long **B**

4. A 1950s necklace, the pendant set with faux pearls and diamantés. 17in (43cm) long **D**

5. A necklace and earrings set, with faux aquamarine and cobalt blue stones, marked "Robert." Earrings 1.25in (3cm) long **D**

NETTIE ROSENSTEIN

Nettie Rosenstein was born Nettie Rosencrans in Salzburg, Austria, in 1890. The family moved to New York City in the late 1890s, where her parents opened a dry-goods store. Her sister Pauline had a milliner's boutique next door and Nettie began working with her before moving on to dress design. In 1916, after her marriage to lingerie-manufacturer Saul Rosenstein, she set up her own company making clothes. By 1921 she employed 50 dressmakers. Nettie Rosenstein is seen as a leader in democratizing women's fashion.

She retired from fashion in the late 1920s, only to return in 1931 as a designer for fashion house Corbeau & Cie, creating jewelry, handbags, perfume, and lingerie. Before long, she had re-established her own company, which was again hugely successful, grossing $1million in 1937. Attention to detail was crucial to Rosenstein's jewelry concepts. Notable pieces include her brightly colored pavé-set rhinestone earrings and pins, while her striking enamel and silver work in the Art Deco style from the 1930s and 1940s is avidly sought and fetches the highest prices.

Rosenstein discontinued her fashion line in 1961, but kept the jewelry and accessories business in operation until 1975. She died in 1980. Her pieces were signed in script "Nettie Rosenstein" or "Sterling Nettie Rosenstein" between 1942 and 1946.

1. A Nettie Rosenstein "Pied Piper" fur clip, in vermeil sterling silver, with enamel and rhinestones. 2.75in (7cm) long **E**

2. A 1940s Nettie Rosenstein mandolin player pin, in faux ivory, gilt, and diamanté. 1.75in (4.5cm) long **E**

3. A pair of 1950s earrings, attributed to Rousselet, comprised of multi-colored glass drops, on gold-tone chains. 2.75in (7cm) long **C**

"It's what you leave off a dress that makes it smart."
Nettie Rosenstein

ROUSSELET

Louis Rousselet (1892–1980) was born in Paris where he learned to manufacture lamp-work beads. In 1919, he opened a factory in the Paris suburb of Menilmontant and began manufacturing glass and Galalith beads, and imitation pearls. By 1925 he employed around 800 workers and his beads were shipped all over the world, many going to famous costume jewelry designers including Coco Chanel. Rousselet's own jewelry was composed of glass beads in a wide variety of colors and styles; some were foiled, some iridescent, and some filled with lamp-wound multi-colored swirls. Many of the collections were designed by Rousselet's daughter, Denise, particularly after 1965 when she took over from her father as chief designer. The last trained worker left in 1975.

1. A pair of 1970s/1980s Yves Saint Laurent flower earrings, in gilt metal, marked "made in France, YSL," with original box. 1.75in (4.5cm) wide **D**

2. A mid-1980s Yves Saint Laurent limited-edition charm necklace, in gold-plate, with framed Lucite "stones," marked "Yves Saint Laurent." 16in (38.5cm) long **F**

3. An Yves Saint Laurent "Rive Gauche" necklace, the large irregular pastes in gilt-metal clawed mounts, 1987. 10in (25.5cm) diam **M**

YVES
SAINT LAURENT

Yves Saint Laurent (1936–2008) became Christian Dior's chief designer (see pages 80–5) at the age of 21 in 1958, and established his own fashion house in 1961. Although his early work caused outrage, by the 1980s Saint Laurent's designs were considered fashion classics. His jewelry, introduced in the 1970s, is as theatrical and colorful as many of his wildest clothing lines, including large ethnic beaded pieces, metal medallions, and whimsical enamels. Such pieces were manufactured by a variety of companies, including Monet, but Saint Laurent maintained creative control. In general, his catwalk jewels are most sought-after, although glass, plastic, and Lucite pieces are gaining in value and may prove to be good investment buys.

SANDOR

Sandor Goldberger's small New York City company produced delicate sterling silver jewelry from the mid- to late 1930s until 1972. His signature floral designs are delicately modelled and decorated with cold enamelling in pastel colors and a mix of high-quality rhinestones which simulated semi-precious stones. Some beaded, faux pearl, and coral pieces in the style of Miriam Haskell were also made, as was figural jewelry. The latter was produced in very small numbers, and such pieces are now rare, but all Sandor jewelry is sought after for its craftsmanship and aesthetic qualities. Most pieces are marked "Sandor," although those produced in 1939–40 are marked "Sandor Goldberger."

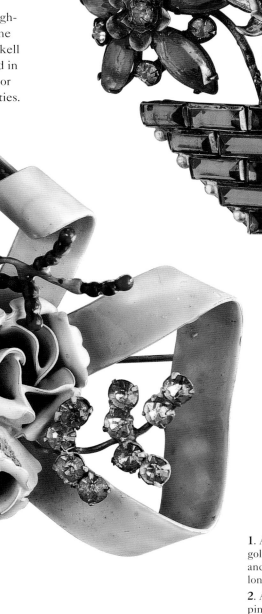

1. A 1930s Sandor flower-pot pin, in gold-tone metal, with amber, green, and colorless rhinestones. 3in (7.5cm) long **I**

2. A 1930s Sandor ribbon and flowers pin, in enameled metal, with colorless rhinestones. 3.5in (9cm) long **F**

1. A 1950s Selro necklace and earrings set, in gold-tone metal, with flat purple and faceted aurora borealis rhinestones. Necklace 16in (40.5cm) long **D**

2. A mid-1950s Selro "Samurai warriors" bracelet and earrings set, in gilded metal, with plastic heads and green and purple crystals. 7in (17.5cm) long **D**

3. A pair of 1960s Selro earrings, in silver-tone metal, with blue rhinestone with confetti Lucite cabochons. 0.75in (2cm) long **B**

SELRO & SELINI

Best known for jewelry incorporating brightly colored plastic faces, Selro was founded by Russian immigrant Paul Selinger in New York City in the late 1940s and remained open until the 1960s. As well as the "head" jewelry, delicate and feminine pieces were also produced. Selini jewelry was made by Selro, and many pieces were signed with both names. Pieces marked "Selan" may also have been Selro products. Most Selro jewelry was unsigned, but pieces can be identified by the settings, herringbone chain used on lariat necklaces, and the bracing structure on the back.

DESIGN

Western jewelry has been influenced by Japan's art and culture for centuries. The particular surge of interest in the late 19th century was due to Japan's trading links with the West re-opening in 1853.

SETTING

The pale faces are in striking contrast with the warm gilt metal and the dark stones. Typically the heads are in bright colors, such as deep red or turquoise, which are sought-after colors.

MOTIF

The Noh Samurai warrior/devil face used on this bracelet is one of the three most common Selro faces. The others are an Asian woman (sometimes known as "Thai girl") and an African man.

STONES

While Selro's plastic faces typically represent exotic cultures, the colors of the stones used in this bracelet are more associated with the Tudor royalty of Britain. This humorous contrast of styles gives the piece interest.

SHERMAN

Canada's most renowned costume jewelry designer, Gustave Sherman, set up his factory in 1947 in Montreal. Previously he had been a jewelry salesman, and he now used his knowledge of the market to create superior pieces. These were sold in department stores, with his most elaborate designs sold in boutiques.

Sherman used high-quality Swarovski rhinestones and crystal beads, which were often navette- or marquise-cut. These were set in heavy rhodium, gold-tone or (more desirable) japanned settings.

Desirability is dependant on the color of the stones, with purple, fuchsia and red, black and yellow especially sought after, particularly those in "Siam Red." Blue is a more common color, and less desirable. Form is also important. Bracelets are typically rare and sought after. Such pieces typically have interlocking crystals over the clasp, making it difficult to tell where the bracelet starts. In the 1970s fashion trends turned towards silver and gold, and Sherman began to make pieces in precious metals set with gemstones. The company closed in 1981.

1. A demi-parure, comprising a necklace, bracelet, and pair of earrings, with light and dark blue spherical glass cabochons. Earrings 1.5in (4cm) long **G**

2. A pair of "chandelier-style" drop earring, with faceted colorless rhinestones. 3in (7.5cm) long **G**

3. A stylized floral pin and earrings set, with prong-set faceted red and colorless rhinestones. Pin 2.5in (6.5cm) wide **F**

4. A stylized foliate pin, with prong-set iridescent blue rhinestones. 3in (7.5cm) long **E**

5. A pin, with prong-set iridescent faceted rhinestones. 2.5in (5cm) long **D**

6. A bracelet, set with alternating small and large circular and oval iridescent rhinestones. 7.75in (17cm) long **D**

7. A flower pin and earrings set , with prong-set red and colorless rhinestones. 2.5in (5cm) long **C**

8. A pair of drop earrings, with prong-set faceted rose pink rhinestones. 2in (5cm) long **D**

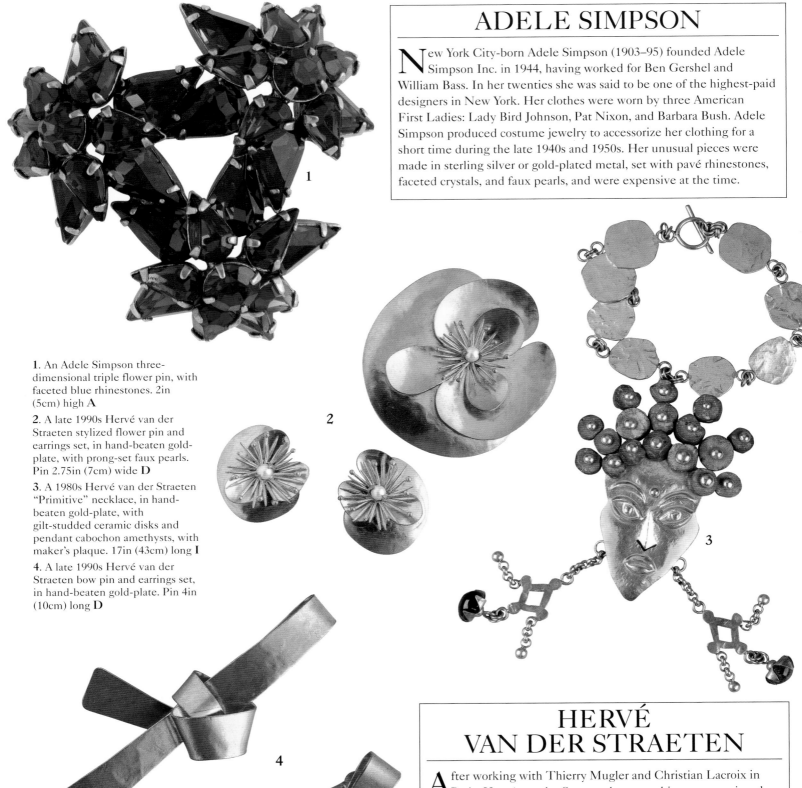

ADELE SIMPSON

New York City-born Adele Simpson (1903–95) founded Adele Simpson Inc. in 1944, having worked for Ben Gershel and William Bass. In her twenties she was said to be one of the highest-paid designers in New York. Her clothes were worn by three American First Ladies: Lady Bird Johnson, Pat Nixon, and Barbara Bush. Adele Simpson produced costume jewelry to accessorize her clothing for a short time during the late 1940s and 1950s. Her unusual pieces were made in sterling silver or gold-plated metal, set with pavé rhinestones, faceted crystals, and faux pearls, and were expensive at the time.

1. An Adele Simpson three-dimensional triple flower pin, with faceted blue rhinestones. 2in (5cm) high **A**

2. A late 1990s Hervé van der Straeten stylized flower pin and earrings set, in hand-beaten gold-plate, with prong-set faux pearls. Pin 2.75in (7cm) wide **D**

3. A 1980s Hervé van der Straeten "Primitive" necklace, in hand-beaten gold-plate, with gilt-studded ceramic disks and pendant cabochon amethysts, with maker's plaque. 17in (43cm) long **I**

4. A late 1990s Hervé van der Straeten bow pin and earrings set, in hand-beaten gold-plate. Pin 4in (10cm) long **D**

HERVÉ VAN DER STRAETEN

After working with Thierry Mugler and Christian Lacroix in Paris, Hervé van der Straeten began making costume jewelry in the 1990s and continues to do so today. His pieces are primarily made from gold- or silver-plated hammered brass, wood, and enamel in bold shapes that combine contemporary and baroque styles. These are already rare and collectible. Van der Straeten is also known for designing interiors, furniture, and perfume bottles.

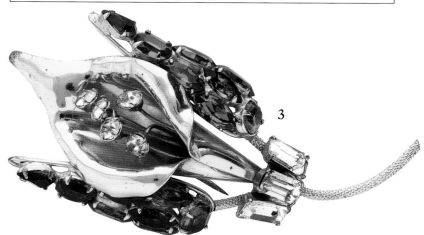

TORTOLANI

Francisco Tortolani began making jewelry in Rhode Island, U.S.A., under the name Mastercraft Jewelry Co., before moving to Los Angeles and founding Tortolani Jewelry in 1950. The pieces he created were often three-dimensional, cast in pewter and plated with gold or silver. The company ceased production in 1976, but has since begun re-releasing old pieces.

VOGUE

Founded by Harold Shapiro, Jack Gilbert, and George Grant in 1936, Vogue is best known for the high-quality crystal bead rope necklaces it produced during the 1950s. The patriotic flag and figural pins it made in the 1940s are rare and sought after today. The Shapiro family sold its interest in Vogue in 1962, but the company continued to operate until 1973, producing jewelry that was sold in stores such as the American department store chain I. Magnin.

1. An early 1960s Francisco Tortolani cherub cuff bracelet, in gold-plate. 3in (7.5cm) wide **C**

2. A 1950s Vogue two-strand necklace and earrings set, of faux pearl and colorless rhinestone rondelles and spheres. Necklace 23in (58cm) long **C**

3. A rare 1930s Vogue lily corsage pin, in vermeil sterling silver, with green rhinestone and diamanté, marked "STERLING." 3.25in (8cm) long **E**

LARRY
VRBA

Larry Vrba's jewelry career began in 1969 when he was aged 18. Following service in the army, he left his home in Lincoln, Nebraska, and moved to New York City with the aim of working for Miriam Haskell whose work he admired. After several visits to the company's offices he met the then owner, Sandy Moss, who gave him a job preparing the components for each piece of jewelry ready for the makers to assemble it. Within six weeks he was a designer, making jewelry for one day a week.

Two years later he followed Haskell's head designer Bob Clark to William De Lillo and then worked for Castlecliff from 1970 to 1972.

Vrba returned to Miriam Haskell in 1973 as head designer, a position he held until 1981. He created over a thousand different lines for Haskell. These typically had an exotic twist to their traditional styling. Vrba then worked for Les Bernard (owned by Bernard Shapiro and Lester Joy) for two years, before setting up his own company in 1983.

His own pieces are large (typically 4in/10cm wide or more), colorful and often three-dimensional. At his New York City studio, he incorporates both contemporary and antique materials (for example, vintage beads and rhinestones) into beautiful and extravagant one-of-a-kind pieces. Each piece is hand-made, typically with prong-set stones with a gold-tone or pewter metal base.

Vrba's jewelry is particularly sought after by the transvestite community (particularly for New York's annual charity drag balls) because it is often so big and bold. For similar reasons Broadway's theater designers also seek him out, and some of Vrba's most recent work can be seen worn in the musicals *Hairspray* and *Wicked*.

1. A 1990s sultan pin, with Lucite face, faux pearls, carved glass, and diamanté. 7in (18cm) long **D**

2. A pair of 1990s earrings, with faux topaz, faux pearl, and aurora borealis, and faux pearl drops. 3in (7.5cm) long **D**

3. A late 1980s sautoir necklace, with 1930s pendant, with art glass, marble, faux pearls, and red pumpkin glass beads. Beads 21in (53.5cm) long **F**

4. A late 1990s bow pin, in ruthenium-plate, with colorless rhinestones. 4in (10cm) wide **D**

5. A mid-1990s three-dimensional floral pin, with a multicolored glass stones and faux pearls. 5in (25cm) long **D**

6. A late 1980s sautoir necklace, with 1930s pendant, with baroque pearl, coral, turquoise, jet, and crystal rhinestones. Beeds 21in (53.5cm) long **F**

1. A 1950s Warner butterfly pin, with turquoise, blue, and red rhinestones. **C**

2. A 1940s Warner mechanical "night and day" flower pin, in gold-tone metal, with opening and closing petals. 2.5in (6cm) long **C**

WARNER

Joseph Warner's company, founded in around 1953, is known for high-quality costume jewelry in gold-tone or particularly japanned metal, set with colorful rhinestones. Typical pieces are shaped like flowers, fruit, and insects, although novelty shapes, such as umbrellas, were also produced. "Night and day" flowers, which feature a mechanism that opens and shuts the petals, are particularly sought after. Production ceased in 1971.

3. A 1980s Vivienne Westwood royal orb choker, in silver-tone metal, with colorless rhinestones, with three strands of faux pearls. 13.5in (34.5cm) long **C**

4. A Vivienne Westwood heart pin, in gold-tone metal, with trademark orb and red enamel ribbon, with ring fitting for necklace, contains Boudoir perfume, c2000. 2in (5cm) long **B**

5. A 1980s Vivienne Westwood royal orb pendant necklace, in gold-tone metal, with rhinestones. Pendant 1.25in (3.25cm) long. **D**

VIVIENNE WESTWOOD

Famous for her collections of punk rock and bondage-inspired clothing, Vivienne Westwood (born 1941) began designing professionally in 1971. Before this she had been a primary school teacher, designing jewelry in her spare time, which she then sold at a stall on Portobello Road, London. Later during the punk era, Westwood's outfits included safety pins, bicycle chains, and spiked dog collars worn as jewelry. Her 1980s jewelry was tame in comparison, often featuring bows, hearts, and traditional royal symbols, for example crowns and orbs. Such pieces were crafted from silver or gold-plate pewter, and decorated with Swarovski crystals and faux pearls.

1. A 1970s Whiting & Davis disco necklace, in gold-tone mesh, with diamanté. Mesh 7in (18in) square **B**

2. A 1960s Whiting & Davis coiled snake bangle, in gold-tone expandable metal mesh, with a solid punched and engraved head. 12in (30.5cm) circ **B**

3. A 1960s Whiting & Davis bracelet, in white metal, with central mother-of-pearl disk, and original swing label. 2.5in (6cm) diam **B**

WHITING & DAVIS

W hiting & Davies was founded in 1876 in Massachusetts and initially produced finely woven mesh evening bags. From 1907 jewelry was added to the range, and this proved successful. The line included iridescent glass jewelry, but most pieces were made from silver, gold-plate, or silver-plate, sometimes with porcelain or cameo-style additions. These pieces, which often display Victorian or Art Nouveau influences, are typically impressed "Whiting & Davis" in the metal, sometimes within a cartouche. The company's delicate mesh chokers are popular today, but the most sought after pieces are mesh bangles adorned with snake heads. Bags and accessories are still made, but the jewelry line was discontinued in 1983.

Austrian Jewelry
Plastic Jewelry
Christmas Tree Pins
Czech Jewelry
Double Clips
Jelly Bellies
Unsigned gems

Galleries

AUSTRIAN JEWELRY

A ustria has been famed for the brilliance and sparkle of its glass (particularly rhinestones) since the early 18th century — indeed the famous Swarovski Company was founded (in 1895) and is still based in Austria. After 1915, a number of costume jewelry producers settled in Austria and the combination of their technical skills and Austrian glass and aesthetic resulted in some extremely fine pieces. One of the best-known Austrian forms is the fruit pin, which was produced during the 1940s and 1950s. These come in a wide variety of fruits (with strawberries, cherries, pears, and grapes most common) and vibrant colors, which are further enhanced by gold- or silver-foiling. These extremely desirable pieces typically have leaves and stems of silver, gilt or japanned metal, which are sometimes enameled or decorated with Austrian crystals.

1. An articulated leaf and grape pin, in gold-tone metal, with faceted brown crystals. 2.75in (7cm) high **B**

2. A 1950s strawberries fruit pin, in black enameled metal, with red glass strawberries and green rhinestones. 2.5in (6cm) wide **C**

3. A 1950s square pin and earrings set, with clear navette-cut rhinestones. Pin 1.5in (4cm) wide **C**

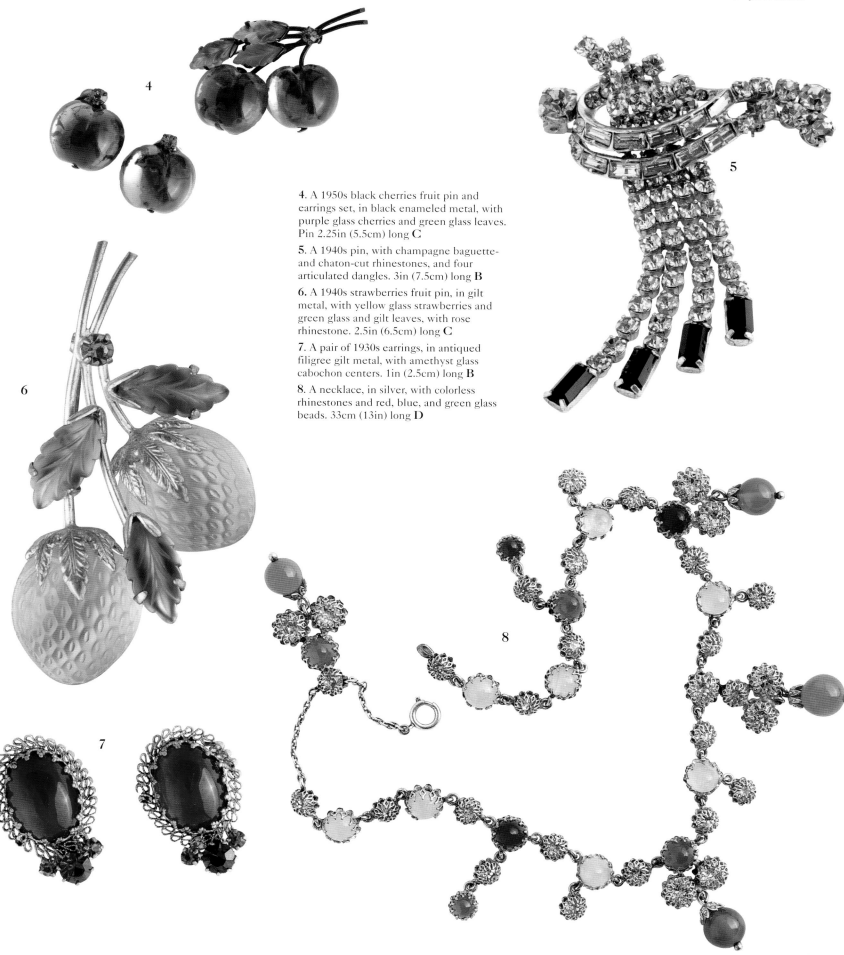

4. A 1950s black cherries fruit pin and earrings set, in black enameled metal, with purple glass cherries and green glass leaves. Pin 2.25in (5.5cm) long **C**

5. A 1940s pin, with champagne baguette- and chaton-cut rhinestones, and four articulated dangles. 3in (7.5cm) long **B**

6. A 1940s strawberries fruit pin, in gilt metal, with yellow glass strawberries and green glass and gilt leaves, with rose rhinestone. 2.5in (6.5cm) long **C**

7. A pair of 1930s earrings, in antiqued filigree gilt metal, with amethyst glass cabochon centers. 1in (2.5cm) long **B**

8. A necklace, in silver, with colorless rhinestones and red, blue, and green glass beads. 33cm (13in) long **D**

PLASTIC JEWELRY

In the period after the Great Depression and before World War II, brightly colored plastic jewelry became incredibly popular, due to its modest price. Inexpensive in its day, such jewelry was often carelessly discarded, and is therefore highly sought after now.

Three basic types of plastic were used for costume jewelry. The two earliest — pyroxylin (such as celluloid) and casin (such as Galalith) — were created from naturally found proteins. The third, known as cast phenolic, is entirely synthetic. The first example of this plastic was patented in 1907 by Dr. Leo Baekeland and was called Bakelite. This exciting new material could be polished to a high sheen, and colored — initially with a limited range of shades (of which black, white, red, brown, and yellow were the most popular), but soon more than 200 existed, with witty names such as "apple juice." It could also be easily shaped and carved, making it perfect for both geometric Art Deco shapes and later figural forms.

Today much plastic costume jewelry is referred to as "Bakelite" no matter which type of plastic it is made of.

1

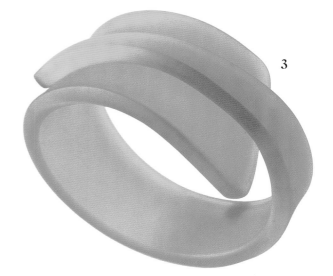

2

3

1. A 1930s American leaves necklace, in orange celluloid, with celluloid chain. 14.5in (37cm) long **D**

2. A swordfish pin, in carved black plastic. 4in (10cm) wide **E**

3 . A curling bangle, in matte yellow plastic. 3.25in (8.5cm) diam **B**

4. A late 1930s bracelet and dress-clips set, in green Bakelite, with applied brass detailing. 3in (7.5cm) diam **F**

5. A leaf pin, in carved cherry red plastic. 3.75in (9.5cm) long **G**

6. A 1930s flamingo pin, in carved "creamed corn" Bakelite, with black Bakelite beak and inlaid green rhinestone eye. 4.25in (11cm) high **F**

7. A 1950s ring, in laminated orange and clear Lucite. 1.5in (3.5cm) high **A**

8. A hollow bangle, in sterling silver, with black Bakelite "injected" panels. 3.5in (8.5cm) diam **F**

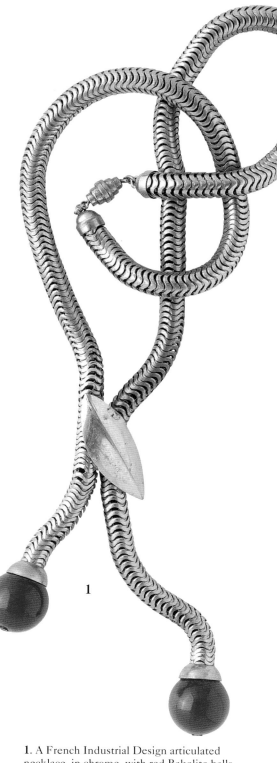

INSPIRATION

This pin is probably based on singer and dancer Josephine Baker. In 1925 she took Paris by storm in the *Revue Nègre*, an African-American song-and-dance review, and subsequently became a pin-up of the Jazz age.

BAKELITE

The textured quality of the "fur stole" contrasts well with the smooth Bakelite of the rest of the piece, and the brass detailing of her "jewelry." This mixing of Bakelite with other materials was a European fashion.

DESIGN

Strong and easily shaped, Bakelite could be used for small, protruding parts of a piece of jewelry without the risk of damage. Here the singer's outwardly bent hands evoke a strong sense of movement.

1

2

3

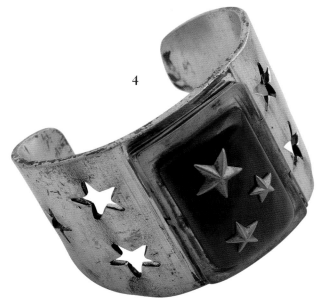

4

1. A French Industrial Design articulated necklace, in chrome, with red Bakelite balls. 14.5in (37cm) long **F**

2. A late 1920s French Josephine Baker pin, in Bakelite, with brass and painted details. 3in (7.5cm) long **C**

3. A 1940s "Bambi" pin, in "creamed corn" Bakelite, with painted details. 3.5in (8.5cm) long **D**

4. A 1940s star photo-locket cuff bangle, in silver, with cut-out and applied stars, and Bakelite locket. 3in (7.5cm) diam **C**

5. A 1950s Donald Hedger necklace, in two-tone Bakelite. 6.25in (16cm) diam **G**

6. A large flower pin, in carved yellow plastic. 3.25in (8cm) diam **E**

7. A heart clip, in carved red plastic. 2in (5cm) long **C**

8. A pair of 1930s American Art Deco earrings, in black and marbled Bakelite. 2in (5cm) long **B**

9. A rare gazelle pin, in wood and green Bakelite. 2.5in (6cm) long **E**

10. A horse-theme charm bracelet, in brass, with red Bakelite charms with brass insets. 7in (18cm) long **E**

1

2

3

1. A dress clip, in carved green Lucite. 3.25in (8cm) long **B**

2. An early 1920s cicada pin, in plastic, probably Galalith, with rhinestones, metal studs, and gold paint. 3in (7.5cm) long **B**

3. A cherry bar pin, in red and green carved plastic, the stringing replaced. 3.25in (8.5cm) long **F**

4. A pair of cube earrings, of green Bakelite. Dangler 2.5in (6.5cm) long **D**

5. A floral hinged bracelet, in coral-colored Bakelite, hinge loose and missing pins. 3in (7.5cm) diam **D**

4

5

6. A 1930s pendant necklace, in carved "apple juice" Bakelite, with rhinestones. Pendant 2.25in (5.5cm) long **D**

7. A pair of flower and leaf dress clips in, peach Bakelite on wood. 2.25in (6cm) long **C**

8. A 1930s lifesaving ring pin, in black bakelite, with original woven two-colour gimp "rope." 1.75in (4.5cm) diam **D**

9. A reverse-carved pin, in Lucite, with paint highlights and metal backing, c1935–40. 2.5in (6.5cm) long **C**

10. An Art Deco bow pin, in green and black carved Bakelite, with brass ribbed center. 3.75in (9.5cm) long **D**

11. A sword pin, in carved yellow Bakelite, with black paint, wire, and pressed brass dangles. 3.25in (8cm) long **D**

CHRISTMAS TREE PINS

The Christmas tree pin phenomenon began in the early 19th century, when fashionable ladies decked out their lapels with festive corsages of cloth and ribbon. These fragile ornaments were replaced in the 1940s by more durable metal-framed Christmas jewelry, but such pieces were not really popular until 1950. That Christmas many American men were away fighting in the Korean War, and so their wives and mothers sent them small Christmas tree pins as a symbol of peace, and in the hope of their safe return.

From then on, designers and manufacturers released new pins annually, typically in silver- or gold-tone metal, adorned with red and green beds, stones, or enamel. Christmas tree pins quickly grew into a collecting phenomenon in America, and have since become internationally sought after. Some unsigned trees are inexpensive, but rare examples by notable makers are highly valuable.

1. A Larry Vrba Christmas tree pin, with large aurora borealis and round-cut colorless rhinestones, and square-cut Montana blue rhinestones, 1990s. 4.5in (11.5cm) long **C**

2. A Cristobal Christmas tree pin, with red and green rhinestones. 2.75in (7cm) long **B**

3

4

3. A Cristobal Christmas tree pin, with 1950s Swarovski rhinestones, with peridot and emerald green glass. 3.25in (8cm) long **B**

4. A 1950s Stanley Hagler Christmas tree pin, with red glass flowers and frosted fan-shaped shells. 3in (7.5cm) long **C**

5. A 1980s Stanley Hagler Christmas tree decoration, with glass beaded leaves and trinkets. 4in (10cm) long **D**

6. A Stanley Hagler Christmas tree pin, with red glass beads, pearl bell flowers, green rhinestones, red glass flowers, jadeite beads, and gold-plated filigree backing. c1990 2.75in (7cm) long **D**

5

6

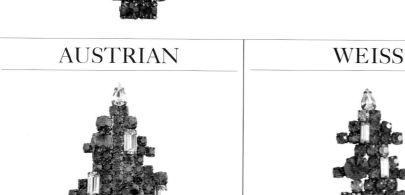

AUSTRIAN | WEISS

UNNAMED vs NAMED

These two pins clearly show the value of a good, named manufacturer. The designs are similar, with some features of the Austrian example arguably superior to the Weiss: for example, the green rhinestones are more densely arranged in the Austrian piece, making the "candles" stand out. However, there is a greater variety of color in the Weiss pin, the red "baubles" are more prominent than the purple, and the orange "flames" add a seasonal warmth. Both pins are 2.75in (7cm) long, but the unmarked Austrian example is only worth $60-80 (£35-45). The Weiss piece, which appeals to collectors of that maker as well as collectors of Christmas tree pins, is worth more than twice that, at $130-180 (£80-120).

1. A Mylu Christmas tree pin, with pink and green stones, and diamanté. 2.75in (7cm) long **E**

2. A late 1990s Atwood & Sawyer snowman pin, in gold-plate, with green and blue enamel, and ruby and pavé-set colorless rhinestones. 1.4in (3.5cm) long **B**

3. A late 1980s Monet Christmas tree pin, in gold-tone metal, with enamel. 2in (5cm) long **B**

4. A JJ Christmas tree pin, in gold-tone metal, with multi-colored glass rhinestones. 2.25in (5.5cm) long **A**

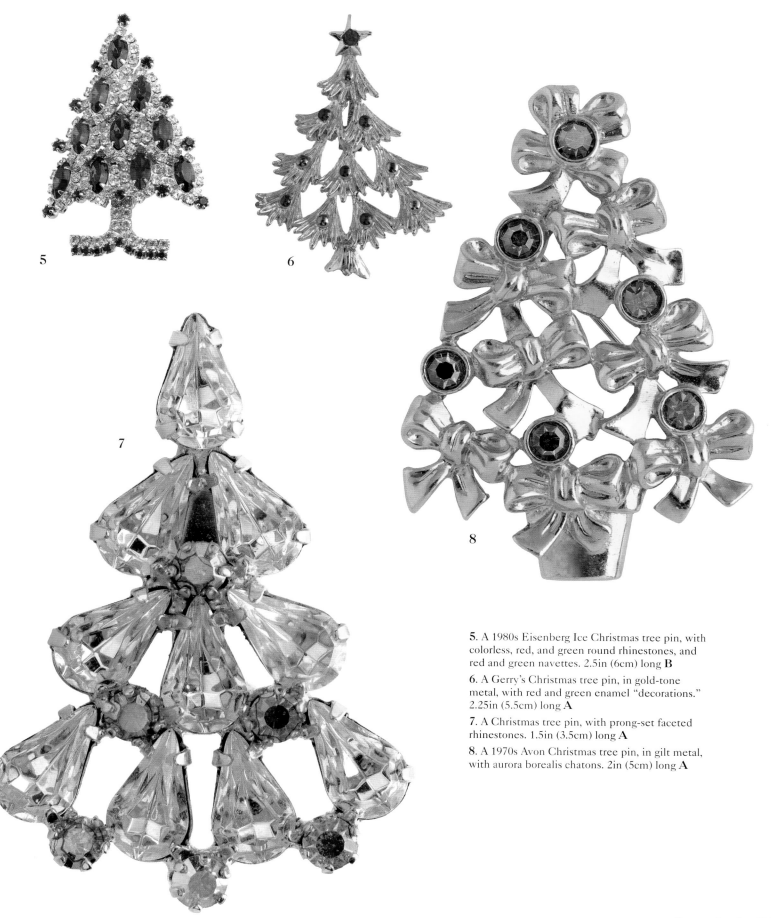

5. A 1980s Eisenberg Ice Christmas tree pin, with colorless, red, and green round rhinestones, and red and green navettes. 2.5in (6cm) long **B**

6. A Gerry's Christmas tree pin, in gold-tone metal, with red and green enamel "decorations." 2.25in (5.5cm) long **A**

7. A Christmas tree pin, with prong-set faceted rhinestones. 1.5in (3.5cm) long **A**

8. A 1970s Avon Christmas tree pin, in gilt metal, with aurora borealis chatons. 2in (5cm) long **A**

CZECH JEWELRY

From the 1890s to the late 1930s, intricate jewelry was created in northern Czechoslovakia. No single large corporation had control over the production of this jewelry as it was made by numerous small factories. Yellow-metal filigree settings and findings were created at Harachov and Liberec, but the stars of the show were the glass stones produced at the nearby town of Jablonec. The "stones," which are typically found in rich purples or delicate pastels, had an almost unrivaled clarity of brilliance. Styles ranged from Art Nouveau, which is most typical, to Egyptian Revival and Art Deco. Unfortunately the Soviet era (1935–89) placed an emphasis on practical crafts and, although Jablonec is still one of the world's major producers of costume jewelry, its heyday was over.

Early 20th-century Czech jewelry, which is often unsigned, was extremely popular across Europe, and is a favored collecting area today. It is very desirable, with higher prices going to complex pieces and necklaces, which are relatively rare.

1. A 1960s pin, in gold-plate, with blue rhinestones. 2.75in (7cm) wide **C**

2. An early 1920s sautoir necklace, of lapis glass, with faux filigree backings. 30in (75cm) long **D**

3. A 1930s necklace, of ruby glass and diamanté, stamped "CZECHOZLOVAKIA.". 10.5in (27cm) long **C**

4. A pair of 1950s earrings, with large purple glass cabochons and pale blue rhinestones. 1in (2.5cm) long **B**

5. An Art Deco Egyptian Revival necklace, in gold-tone metal, with green glass, c1925. 18in (46cm) long **M**

6. An Art Nouveau bracelet, in gilt brass filigree, with large hand-faceted red stones, c1900. 7in (17.5cm) long **D**

7. An Art Nouveau pin, with enamel and large pink glass stone, c1910. 2.5in (6.5cm) long **C**

DOUBLE CLIPS

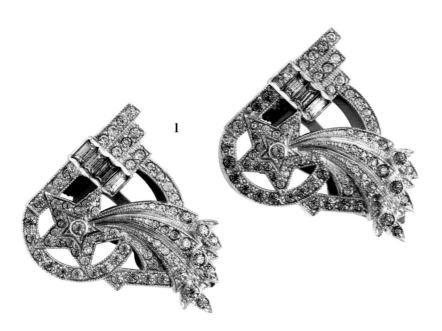

The idea for the clip pin supposedly came to French jeweler Louis Cartier as he watched a peasant woman hanging out her washing with wooden clothes pegs. This then evolved into a series of clip variations, including the double clip: two fur clips that could be worn separately or together attached to a frame. Cartier patented this idea in 1927, and it soon became extremely popular across Europe and America as a result of its incredible versatility. The most successful example, which largely dominated production, was made by the American company Coro, which patented its "Duette" in 1931.

According to Loelia Linsey, Duchess of Westminster, "By the end of the Twenties, it had become essential to possess a pair of diamond, or pseudo-diamond, clips. They were clipped not only to hats but on to everything else, even the small of the back, where they served to keep underclothes out of sight." Other celebrities of the day were also known to endorse the double clip: Mrs Cole Porter commissioned a Cartier "tutti frutti" double clip in 1935, and Princess Elizabeth (later Queen Elizabeth II) was given Cartier diamond and aquamarine clips in 1944 by her parents.

The double clip remained popular until the 1950s, graduating in style from Art Deco in the 1920s to a more sculptural naturalism.

1. A pair of rare Art Deco "shooting star" dress clips, in silver-tone metal, with diamanté. 1.5in (3.5cm) long **C**

2. A 1930s Trifari Clip-mate, in silver-tone metal, with moonstone and colorless rhinestones. 3.5in (9cm) long **J**

2

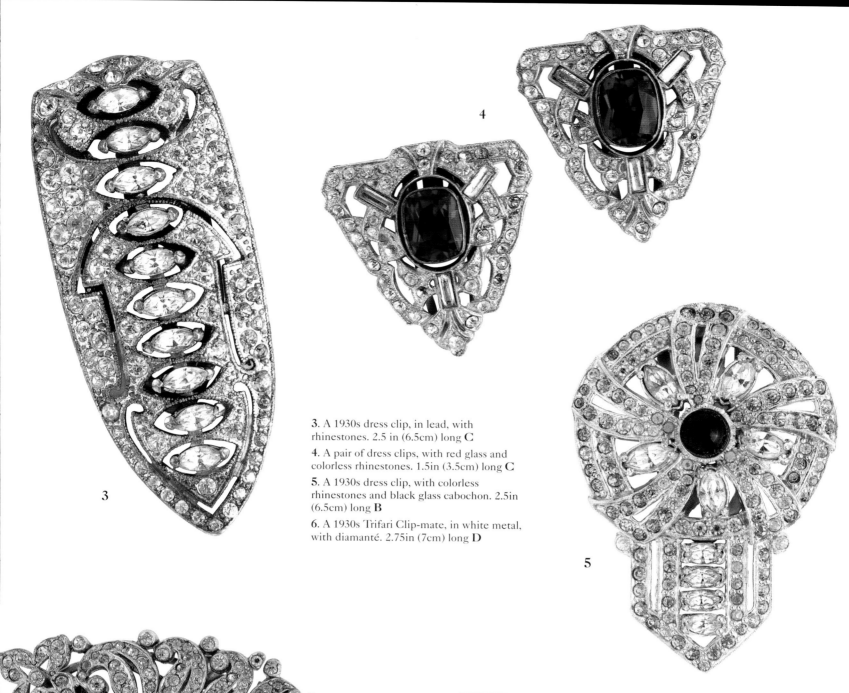

3. A 1930s dress clip, in lead, with rhinestones. 2.5 in (6.5cm) long **C**

4. A pair of dress clips, with red glass and colorless rhinestones. 1.5in (3.5cm) long **C**

5. A 1930s dress clip, with colorless rhinestones and black glass cabochon. 2.5in (6.5cm) long **B**

6. A 1930s Trifari Clip-mate, in white metal, with diamanté. 2.75in (7cm) long **D**

TRIFARI CLIP-MATE

Although Coro held the patents for the "Duette" (see pages 78–9), this did not stop other manufacturers producing their own double clips. The most successful of these was the Trifari "Clip-Mate." Rather than folding into the frame like the Duette, Trifari's two clips slid onto their frame in a closed-up position. This mechanism was less versatile than the Duettes, but the result invariably looked more like precious jewelry, aided by the fact that Trifari favored abstract forms over Coro's cheerful figurals. Most examples are marked "Clip-mates" inside the mechanism, and Clip-mates made from 1936 to the end of 1937 should also be marked "TKF."

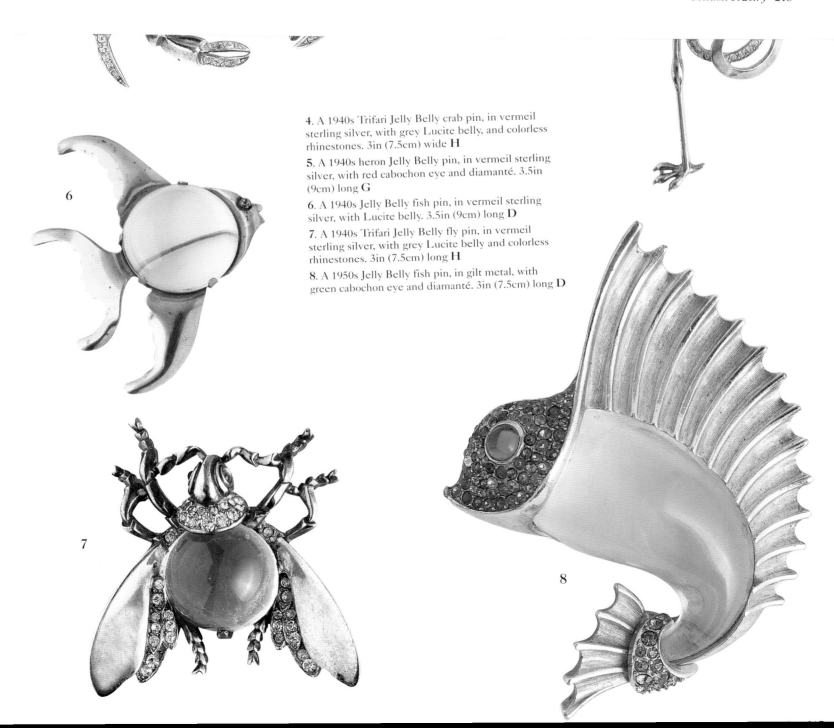

4. A 1940s Trifari Jelly Belly crab pin, in vermeil sterling silver, with grey Lucite belly, and colorless rhinestones. 3in (7.5cm) wide **H**

5. A 1940s heron Jelly Belly pin, in vermeil sterling silver, with red cabochon eye and diamanté. 3.5in (9cm) long **G**

6. A 1940s Jelly Belly fish pin, in vermeil sterling silver, with Lucite belly. 3.5in (9cm) long **D**

7. A 1940s Trifari Jelly Belly fly pin, in vermeil sterling silver, with grey Lucite belly and colorless rhinestones. 3in (7.5cm) long **H**

8. A 1950s Jelly Belly fish pin, in gilt metal, with green cabochon eye and diamanté. 3in (7.5cm) long **D**

JELLY BELLIES

During World War II, Trifari converted some of its factories to produce Lucite windshields and turrets for American fighter planes. The rejects were thrown away until someone (possibly chief designer Alfred Philippe) had the bright idea of cutting the discarded Lucite into cabochons and using them as the "bellies" of sterling silver animal pins. Roosters, penguins, and seals are among the more common animals, with poodles being especially rare and desirable. Most were designed by Philippe.

As Jelly Bellies proved very popular, other manufacturers—notably rival company Coro—soon began releasing their own versions. Coro's Jelly Bellies were designed by Adolph Katz, and could be found singly or mounted on a Duette double clip.

Jelly Bellies have seen a dramatic rise in price recently, with signed examples in rare shapes commanding up to $1,000 (£500).

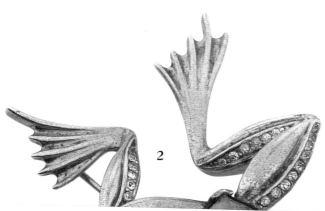

1. A 1950s Trifari sparrow Jelly Belly pin, in gilt metal, with Lucite belly, red cabochon eye, and diamanté. 2in (5.5cm) long **D**

2. A Trifari Jelly Belly frog pin, in vermeil sterling silver, with Lucite belly, marked "Trifari" and "STERLING," 1943. 2.75in (7cm) long **F**

UNSIGNED GEMS

So much attention is given to jewelry made by famous designers it is possible to lose sight of the fact that the majority of vintage pieces were never marked with the name of the designer or maker. For many years collectors tended to ignore "unsigned" pieces in favor of those made by named designers. However, this has changed in recent years due to rising prices for designer work. Buyers appreciate design, materials, and craftsmanship. Examples that are typical of their era and show a strong design aesthetic are rising in value and popularity.

An experienced dealer or collector can sometimes tell if a piece is an unsigned jewel by a famous name such as Trifari or Coro, but often only days of painstaking research looking at patents and original advertisements, and comparing materials and methods of manufacture, can lead to identification.

The best unsigned pieces feature exceptional design and quality materials and show superb craftsmanship.

1. A 1920s French iris pin, possibly by Maison Burma, in silver, with enamel and diamanté, with French touch mark. 4in (10cm) long **K**

2. A late 1910s crown pin, in silver, with white and red crystals. 1.5in (4cm) long **D**

3. A possibly French open pierce-work bar pin, in silver, with colorless rhinestones and large central faux emerald, c1910. 3in (7.5cm) long **D**

4

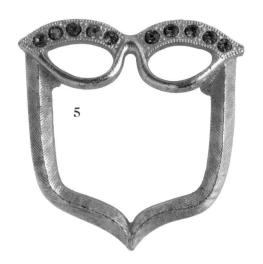

5

6

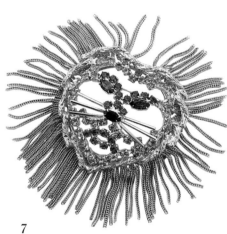

7

8

4. A strawberry fruit pin, in faux pearl and colored rhinestones. 1.75in (4.5cm) long **A**

5. A spectacles pin, in gold-plate, with blue rhinestones. 1.25in (3cm) high **A**

6. A cat head pin, in gold-plate. 1.5in (4cm) wide **A**

7. A late 1950s lion's head tassel pin. 3in (7.5cm) long **C**

8. A 1940s crown pin, in sterling silver, with faceted yellow and ruby red glass tones, marked "Sterling." 1.5in (3.5cm) long **B**

9. A leaf pin, in gold-plate, with green faceted rhinestone. 2.75in (7cm) high **A**

10. A 1970s American Stars and Stripes pin, in gold-tone metal, with red, blue, and colorless rhinestones. ein (7.5cm) long **B**

9

10

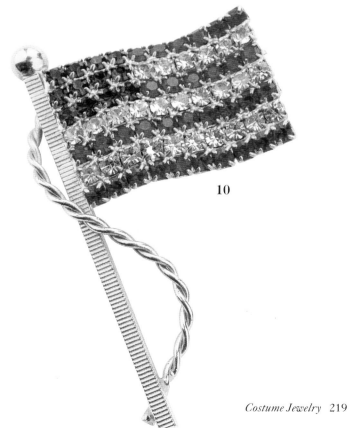

1. A 1930s female African head fur clip, in enameled base metal, with colorless and red rhinestones. 1.75in (4.5cm) long **C**

2. A 1920s/1930s "Fu Manchu" fur clip. 3in (7.5cm) high **B**

3. A 1940s American gondola-shaped watch pin, in gold-tone metal, with enamel and colorless rhinestones. 3in (7.5cm) long **C**

4. A floral spray pin, with red and colorless faceted rhinestones. 2.75in (5.5cm) high **A**

5. A 1960s pear pin, with large oval-cut faux topaz and pavé-set colorless, topaz, and green chaton-cut rhinestones. 3.25in (8cm) long **C**

6. A 1950s monkey pin, in gold-tone metal, with mink body and googly eyes. 3in (7.5cm) long **B**

7. A mid-1930s American "Pumpkin Man" pin. 4in (10cm) long **M**

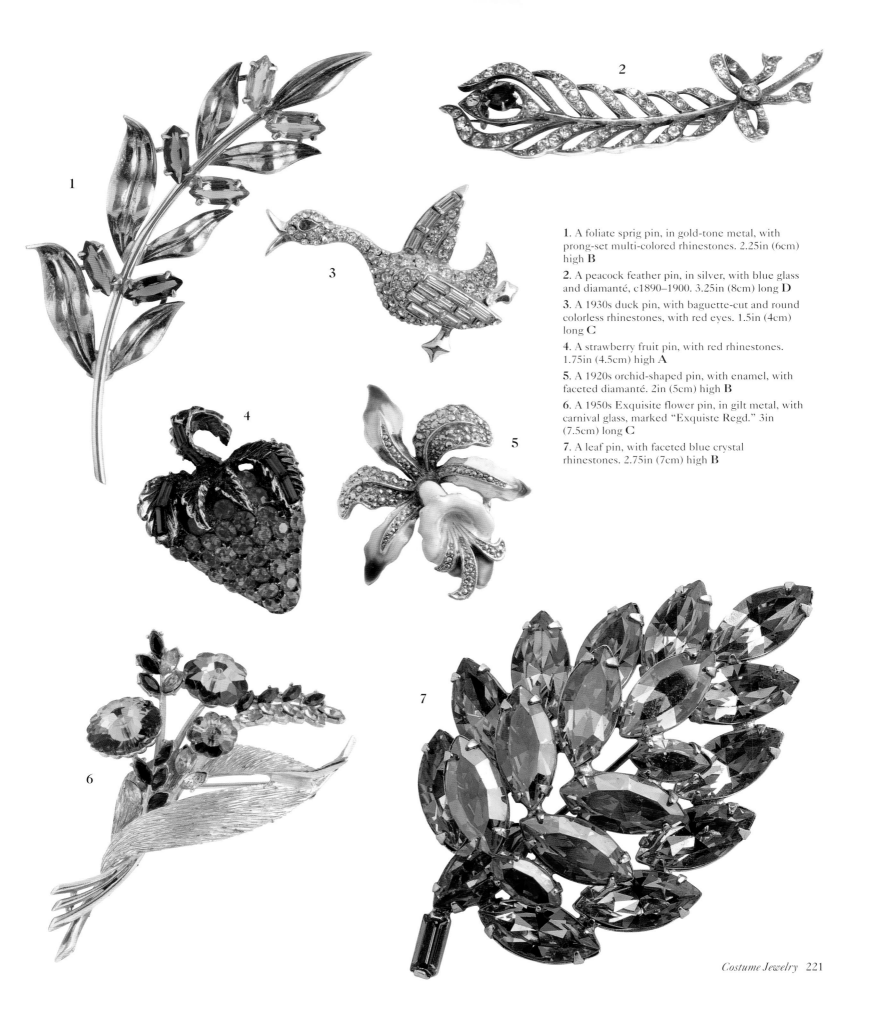

1. A foliate sprig pin, in gold-tone metal, with prong-set multi-colored rhinestones. 2.25in (6cm) high **B**

2. A peacock feather pin, in silver, with blue glass and diamanté, c1890–1900. 3.25in (8cm) long **D**

3. A 1930s duck pin, with baguette-cut and round colorless rhinestones, with red eyes. 1.5in (4cm) long **C**

4. A strawberry fruit pin, with red rhinestones. 1.75in (4.5cm) high **A**

5. A 1920s orchid-shaped pin, with enamel, with faceted diamanté. 2in (5cm) high **B**

6. A 1950s Exquisite flower pin, in gilt metal, with carnival glass, marked "Exquiste Regd." 3in (7.5cm) long **C**

7. A leaf pin, with faceted blue crystal rhinestones. 2.75in (7cm) high **B**

1. A pin, in white metal, prong-set faceted black rhinestones. 2.25in (5.5cm) high **A**

2. A leaf pin and earrings set, in gold-tone metal, with prong-set striped "tiger" rhinestones. Pin 2.75in (7cm) high **C**

3. A 1930s/1940s pin, with aurora borealis rhinestones. 2in (5cm) wide **B**

4. A 1950s top hat and cane pin, in gold-plate, with red rhinestones. 2.5in (6cm) high **A**

5. A scarecrow bar pin, in white metal, with colorless and multi-colored rhinestones. 3in (7.5cm) high **B**

1. A pair of 1920s French earrings, in cast metal, with green glass watermelon-cut drops. 2in (5cm) long **B**

2. A pair of earrings, in gold-tone metal, with cut faux aquamarines and teardrop-shaped brown glass stones. 1.25in (3cm) long **B**

3. A pair of 1960s Pierre Cardin-style earrings. 3in (7cm) long **B**

4. A pair of mid-1970s ethnic-style earrings, in silver, with turquoise. 2.5in (6.5cm) long **B**

5. A pair of earrings, in gold-tone metal, with faceted aurora borealis stones and large faux amber teardrops. 1.25in (3cm) long **B**

6. A pair of earrings, with purple faceted rhinestones. 1.5in (4cm) long **A**

1. A late 1950s necklace, in silver-tone metal, with sapphire glass teardrops and round diamanté. 16in (40.5cm) long **D**

2. A late 1920s French necklace, in silver, with Peking glass (faux jade) and cut-crystal. 16in (40.5cm) long **E**

3. A 1920s sautoir necklace, of Venetian glass, the pendant of millefiori, with beads in jade and lapis lazuli colors. 30in (75cm) long **D**

4. A 1930s geometric necklace, in phenolic/catalin. Pendant 2.5in (6.5cm) long **D**

5. A mid- to late 20th-century necklace, in gilt metal, with black pastes. 18in (46cm) long **C**

6. A mid-1920s French sautoir necklace, in faux pearl, with central plaque of intaglio-carved glass. 30in (7.5cm) long **E**

7. A 1950s necklace, retailed by Du Boyes, with jonquil diamanté and caramel cabochon poured glass, with original swing tag. 14.5in (37cm) long **C**

8. A 1950s Austrian Edwardian Revival choker collar, in gold-tone metal, mandolin panels adorned with blue and topaz rhinestones. 15in (38cm) long **D**

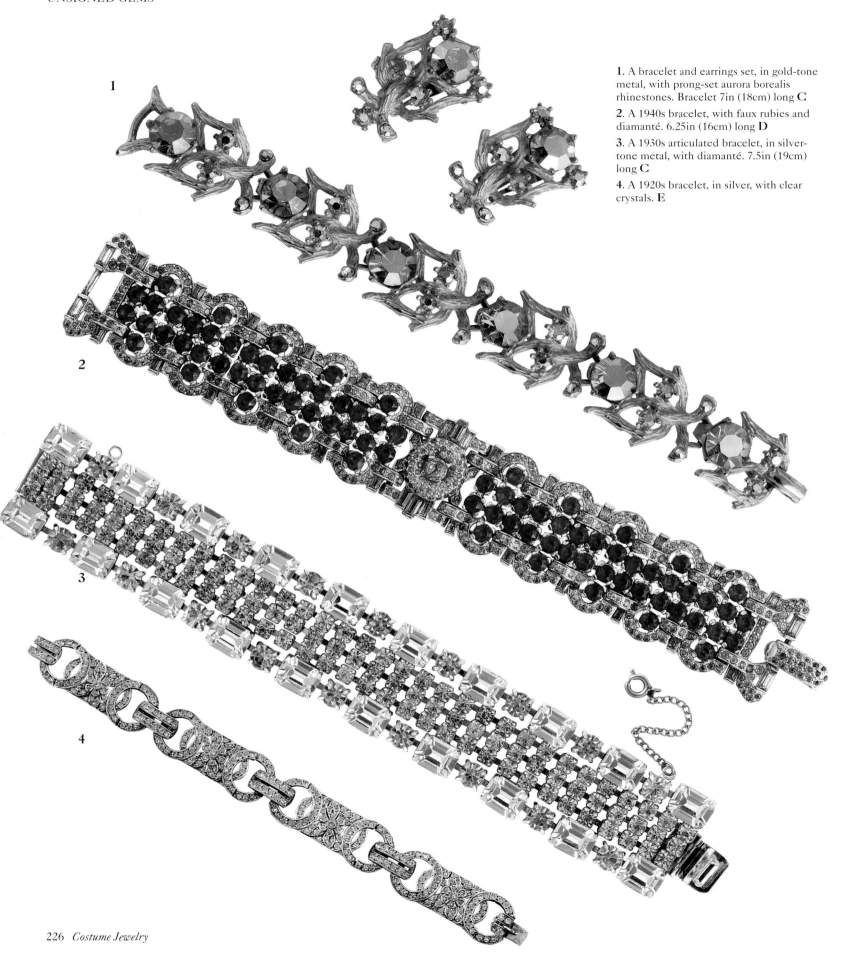

1

2

3

4

1. A bracelet and earrings set, in gold-tone metal, with prong-set aurora borealis rhinestones. Bracelet 7in (18cm) long **C**

2. A 1940s bracelet, with faux rubies and diamanté. 6.25in (16cm) long **D**

3. A 1930s articulated bracelet, in silver-tone metal, with diamanté. 7.5in (19cm) long **C**

4. A 1920s bracelet, in silver, with clear crystals. **E**

5. A 1960s bracelet, in copper, with ball and curving wing design. 2.75in (7cm) wide **A**

6. A scarab bangle, in brass, with carved cast phenolic scarab, gold paint and faux jewel. Scarab 2in (5cm) high **D**

7. A 1960s American stylized mythical lion cuff bracelet, in gilded metal, with enamel and paste. 3in (7.5cm) wide **E**

Hanna Bernhard
Bijoux Heart
Alexis Bittar
Lara Bohinc
Eddie Borgo
Sabrina Dehoff
Erickson Beamon
Dana Lorenz
Mawi
Simon Mower
St Erasmus
Tatty Devine
Marion Vidal
Scott Wilson

Future Designers

HANNA
BERNHARD

Husband-and-wife team Nathalie and Fernand Bernhard create extravagant, sculptural jewels embellished with vintage Swarovski crystals for their Hanna Bernhard range. The couple, who live and work in Paris, and share a passion for color, designed their first collection in the early 1990s. They have gone on to create an ever-growing menagerie of handcrafted rhinestone animals including horseshoe crabs, spiders, snakes, parrots, and flamingos.

Their influences come from a number of sources: Nathalie's father was a natural sciences teacher who encouraged her to hunt for butterflies, insects, and fossils; her mother took her hunting for antiques. One day she found an enormous pineapple pin at an antiques fair and was inspired to learn to make jewelry. Fernand spent his childhood on the island of Corsica where he studied sea creatures. As an adult he became an expert in dental prosthetics and now uses these sculpting skills to make the three-dimensional forms which are the base of Hanna Bernhard jewelry.

Each piece is unique and many are designed with a special display stand so they can be admired as sculpture when they are not being worn. The long snake and flamingo necklaces mold to the body as they are worn.

1. A snake necklace, in bronzed metal, with colorless, Siam red and black rhinestones, and vintage black glass cabochon eyes. 29in (73.5cm) long **M**

2. A cross with mistletoe necklace, in bronzed metal, with faux pearl, vintage faux coral, and vintage amber and green rhinestones, vintage stampings. 29in (73.5cm) long **J**

3. An articulated spider pin, in gold-tone metal, with red pear-shaped glass stones, and vintage gren and black rhinestones. 8in (20.5cm) long **M**

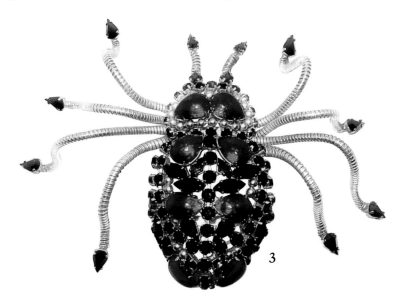

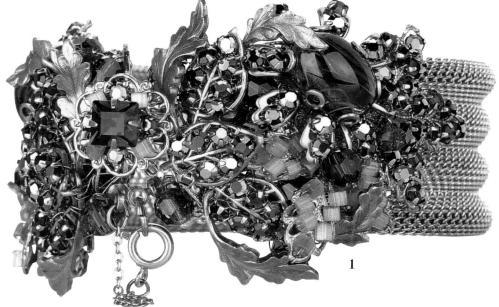

BIJOUX HEART

Designer Tracy Graham creates glamorous and complex pieces which recall the golden age of costume jewelry. Her opulent work uses vintage stones and components combined with modern crystals, semi-precious stones and Venetian glass in a style which is partly inspired by Art Nouveau and Art Deco pieces.

Tracy began Bijoux Heart in Yorkshire, England, in 1990 with her partner Robert. They combine her eye for color and form with his goldsmithing skills to produce intricate jewelry featuring a level of craftsmanship usually only seen in precious pieces.

During the 1990s Bijoux Heart made couture bridal tiaras, which won several Condé Nast British Bridal Awards. More recently they have created a limited number of jeweled headdresses for evening wear.

Tracy has made pieces for fashion designers Vivienne Westwood and Catherine Walker, and unusual bag handles and clasps for Lulu Guinness. Since 2007 she has collaborated with burlesque star Dita von Teese, producing headdresses and earrings for her stage work which emulate the detailed beadwork on her gowns. In 2008 Tracy created a huge pearl and crystal brooch and earrings demi-parure in collaboration with Dita for the opening of the Bollinger Jewelry Gallery at the Victoria & Albert Museum in London.

In 2009 *pâte-de-verre* pieces were added to the Bijoux Heart range. In 2010 the company began working on a collaboration with Swarovski, and loaned pieces for the film *Sex and the City 2*.

1. A "Montana Crystal and Dove Grey" bracelet, in gold-plate, with vintage cabochons, swirled Montana glass, and pavé set aurora borealis stones. 6.5in (16.5cm) long **H**

2. A collar with vintage faux topaz pendant, in gold-plate, with vintage blue cabochons and gold rose montées. 10.5in (27cm) long **M**

3. A pair of "Garland" earrings, in gold-plate, with pavé-set colorless crystal leaves, and prong set cubic zirconia. 3.5in (8cm) long **E**

4. A "Montana Crystal and Dove Grey" Whiplash ring, in gold-plate, with vintage stones, Montana glass, and aurora borealis stones. 1.5in (3.75cm) high **E**

5. A model wearing a three-dimensional necklace, in gold-plate, with jade, opals, Swarovski crystal, seed pearl, and baroque pearls. **M**

ALEXIS BITTAR

In 1990, at the age of 22, Alexis Bittar began hand-carving Lucite jewelry, having been inspired by the Bakelite jewelry of the 1930s. He started selling it on the streets of New York City, and was spotted by Dawn Mello, the fashion director of the Bergdorf Goodman department store.

Subsequently Bittar's career prospered. *Vogue* stylists, Grace Coddington and Patti Wilson asked him to produce bespoke pieces for their shoots. He designed Burberry's first couture jewelry collection in 1999, and went on to work with Patricia Field in 2002 on the jewelry for the *Sex and the City* television series. In 2004, he opened his first New York boutique, with a third opening in 2010. 2010 also saw 1980s icon Joan Collins used for an Alexis Bittar advertising campaign.

Currently Bittar's jewelry is split into three lines. The main line, "Lucite," features hand-painted chunky cuffs, and large earrings and rings, adorned with crystals, studs, or gilding. 1980s-style whimsical pieces also feature in this collection, including pieces such as ice cream cone necklaces. "Miss Havisham" is a more sculptural line, deriving its influences from Art Deco and, again, 1980s punk. "Elements" is a softer, more feminine range, inspired by 1960s and 1970s costume jewelry, featuring precious and semi-precious stones and antique-style hammered metalwork. All of these collections display Bittar's appreciation for form, texture, color, and light.

1 An "Elements" "Gold Vendome Coral & Pearl" necklace, of Lucite beads, hydro quartz stones and gold-plate. 23in (58.5cm) long **E**

2 A "Lucite" Mantauk hinge bracelet, in turquoise. 2.5in (6.5cm) diam **F**

3 Joan Collins in the 2010 advertising campaign, wearing "Miss Havisham" pieces.

1

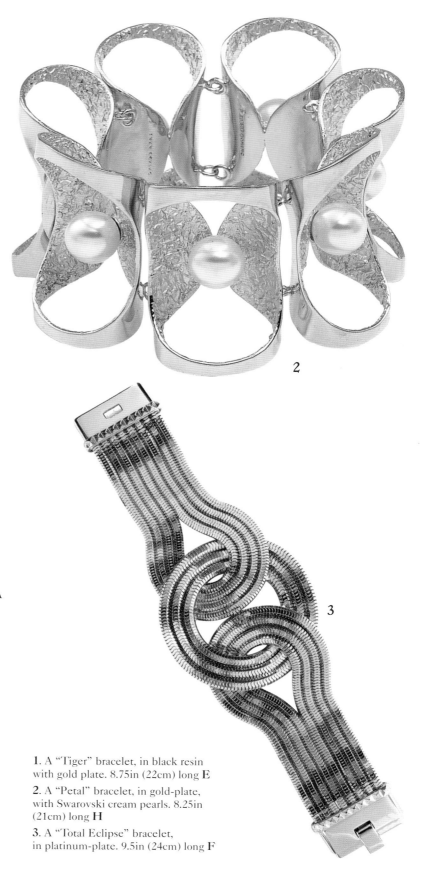

2

LARA BOHINC

Born in Slovenia, Lara Bohinc graduated from Ljubljana Academy of Fine Arts with a degree in industrial and graphic design. In 1994 she moved to London (where she is now based) and took an MA in jewelry and metalwork. She launched her own range of jewelry and leather accessories three years later, under the name Lara Boeing 747—a name she was soon forced to change. Although her name had not been a success, her designs were, and Bohinc won a New Generation Design Award at London Fashion Week that same year.

All Bohinc's jewelry is designed on a computer, and typically employs other techniques from her industrial background, such as laser cutting. Many pieces display industrial forms, although Bohinc is also influenced by nature. Her pieces are typically made from gold-and rhodium-plated brass cast in repeated geometric patterns juxtaposed with elegant curves and spheres.

Design consultant to Cartier since 2001, Bohinc has also worked with Gucci, Lanvin, Exte, Guy Laroche, Julien McDonald, and Costume National. However, she was still relatively unknown until 2009, when British popstar Cheryl Cole wore one of her necklaces on *The X Factor*; and Samantha Cameron, wife of British Prime Minister David Cameron (then Conservative leader), gave American First Lady Michelle Obama a woven Bohinc cuff at the G20 Summit.

3

1. A "Tiger" bracelet, in black resin with gold plate. 8.75in (22cm) long **E**

2. A "Petal" bracelet, in gold-plate, with Swarovski cream pearls. 8.25in (21cm) long **H**

3. A "Total Eclipse" bracelet, in platinum-plate. 9.5in (24cm) long **F**

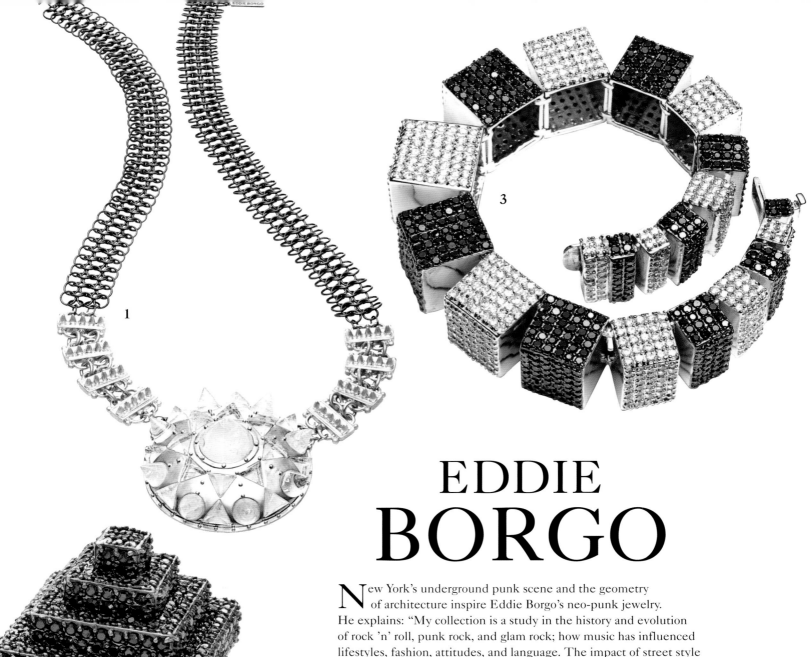

EDDIE BOROGO

New York's underground punk scene and the geometry of architecture inspire Eddie Borgo's neo-punk jewelry. He explains: "My collection is a study in the history and evolution of rock 'n' roll, punk rock, and glam rock; how music has influenced lifestyles, fashion, attitudes, and language. The impact of street style and its trickle-up effect into the luxury market are also constant sources of inspiration. I hope to show a meeting of high end and street in every piece I create."

Eddie studied Art and began designing one-off pieces for magazine editors and fashion stylists. He soon became a consultant for different jewelers in New York City, learning the techniques of jewelry making as he went along.

In 2008 he was commissioned to create pieces for American fashion house 3.1 Phillip Lim, and a year later he launched his own line. That same year he also created ranges for Marchesa (in collaboration with Pamela Love), Camilla Staerk, and Jen Kao.

Eddie Borgo's elegant and classic pieces have great clarity of form, created from unexpected materials. Studded cuffs, oversized medallions, and two-finger rings made from crystals, brushed gunmetal, chainmail, and brushed glass studs, are typical Borgo pieces. He designs ranges for women and men and his jewelry is made in the USA.

1. A "Star" necklace, in silver-plate and rock crystal. 15in (38cm) long **G**

2. A "Block Pyramid" ring, in gun-metal plate, with pavé-set black crystals. 1.5in (3.5cm) wide **E**

3. A "Step" bracelet, in silver-plate, with pavé set black and colorless crystals. 7in (17.5cm) long **G**

1

2

1. A "Mouth" necklace, in red leather, with gold chain. Pendant 3in (7.5cm) wide **D**

2. A "Smile" necklace, of multicolored wooden beads, on sterling silver chain. 16in (40.5cm) long **C**

3. A 'Unification' braclet, of six purple cords, with gold-plate clasp and details. 7in (17.5cm) long **C**

3

SABRINA
DEHOFF

Whimsical jewelry designer Sabrina Dehoff graduated with a degree in women's wear from the Royal College of Arts in London in 1996. After working as a design assistant for Guy Laroche and Lanvin in Paris for several years, she returned to her native Berlin in 2005 to start her own fashion consultancy company vonRot. The same year, she founded Sabrina Dehoff Accessories, for which she created her own line of jewelry.

Her first collection, "Little Helpers," was a range of soft leather pendants, shaped as doves, guitars, masks, and hearts, hung on silver and gold chains. Later collections have been given equally fanciful names, such as "Erratic Blocks from the Trip to the Moon" (2007), "Epigenetics Vs Atomists" (2008), "MEpairedYOUunited" (2008), and her most recent collection, "Hush Hush" (Fall Winter 2010). Each of these collections is demonstrably different from the others, and hand-created in Dehoff's studio from completely different materials, such as leather, acrylic, and precious metal, pompoms, silk and wood. Despite their differences, all these collections display her playful approach to jewelry design.

This approach is further reflected in the *Lookbooks* (or catalogues) she produces for each collection. Beautifully presented, these include illustrations, photographs, sayings, explanations, or poetry snippets intermingled with photos of Dehoff's jewelry.

1

2

ERICKSON BEAMON

Detroit-born Karen Erickson and Vicki Beamon moved to New York in the late 70's and soon became part of the city's fashion scene. While working together on a friend's catwalk show in 1983, they were inspired to create their own jewellery from suede, crystals, and beads as no other Manhattan jeweller was producing the type of pieces which they were looking for. Soon afterwards they had a photographer friend shoot one of their pieces and an advertisement was placed in Andy Warhol's *Interview* Magazine. This attracted considerable interest from some of the most prestigious stores in New York. After the great success in America, Vicki Beamon moved to London in 1985, to oversee and manage the brand's European expansion. In 1995 a flagship boutique in Belgravia was opened.

The company produces a vast collection each season with a wide range of mini-collections. Their signature looks are intricately beaded necklaces and large 'chandelier' earrings, a phrase that they are credited with coining. Each of their fantasy pieces is hand-made by a team of craftspeople in their studios in New York and London using a variety of techniques, such as macramé, beading, and soldering.

A range of fine jewellery, Diamonds by Erickson Beamon, was launched in 2003, to coincide with the brand's 20th anniversary. This was celebrated with a retrospective exhibition for the windows of Barney's department store in New York City, curated by the store's Creative Director, Simon Doonan.

Erickson Beamon's designs, which today include sunglasses and home-ware such as chandeliers, mirrors and frames, are now sold in over 600 stores in 75 countries. Their jewellery can be seen on a wide range of celebrities, including Lady Gaga, Madonna, Sarah Jessica Parker, and Michelle Obama. Other pieces can be found in museum collections. A pair of 'Dollhouse' chandelier earrings is permanently housed at the Victoria and Albert Museum in London and the Costume Institute of the Metropolitan Museum of New York.

As well as creating their own collections, Erickson Beamon have collaborated with many high-end fashion houses, such as Donna Karan, John Galliano, Dries Van Noten, Zac Posen, and Anna Sui. At the other end of the scale, they have produced lines for high-street stores, including Britain's Debenhams and America's Target.

1. An Erickson Beamon "Mist of Avalon" vest and neckpiece commissioned for Italian 'Vogue'. **M**

2. An Erickson Beamon for Anna Sui "Fatal Attraction" floral necklace, for the FW2010 catwalk. Pendant 4in (10cm) diam **M**

3. An Erickson Beamon "Tropical Punch" floral necklace. 17in (43cm) long **M**

4. A pair of Erickson Beamon "Dune" earrings. 3in (7.5cm) long **M**

DANA LORENZ

After training as a painter, Dana Lorenz began working for the fashion houses Gucci and Donna Karan. She launched Fenton, her first independent jewelry collection, in 2006 to great success. Fenton pieces are created from diverse materials, including rope, crystals, chains, and pearls, typically twisted and bound together into unique jewelry. A lower-priced but even more brazen range, Fallon, was introduced soon afterwards. Pieces in this line range from studded brass bangles to necklaces of shark's teeth and crystals. Lorenz's extravagant pieces are sold by top retailers worldwide including Barney's in New York and Liberty in London, and in her own flagship store, which opened in New York City in 2009.

5. A Dana Lorenz Fenton "Divorcee multi" necklace, in mink fur, base metals and crystal. 19in (48cm) long **H**

6. A Dana Lorenz Fenton "Excavation" choker, with glass beads and brass chains. 16in (40.5cm) long **H**

MAWI

Mawi puts an emphasis on luxurious statement pieces that combine contemporary style with traditional influences. Designer Mawi Keivom was born in India and spent her childhood living in countries such as Saudi Arabia, Burma and New Zealand. Graduating from Auckland Institute of Technology in Fashion Design (Womenswear) she worked with fashion designer Isaac Mizrahi before moving to London, England and setting her own accessories label with her partner Tim Awan.

Initially focusing on handbags, Mawi made her jewelry debut at London Fashion Week, in 2003. She was an immediate success winning the British Fashion Council's New Generation award for three consecutive seasons.

The brand's vision has subsequently split into two distinct paths: "Costume Luxe" draws inspiration from architecture, sculpture, industrial and futuristic forms. Shiny, hard edges combined with Swarovski crystals and pearls result in dramatic pieces.

"Heirloom" continues to draw inspiration from its early beginnings harking back to the past taking inspiration from estate jewels, royal and historic influences and found objects. Focusing on themes such as Punk Rock, Victorian and Art Nouveau, Heirloom mixes "granny jewels" with punk inspired edginess and delicate feminine detailing. Typical pieces include "old-fashioned" pearls, engraved lockets, cameos, skulls and crowns.

1

2

3

1. A Mawi "Box Chain" bracelet, in gold-plate, with faux pearls. 7.5in (19cm) circ **E**

2. A Mawi "Multi Set Dome" necklace, in gold-plate with Swarvoski crystal and faux pearls. 13in (33cm) long **G**

3. A Mawi "Dynamite, Dome and Spiral" necklace and "Dynamite" earrings, in gold-plate. Necklace 9.75in (25cm) long **I**

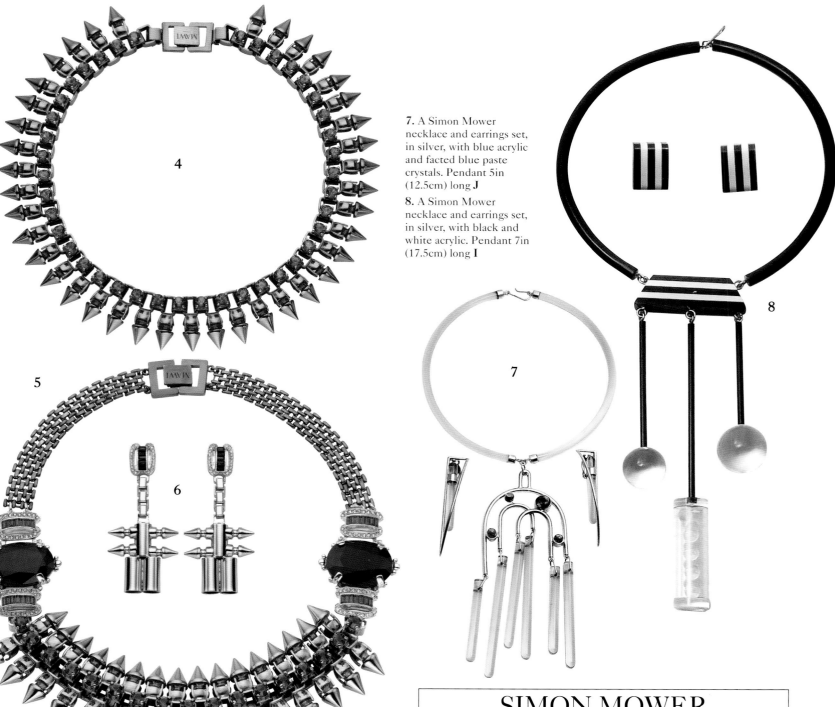

7. A Simon Mower necklace and earrings set, in silver, with blue acrylic and facted blue paste crystals. Pendant 5in (12.5cm) long **J**

8. A Simon Mower necklace and earrings set, in silver, with black and white acrylic. Pendant 7in (17.5cm) long **I**

SIMON MOWER

Essex-born Simon Mower has spent many years restoring the Art Nouveau and Art Deco jewelry and objects he is passionate about. He started producing his own jewelry in London in 1992, creating pieces which are often inspired by those early 20th century styles. Mower's jewels frequently incorporate period techniques with his own modern twists to make them practical for today's wearers. His jewelry is typically produced in a combination of plastics and resin, enamel, wood, glass, precious metals, and gemstones. Such pieces, which have been made for Madam Tussaud's waxworks and a variety of celebrities, are all limited-edition or one-offs.

4. A Mawi "Punk Rajah" double claw set spike necklace, with onyx and Swarvoski crystal. **G**

5. A Mawi "Punk Rajah" claw set crystal and spike necklace, with Swarvoski crystal. 10in (25.cm) long **F**

6. A pair of Mawi "Punk Rajah" tube and spike earrings, in gold-plate, with Swarvoski crystals. 3in (8cm) long **D**

1

2

ST ERASMUS

Distinctive St Erasmus jewelry is the creation of Pieter Erasmus. Born in South Africa, Erasmus moved to London, UK in 1995, where he worked in a pub, before landing a job at the London branch of Erickson Beamon in 1997. There he designed and created jewelry for fashions houses such as Givenchy and Alexander McQueen.

After seven years at Erickson Beamon, Erasmus left to found his own company, which initially made bags, belts, and sandals, before moving into jewelry. His sophisticated three-dimensional pieces are primarily inspired by Erasmus's native Africa, where, he explains, people make jewelry out of anything: "straws, […] buttons, branches, flowers, glass bottles." Other influences have been cited as the retro modernism of Fritz Lang's *Metropolis*, and traditional arts and crafts techniques, as well as the art of India, where he lives for half of the year. His 2010 line was inspired by the 18th century jewelry worn at the Nizam's court in Hyderabad. However, rather than look at that opulent jewelry, Erasmus was inspired by reading about it in William Dalrymple's books.

In New Delhi, India, he heads a production team of 15 craftspeople. Using the brand's signature crocheted Zari thread (a fine metallic wire thread usually woven into Indian garments), Swarovski rhinestones, and freshwater pearls, the production team create intricate, layered bib-necklaces, long necklaces, cocktail rings, cuffs, pins and earrings.

St Erasmus was pushed into the spotlight after American First Lady Michelle Obama wore one of the necklaces from the 2009 spring/summer collection "Ancient Tribes" (since renamed the "Mobama" necklace) to a White House correspondents' dinner in 2009. But even prior to this, St Erasmus's designs had been seen on global catwalks and in displays at Harrods and Harvey Nichols in Britain, as well as top-end stores in Hong Kong, Qatar, Singapore, Zurich, Mumbai, and Tokyo.

4. A model wearing a flower necklace and pin (in hair), with fresh water pearls, inspired by Bollywood movie 'Dev D'. Necklace 10in (25.5cm) wide **D** Pin 5in (12.5cm) wide **D**

1. A bib necklace, of Zari thread crochet, tiger's eye beads and Swarovski crystals, inspired by the Nizam's court. 6.5in (16.5cm) wide **F**

2. A bangle, with faux pearls, inspired by Audrey Hepburn. 1.5in (4cm) wide **D**

3. A bangle, with pewter color crocheted Zari thread, embroidered with black fuax pearls, hematite and glass beads, inspired by Metropolis. 1in (2.5cm) wide **C**

3

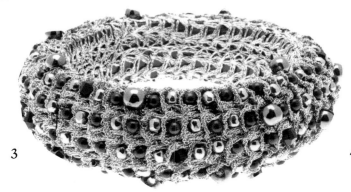

4

1. A "Lolly" necklace, in translucent red acrylic and base metal. Pendant 2.75in (7cm) long **B**

2. A "Dinosaur" necklace, in gold acrylic and base metal. 12.25in (31cm) long **D**

3. A pair of "Pen Nib" earrings, in gold acrylic, with black Swarovski crystal. 1.75in (4.5cm) long **B**

TATTY DEVINE

Harriet Vine and Rosie Wolfenden studied fine art at Chelsea School of Art in London. They sold their first jewelry—ornamented leather wrist-cuffs—at London's weekend market in 1999, and soon began making a considerable profit. Their big break came when a *Vogue* stylist admired a Tatty Devine headband worn by Wolfenden, and asked her to bring her collection in for a shoot in the millennium issue of the magazine. Six months later Tatty Devine's jewelry could be seen in UK shops such as Whistles and Harvey Nichols. The company has since worked with Selfridges, the Tate, screen printer Rob Ryan, and artists Gilbert & George.

Typical Tatty pieces are found in brightly colored acrylic shapes (such as 3D glasses and moustaches), but textiles, reclaimed wood, leather, and veneers are also used. All these pieces are assembled by hand in London.

Famous fans of Tatty Devine include Katy Perry and Kate Moss.

1 A Marion Vidal necklace, of red and white glazed ceramics, with satin ribbon and gilded lock. Winter 2010/11 17in (43cm) long **E**

2 A Marion Vidal necklace, of red glazed ceramic beads, with satin ribbon, and gilded lock. Winter 2010/11 17in (43cm) long **E**

3 A Marion Vidal bracelet, in gilt brass, with black cord. 7in (18cm) long **E**

MARION VIDAL

Marion Vidal studied architecture in Paris and Milan before she moved into fashion, graduating form the Royal Academy of Fine Arts of Antwerp in 2003. These two disciplines can be seen in her jewelry, which is often large and well balanced, featuring a confrontation of materials and colours. Her first collection of womenswear was released in 2004, and her first accessories-only line in 2006. Typical materials are include leather, wood, and particularly ceramics, which she used in her 2007 "Lucky Charm" collection for the fashion house Céline. Another collaboration with Murano glass manufacturer Salviati resulted in two collections created from glass beads.

3

4

SCOTT WILSON

While studying for a Masters in millinery and womenswear at the Royal College of Art in London, Scott Wilson won a work placement with Karl Lagerfeld in Paris. There he was given the task of creating 'mystical' wire head and body pieces for Lagerfeld's 1996 spring/summer show.

Following his graduation, Wilson launched his own jewelry label to critical acclaim. Inspired by foreign civilizations and Modernist architecture, Wilson's jewelry is typically bold and sculptural. His AW10 collection, for example, is comprised of heavy chain necklaces with large ring and drop pendants, as well as Cubist-style pieces set with large acrylic stones and metallic balls and cubes. His catwalk pieces, which have been created for fashion houses such as Thierry Mugler, Hussein Chalayan, Matthew Williamson, Jean Paul Gaultier, Valentino, Givenchy Couture, and Burberry, are even more opulent.

Many Scott Wilson pieces are available to buy at major department stores, such as Dover Street Market in London and Henri Bendel in New York City; however, other one-off pieces have been created for celebrities such as Nicole Kidman, Kylie, and Madonna.

Wilson's jewelry is regularly seen in the pages of Vogue, and his work has been exhibited at London's Victoria & Albert Museum.

4 A Scott Wilson necklace, in gunmetal-plate, with large reducing ring pendant, and three strand chain. Pendant 3.25in (8cm) long **K**

5 A Scott Wilson irregular folded cuff, in silver- and gold-plate with large acrylic facted stone, and gunmetal-plate ball. 3.25in (8.5cm) wide **K**

6 A Scott Wilson necklace, in silver- and gold-plate, with large acrylic facted stone and gunmetal-plate ball. 10in (25cm) long **K**

7 A Scott Wilson medium double mixed chain bracelet, in gunmetal- and gold-plate. 8in (20cm) long **F**

Dealers & Stockists
Glossary
Jewelers' Marks
Index
Acknowledgments

Resources

DEALERS & STOCKISTS

The following dealers all contributed pieces for this book. The page and position of the pieces they supplied are listed after their contact details. Please note that inclusion in this book in no way constitutes or implies a contract or a binding offer on the part of any contributing dealer, auction house, or stockist to supply or sell the pieces illustrated, or similar items, at the prices stated.

ANCIENT ART
85 The Vale, London, N14 6AT, UK
www.antiquities.co.uk
11 (2 & 3)

ANTIQUES EMPORIUM
29 Division Street, Somerville, NJ 08876, USA
90 (4), 97 (3), 111 (4), 112 (1), 116 (2), 144 (2),
211 (6&7), 219 (6&9), 220 (4), 221 (4), 222 (5),
223 (6)

AURORA BIJOUX
www.aurorabijoux.com
51 (4, 5, 6), 78 (4), 123 (5), 127 (4), 129 (5), 160
(3), 161 (2), 168 (5), 171 (3), 174 (2&3), 177
(4&6), 217 (6)

LINDA BEE
Stand L18-21, Grays Antique Market,
1-7 Davies Mews, London, W1K 2LP, UK
198 (5)

HANNA BERNHARD
www.french-bakelite.com

BIJOUX HEART
bijoux-heart.com

ALEXIS BITTAR
www.alexisbittar.com

BARBARA BLAU
South Street Antiques Market,
615 South 6th Street, Philadelphia,
PA 19147-2128, USA.
61 (6), 125 (5), 150 (2&3), 151 (5), 169 (2), 170
(2), 174 (6), 181 (3), 186 (1), 200 (1), 202 (3), 206
(3), 211 (8), 212 (1), 219 (4, 5, 8), 219 (8), 220 (2),
221 (1&7), 222 (1&4), 226 (3&4), 227 (5&6)

BLOOMSBURY AUCTIONS
24 Maddox Street, London, W1 S1PP, UK
www.bloomsburyauctions.com
10

LARA BOHINC
www.larabohinc.com

EDDIE BORGO
www.eddieborgo.com

BUTLER & WILSON
20 South Molton Street, London, W1K 5QY UK
www.butlerandwilson.co.uk
130 (1)

CHIAGO SILVER
www.chicagosilver.com
23 (2)

CIRCA 1900
6 Camden Passage, London, N1 8ED, UK
www.circa1900.org
22 (1)

CRISTOBAL
26 Church Street, London, NW8 8EP, UK
www.cristobal.co.uk
5 (bottom), 28 (5), 30, 40, 41, 43 (3, 4, 5, 7), 45,
46 (1), 47 (6&7), 48 (1 and box), 49 (3, 4, 6, 7), 51
(box), 52 (1), 53 (6), 54 (1&2), 55 (4&5), 56, 57
(5&6), 58, 59 (4, 5, 6, 8), 60 (1), 62, 63, 64, 65, 66,
67, 68, 69 (2, 3, 4, 5), 70 (1&3), 71, 73 (4&6), 75
(4&6), 78 (2), 79 (5, 6, 8), 81 (5), 86, 87 (3&4), 88
(2), 89, 90 (1, 2, 3, box), 91 (6&7), 93 (5), 96, 97
(4&6), 98, 99 (2, 4, 5, 6), 100, 101 (5, 6, 7, 8), 102,
103 (4&6), 109 (4), 111 (3), 112 (2), 113 (5&6),
114 (3), 119 (2, 3, 5, 6), 120 (1&3), 121 (5, 6, 7),
122, 123 (4), 125 (3), 127 (5&6), 131 (3), 133 (3),
137 (3&7), 138 (2), 139 (8), 140, 141 (3, 4, 5), 144
(1), 145 (5&6), 147 (2, 3, 4, 5, 6, 7), 148, 151 (4,
6, 7, 8), 154 (3), 155 (2), 162 (1), 163, 168 (2), 170
(1), 172 (2), 178 (1&2), 179 (5, 6, 7) 180, 181 (4),
182 (1, 2, 3), 185 (2&3), 189 (1), 194 (2&4), 196,
197, 198 (2), 200 (2), 201 (4&6), 204 (4), 208,
209, 210 (2, 3, 4), 211 (5), 213 (4), 215 (6), 216
(1), 217 (5&8), 218 (1&3), 221 (3), 226 (1)

DAWSON & NYE
128 American Rd, Morris Plains, NJ 07950, USA
www.dawsons.org
206 (5)

DECO DAME
853 Vanderbilt Beach Road,
PMB 8, Naples, FL 34108, USA
www.decodame.com
26, 27 (3), 28 (5), 29 (6), 52 (3), 53 (4), 95 (2&4),
167 (2), 214 (2)

SABRINA DEHOFF
www.sabrinadehoff.com

THE DESIGN GALLERY
5 The Green, Westerham, Kent, TN16 1AS, UK
www.designgallery.co.uk
82 (1), 84 (1, 2), 85 (5), 112 (3), 126 (2), 133 (4),
158, 169 (3), 170 (3), 187 (1), 213 (5), 221 (2&6),
225 (5)

DREWEATT'S
Donnington Priory Salerooms, Donnington,
Newbury, Berkshire, RG14 2JE, UK
www.dnfa.com
25 (2)

ECLECTICA
www.eclectica.biz
123 (3), 201 (8)

LARRY & DIANNA ELMAN
P.O. Box 415, Woodland Hills, CA 91365, USA
74 (1)

ERICKSON BEAMON
www.ericksonbeamon.com

RICHARD GIBBON
neljeweluk@aol.com
2, 50 (1), 81 (4&6), 87 (6), 94, 95 (3), 97 (7), 141
(7), 167 (3&4), 184 (5)

GLITZ UK
www.glitzuk.co.uk
5 (top), 48 (2), 59 (7), 77 (8&9), 85 (6), 93 (7),
110, 111 (5&6), 113 (7), 115, 117 (4&5), 123 (6),
135 (2&6), 139 (4), 143 (2&5), 156 (2&3), 157,
159 (2), 160 (1), 162 (2&3), 164 (2), 165 (3, 5, 6,
7), 168 (1&3), 169 (1), 173 (1), 174 (1, 4, 5), 178
(3), 183 (7), 189 (3), 195 (2), 199 (7&8), 200 (3),
201 (5), 204 (8), 211 (8), 220 (5), 225 (7&8)

GRIFFIN & COOPER ANTIQUES
South Street Antiques Centre,
615 South 6th Street, Philadelphia, PA 19147-
2128, USA
194 (1)

JUNKYARD JEWELER
www.junkyardjeweler.com
76 (1, 2, 3), 77 (6), 125 (4), 127 (3), 129 (2), 145
(3), 156 (1), 160 (2), 166 (2&3), 199 (6), 201 (7)

EVE LICKVER
California, USA
202 (2), 204 (3), 205 (5, 6, 7, 9, 10), 207 (7, 10,11)

DANA LORENZ
www.danalorenz.com

LYON & TURNBULL
33 Broughton Place, Edinburgh, EH1 3RR, UK
www.lyonandturnbull.com
12, 14

MARIE ANTIQUES
G107 & 136–137 Alfies Antique Market,
13 Church Street, London NW8 8DT, UK
www.marieantiques.co.uk
19 (3)

MARKOV & BEEDLES
markov@btopenworld.com
6 (bottom)

FRANCESCA MARTIRE
F131–137, Alfies Antique Market,
13 Church Street, London, NW8 8DT, UK
www.francescamartire.com
149 (2)

MAWI
www.mawi.co.uk

MEROLA
195 Fulham Road, London, SW3 6JL, UK
54 (3), 126 (1), 225 (6)

MILLION DOLLAR BABIES
47 Hyde Blvd., Ballston Spa, NY 12020, USA
77 (5&7), 79 (7), 117 (3, 6, 7), 124 (2), 173 (2),
177 (5)

MOD-GIRL
South Street Antiques Centre,
615 South 6th Street, Philadelphia,
PA 19147–2128, USA.
27 (2), 135 (5), 181 (1&2), 203 (5, 7, 8), 204 (1),
206 (4)

MODERNE GALLERY
111 North 3rd Street, Philadelphia,
PA 19106, USA
www.modernegallery.com
25 (3)

SIMON MOWER
www.scarabantiques.com

THE MULTICOLOURED TIME SLIP
eBay Store: multicoloured timeslip,
154 (1&2)

N&N VINTAGE COSTUME JEWELRY
www.trifari.com
143 (7)

N. BLOOM & SON
www.nbloom.com
21 (3)

PORT ANTIQUES CENTER
289 Main Street, Port Washington,
NY 11050, USA
43 (2&6), 203 (6), 206 (1), 207 (6), 214 (1), 215
(3, 4, 5)

PRIVATE COLLECTION
3, 34, 44 (4), 47 (4), 55 (3), 58 (5&6), 60 (2), 61
(4), 70 (2&4), 76 (4), 80 (1&3), 83 (4,5 and box),
84 (3 and box), 91 (5), 99 (3), 101 (4), 103 (5),
105 (5), 107 (5), 111 (2), 112 (4), 114 (2), 119 (4),
125 (6), 130 (2), 131 (4&6), 132, 134, 137 (5), 139
(6), 151 (9), 155 (3), 167 (1), 172 (1), 181 (4), 182
(4), 183 (5), 185 (5), 186 (3), 194 (1), 198 (4), 216
(3), 220 (1&7), 221 (5), 222 (2&3), 223 (1, 2, 3),
224 (4)

QUITTENBAUM
Hohenstaufenstrasse 1,
D-80801, München, Germany
www.quittenbaum.de
109 (3)

RBR GROUP
158/168, Grays Antique Market, 58 Davies
Street, London, W1K 5LP, UK
17

RELLICK
8 Golborne Road, London, W10 5NW, UK
www.relliklondon.co.uk
198 (4)

MELODY RODGERS
30 Manhattan Art and Antique Center,
1050 2nd Avenue, NY 10022, USA
www.melodyrodgers.com
29 (7), 129 (3&4), 139 (10), 141 (6), 188, 217
(4&7)

JOEL ROTHMAN
Top Banana Antiques Mall, 1 New Church St.
Tetbury Gloucestershire GL8 8DS UK
16, 19 (1&2), 24, 131 (5), 171 (2), 176 (3), 203
(4),
216 (2)

CHARLOTTE SAYERS
313-315 Grays Antique Market,
58 Davies Street, London, W1K 5LP UK
15 (3), 18

SCARAB
www.scarabantiques.com

SYLVIE SPECTRUM
372, Grays Antique Market, 58 Davies Street,
London, W1K 5LP UK
184 (4)

ST ERASMUS
www.st-erasmus.com

ROXANNE STUART
gemfairy@aol.com
7, 50 (2), 51 (3), 53 (5), 60 (3), 74 (2), 91 (9), 93
(8), 121 (4), 136 (1), 139 (9), 141 (2), 143 (4&6),
166 (1), 186 (2), 195 (3), 210 (1), 212 (3), 218 (2)

TADEMA GALLERY
10 Charlton Place, Camden Passage,
London, N1 8AJ UK
108

TATTY DEVINE
www.tattydevine.com

KERRY TAYLOR AUCTIONS LLP
Unit C25 Parkhall Road Trading Estate, 40
Martell Road, Dulwich, London SE21 8EN UK
www.kerrytaylorauctions.com
187 (3), 194 (3)

TRACY TOLKIEN
Private Collection
20, 21 (2), 32, 33 (2&3), 35 (2), 42, 44 (3&4), 46
(2&3), 47 (5), 49 (5), 52 (2), 72 (2), 73 (3), 75
(3&5), 77 (3), 78 (1&3), 83 (2&3), 85 (4), 87
(5&7), 88 (1), 92, 93 (8), 97 (5), 101 (3), 104, 106,
107 (4&6), 114 (1), 116 (1), 118, 120 (2), 124 (1),
135 (3&4), 137 (2, 4, 6), 138 (1&3), 139 (5&7),
141 (8), 143 (3), 145 (4&7), 146, 147 (8), 150 (1),
155 (1), 161 (4), 165 (4), 171 (1), 172 (2), 173 (3),
175 (7), 179 (4), 180 (1), 181 (5), 183 (6), 184
(2&3), 185 (1), 187 (2), 189 (2), 195 (1), 198 (1),
202 (1), 204 (2), 206 (2), 207 (9), 212 (2), 213
(6&7), 219 (7&10), 220 (3&6), 223 (3&4), 224
(1&2), 227 (7)

TORONTO ANTIQUES CENTER 284
King Street, W. Toronto, ON M5V 1J2, Canada
159 (1, 3, 4), 190, 191

VAN DEN BOSCH
123 Grays Antique Market, 58 Davies Street,
London, W1K 5LP UK
www.vandenbosch.co.uk
109 (2&5)

MARION VIDAL
www.marionvidal.com

WILLIAM WAIN
www.williamwain.com
35 (3), 44 (1), 61 (5), 80 (2), 85 (7), 105 (6), 128,
142, 149 (3, 4, 5)

SCOTT WILSON
www.scottwilsonlondon.com

WOOLLEY & WALLIS
51-61 Castle Street,
Salisbury, Wiltshire, SP1 3SU, UK
www.woolleyandwallis.co.uk
23 (3)

BONNY YANKAUER
bonnyy@aol.com
93 (4), 164 (1), 226 (2), 227 (6)

GLOSSARY

Alloy: A combination of two or more different metals.

Art Deco: A style that is characterized by geometric lines and angles. It was popular from the mid-1920s until the late 1940s.

Art Nouveau: A style characterized by flowing, free-form imagery based on organic forms. It was popular from the 1890s until World War 1.

Arts & Crafts: A movement that emphasized the natural beauty and quality of materials. It was popular in the late 19th century.

Aurora borealis: An iridescent, rainbow-effect coating on stones created in the mid-1950s by the Austrian firm Swarovski. The iridescent effect resembles the Northern Lights or Aurora Borealis, hence the term.

Baguette-cut: A cut that produces a rectangular stone.

Bakelite: A strong, attractive and often brightly colored plastic, heavily used 1920s to 1940. The name bakelite is often used to refer to other forms of early plastic.

Bangle: A stiff bracelet.

Baroque pearl: An irregularly shaped pearl.

Base metal: The common, non-precious metals, such as tin and copper, as well as their alloys, including nickel silver. They may be plated with gold or silver.

Berlin ironwork: A style of cast iron-jewelry, first made by the Royal Berlin Foundry in the early 19th century.

Bezel setting: A circular metal setting that is folded over the circumference of the stone.

Bib: A type of necklace, constructed as a substantial band that is wider at the front and tapers towards the back of the neck.

Brilliant cut: A popular cut designed to produce an exceptional sparkle. The standard is 57 facets, or 58 including a flat base.

Cabochon: From the French, a smooth domed gem either circular or oval in shape.

Calibré cut: A stone cut individually to fit the exact outline of an irregular design.

Cameo: A stone or shell carved with a relief design, often in a contrasting color.

Channel setting: A setting where metal is folded over the edges of a rectangular stone, such as a baguette. A number of baguette stones may be set in a row.

Chatelaine: A chain connecting two pins or clips.

Choker: A necklace that sits tightly round the throat.

Claw setting: A setting in which the stone is held in place by small "prongs" or "fingers" of metal—also known as prong setting.

Cold enamel: A paint effect imitating baked enamel. It is less hard-wearing than genuine enamel.

Diamanté: Highly reflective, faceted glass or crystal, resembling gemstones. See "Rhinestone."

Double clip: A pair of pins that can be worn separately or clipped together as one. Also called "Duette."

Duette: See "Double clip."

Enamel: Colored, fused glass powder baked in an oven to achieve a glassy opaque or translucent finish, bonded to the metal.

En tremblant: Used to describe jewelry with spring-mounted parts that tremble as the wearer moves.

Facet: A flat face of a stone.

Figural: A piece of jewelry in the shape of a figure, such as an animal or person.

Filigree: An arrangement of gold or silver wire that has been twisted into a decorative shape.

Findings: The functional parts of jewelry, such as clasps, hooks, and settings.

Foil: A method whereby foil is coated onto the back of a stone, so increasing its brilliance.

Hair-work jewelry: Jewelry containing or made from locks of hair. It was popular in the mid 1800s as a way of remembering loved ones who had died.

Hematite: A dark graphite-colored natural stone.

Fruit salads: Jewelry set with molded red, green, and blue glass or plastic stones.

Fur clip: A large pin with a spring clasp, designed to hold a fur stole in place.

Intaglio: A carving in either glass or natural crystal. The design is carved into the stone rather than standing proud of the surface.

Invisible setting: A technique in which stones are fastened from the back, so it appears as though there is no metal mount.

Japanned: A process that leaves metal colored a dull black.

Jump ring: The small ring that links two components in a piece of jewelry, allowing movement of the piece. Also called "drop ring."

Maltese Cross: A cross with four arms of equal length that increase in width away from the center.

Marcasite: An iron oxide mineral that has a dark metallic finish that can be faceted and polished.

Marquise-cut: A cut that results in an oval-shaped stone, pointed at both ends. Also called "Navette-cut."

Millefiori: A pattern resembling "a thousand flowers," created by cutting a section through numerous fused colored glass rods.

Navette-cut: See "Marquise-cut."

Niello: A method of decoration where a metal surface is engraved with a design and the lines filled with a black metallic alloy of sulfur, copper, silver, and usually lead.

Parure: A matching set of jewelry, usually including a pin, earrings, bracelet, and necklace. A demi-parure consists of only two components, such as earrings and a necklace.

Paste: Invented in the 1730s by the French jeweler Frédéric Strass, a hard versatile compound of glass, which can be given many of the properties of gemstones when certain minerals and oxides are added to it. Pastes have been used in a wide range of colors to make costume jewelry since the 18th century. See "Rhinestone."

Pâte de verre: The French term for "poured glass."

Patina: A subtle sheen or change in color acquired by some metals when exposed to the air and handling.

Pavé: A type of setting in which individual stones are placed, or "paved" in formation, side by side, without any space between neighboring stones.

Pear-cut: A cut that results in teardrop-shaped stones.

Peridot: A natural stone of deep green or yellow color frequently used in Arts & Crafts and Art Nouveau jewelry.

Pinchbeck: A copper alloy, invented by Christopher Pinchbeck in the 18th century, that resembles gold. Also called "false gold."

Plating: Coating one metal with another.

Plique à jour: A form of enamel decoration with an open metalwork frame which allows light to shine through.

Pot metal: An alloy of tin and lead, gray in color, used in early 20th century costume jewelry.

Poured glass: A method in which powdered glass is placed in a metal frame and melted by blow-torch, so that it sets in place with a "poured" effect.

Prong setting: See "Claw setting."

Repoussé: A raised high relief design on the front of a metal object, made by hammering, embossing, or punching the reverse side of the metal to form the design from the back.

Rhinestone: Originally a type of clear quartz used in costume jewelry, but now also used to mean any colorless paste or rock crystal used in costume jewelry to imitate diamonds.

Rhodium: A metal often used to plate silver, giving it a high shine.

Rock crystal: Natural quartz.

Rondelles: Small, round, crystal-set metal links.

Rose montées: Flat-backed stones set into individual metal settings, which are themselves wired into place.

Russian gold plating: A matt coppery finish used first in 1940s films, because it reduced the glare of the studio lights.

Ruthenium: A metal in the platinum group, often used for plating.

Sautoir: From the French for chain or long collar. A long necklace decorated with a pendant and/or tassel.

Seed pearls: Tiny (2mm diam) real or artificial pearls.

Setting: The method of securing a stone in jewelry.

Spacer: A decorative bead that is used between larger beads or pearls in a necklace to separate them and set them off.

Step cut: A rectangular or square-shaped gemstone cut with several facets parallel to the edges of the stone.

Sterling silver: A hard alloy that is 925 parts pure silver, and 75 base metal.

Swarovski crystals: Top-quality brilliant-cut crystal rhinestones made by the Swarovski company.

Trembler: See "en tremblant."

Trifanium: A shiny metal alloy that looked like gold, but did not tarnish. Patented by Trifari.

Vermeil: From the French word for "rosy," silver that has been plated, or covered, with gold. Now used to describe any light gold plating.

JEWELERS' MARKS

Many pieces of costume jewelry are marked by the designer and/or manufacturer. As well as identifying the maker, these marks can help with dating as some companies changed their marks from time to time. Others, notably Christian Dior, included the date of manufacture within the mark. Patent numbers were also stamped on pieces, these enable collectors to research the date of design and more, and offer a fascinating insight into the design process.

ART

Used 1940s until late 1960s. Copyright symbol used after 1955.

BOUCHER

Used 1950s to 1970s. Copyright symbol used after 1955.

BUTLER & WILSON

Used 1970 to the present. Other marks used: BUTLER & WILSON.

CHANEL

Script signature used from early 1930s; not registered as a trademark in US.

CHANEL

Block signature registered in US in 1925. Continues to be used today.

CORO

Coro Pegasus mark used from 1938. A copyright symbol was added in 1955

DEMARIO

Used 1945 until 1965.

CHRISTIAN DIOR

Mitchell Maer designed for the company from 1952–1956.

CHRISTIAN DIOR

Christian Dior mark with date for 1958.

EISENBERG

Eisenberg Original mark 1935–1945.

FAHRNER

Original Fahrner mark with TF trademark introduced in 1901.

GROSSE

Gross and Made in Germany mark dated 1953.

STANLEY HAGLER

Mark used 1983–1996.

MIRIAM HASKELL

Horseshoe mark tends to be used on earlier pieces. This example c1950.

HOBE

This mark used 1958–1983

JOSEFF OF HOLLYWOOD

Block mark used 1938-early 1950s.

JOSEFF OF HOLLYWOOD

Script signature used from 1938.

CHRISTIAN LACROIX

Used from c1980

KENNETH JAY LANE

Mark used c1990.

MCCLELLAND BARCLAY

Used 1935–1943.

REGENCY

Used c1950–1970.

ROBERT

Used 1942–1979. Copyright symbol used after 1955.

YVES ST LAURENT

Monogram used 1960s-present

TRIFARI

Trifari crown mark, used 1918-present. Copyright mark used after 1955.

VENDÔME

Used 1944–1979.

WEISS

Used 1942–1971.

WESTWOOD

Used c2000.

INDEX

A

ACME   154
aigrettes   15
Alcozer   154
Almaraz, Carlos   154
ancient world   10–11
Angeli, Pia   28
Art   144
Art Deco   26–9, 31, 33, 175
   Bengel, Jakob   158
   Bijoux Heart   231
   Bittar, Alexis   232
   Butler & Wilson   130
   Castlecliff   161
   Czech jewelry   212–213
   double clips   214
   Fahrner   26, 108–9
   Mower, Simon   239
   plastic   202
   Rosenstein, Nettie   186
   Weiss   110
Art (ModeArt)   155
Art Nouveau   22–3, 24, 33
   Bijoux Heart   231
   Czech jewelry   212–213
   Simon Mower   239
Arts & Crafts jewelry   24–5, 150
Ashbee, C.R.   24, 25
Atwood & Sawyer   210
aurora borealis stones
   Dior, Christian   31, 82
   Eisenberg   138
   Har   144
   Kramer   117
   Lisner   122
   Regency   182
   Schiaparelli, Elsa   87
   Weiss   31, 110–1
Austin, Larry   54
Austrian jewelry   200–1
Avon   128, 156, 211

B

Bacall, Lauren   169
Bailey, David   132
Bakelite jewelry   28, 33, 202–7
Balenciaga   90, 148
Ball, Lucille   58
Ballet Russes   26
bangles
   Bakelite   202–3, 205
   Coro & Corocraft   73
   Lane, Kenneth Jay   127
   St Erasmus   240
   Whiting & Davis   197

see also bracelets
Bankhead, Tallulah   142
Barack, Clara   25
Barclay, McClelland   175
baroque pearls   54
Barrymore, Drew   176
Bass, William   192
beads
   Coppola e Toppo   148, 149
   Hagler, Stanley   67
   Haskell, Miriam   54, 56
   Rousselet   186
Beamon, Vicki   236
Beaujewels   157
Bengel, Jakob   158
Bérard, Christian   86
Berlin ironwork jewelry   18
Berlin, Kate Ganz   122
Bernhard, Hanna   230
Bijoux, Aurora   36
Bijoux Heart   231
Bing, Samuel   22
Bittar, Alexis   232
black diamonds (Weiss)   112
Blanch Ette Company   174
Blass, Bill   176
Bobley, Joseph   161
Boeres, Patriz   108
Boeuf, André   42
Bogoff   159
Bohan, Mark   32, 82
Bohinc, Lara   233
Bond Boyd   159
Booth, Rose   142
Borgo, Eddie   234
Bosselt, Rudolf   108
Boucher et Cie   92, 94
Boucher, Marcel   27, 92–7, 140
Boulton, Matthew   16–7
Boussac, Marcel   80, 82
Bowman & Foster   157
bracelets
   Alice Caviness   160
   Bakelite   203, 205
   Bengel   158
   Bijoux Heart   231
   Bogoff   159
   Bohinc, Lara   233
   Boucher, Marcel   92, 95
   Butler & Wilson   132
   Carolee   160
   Chanel   104, 106–7
   Ciner   162
   Coppola e Toppo   148
   Coro & Corocraft   75
   Danecraft   166

DeLizza & Elster   165
Eisenberg   138–9
Fahrner, Theodor   109
Hagler Stanley   66
Har   145
Haskell, Miriam   55–6
Hobé   135
Judy Lee   174
Kramer   115, 116–7
Lacroix, Christian   172
Lagerfeld, Karl   172
Lane, Kenneth Jay   129
Lisner   123–4
Mazer & Jomaz   140–1
Napier   178–9
Rebajes   181
Renoir   151
Schiaparelli, Elsa   87, 88, 89
Selro   189
Sherman   190, 191
Stein, Lea   146
Tortolani   193
Trifari   41–3, 46–7, 50–1
unsigned   226–7
Vendôme   119
Weiss   111, 113
Whiting & Davis   197
see also bangles
Braendle, Gustav   108–9
Braendle, Hubert   109
Brania   177
Braque, Georges   118, 121
Brody, Steve   160
Brubach, Holly   107
Brunialti, Roberto   144
buckles
   Fahrner, Theodor   109
   shoe buckles   15, 19
Bulgari   128
Bush, Barbara   192
Butler & Wilson   34, 130–3
   Christmas jewelry   132
   lizard pin   131
Butler, Nicky   34, 130, 132
Byzantine jewelry   11

C

Cadoro   160
Caluwaerts, Thierry   170
cameos, Wedgwood   17
Cameron, Samantha   233
Cardin, Pierre   82, 89
Carnegie, Hattie   142–3, 164
   Antelope pin   142, 143
Carolee   160

Cartier   31, 33, 42, 46, 92, 128, 214, 233
Castlecliff   161
Caviness, Alice   160, 161, 164
Celtic jewelry   11, 24, 25
chains   12
Chanel, Coco   7, 26, 29, 30, 35, 52, 81, 104–7
   CC logo   35, 107
   little black dress   94
   Maltese cross jewelry   104, 106, 107
   original boxes   107
   and Schiaparelli   86, 90, 104
   Total Look   104
chatelaines   16, 17
chokers
   Boucher, Marcel   95
   Haskell, Miriam   52, 53
   Kramer   117
   Trifari   42
   unsigned   225
   Westwood, Vivienne   196
Christmas tree designs
   pins   208–11
   Weiss   110
Christmas themed jewelry   114, 132, 163
Ciner   162
Clark, Robert F.   52, 61, 194
Clément, Jean   89
clips
   Bakelite   203, 205–6, 207
   Boucher, Marcel   26
   Chanel   106
   Coro & Corocraft   31, 73
   De Rosa   167
   double   214–15, 216
   Eisenberg   138
   Rosenstein, Nettie   186
   Trifari   41, 43
   unsigned   220
clock clasps   12
cocktail jewelry   31
Cocteau, Jean   30, 86
Coddington, Grace   232
Cohn & Rosenberger   72
Cole, Cheryl   233
Collins, Joan   232
Coppola e Toppo   148 9
   Bijoux Vogages   148
Coppola, Lydia   89
Corbeau & Cie   186
Coro & Corocraft   31, 42, 72, 110, 140, 164–9
Duettes   31, 74, 76, 78–9, 214,

215, 216
  Emblem of Americas pins   74
  Jelly Bellies   31, 74, 78, 216
  Vendôme   72, 78, 118
coronets   12
Crawford, Joan   29, 30, 52, 58, 142, 146
Cristobal   163, 208
crosses   11, 20
  Chanel   106, 107
  Hagler, Stanley   64
  Lisner   126
cuff bracelets,
  Chanel   104, 106, 107
  Curtis Jere   151
cut steel jewelry   16
Czech jewelry   212 13

D
Daché, Lilly   166
Dali, Salvador   30, 86
Dalrymple, William   240
Danecraft   166
Davis, Bette   81, 134, 136
De Lillo, William   194
de la Renta, Oscar   34, 176
Dehoff, Sabrina   235
DeLizza & Elster (D& E)   164–5
deLizza, Guillermo (William)   164
DeMario, Robert   167, 177
DeMille, Cecil B.   134
DeRosa   89, 167
Di Niscemi, Mimi   177
Diaghilev, Sergei   26
diamonds   13, 14, 21
  all white look   27
  black   122
Dietrich, Marlene   98, 166
Dior, Christian   80 5, 90, 126, 148
  aurora borealis line   31, 82
  floral forms   82, 84
  and Grosse   170
  and Kramer   82, 114 16
  Mitchell Maer   82, 83
  New Look   32, 80, 81, 84, 138
  and Schreiner   136
Doohan, Simon   236
double clips   214 15, 216

E
earrings
  1960s   32
  1980s   34
  Art   155
  Austrian   200, 201
  Beaujewels   157

Bijoux Heart   231
Boucher, Marcel   92–3, 95, 97
Carnegie   142, 143
Chanel   106, 107
Coppola e Toppo   148, 149
Coro & Corocraft   73, 76, 77
Cristobal   163
DeLizza & Elster   165
Dior, Christian   80– 85
eighteenth century   15
Eisenberg   138, 139
Eugene   168
Givenchy   169
Hagler, Stanley   63–71
Har   145
Hobé   135
Hollycraft   171
Iskin, Harry   171
Joseff of Hollywood   99–103
Judy Lee   174
Kramer   115, 117
Lagerfeld, Karl   172
Lane, Kenneth Jay   127, 129
Lisner   123, 124
Marvella   174
Matisse   151
Mazer & Jomaz   140, 141
Haskell. Miriam   53, 56, 58–9
Napier   178, 179
Nettie Rosenstein   186
Panetta   180
Rebajes   181
Regency   182, 183
Réja   184
Robert   185
Saint Laurent, Yves   187
Sarah Coventry   162
Schiaparelli, Elsa   86–91
Schreiner   137
Selro   189
Sherman   190–1
Tatty Devine   241
Tortolani   193
Trifari   41–3, 44–7, 49–51
unsigned   222–3
van der Straeten, Hervé   192
Vendôme   119–21
Vrba, Larry   195
Weiss   111–3
Egypt, ancient   10–11
Egyptian revival   27, 29, 212, 213
eighteenth century jewelry   14, 17
Eisenberg   138–9, 211
Eisenhower, Mamie   37, 42, 45
Elizabeth II, Queen   214
  coronation   40
Ellen Designs   185
Elster, Harold   164
Emmons Jewellers   162
enameling   12, 22
Erasmus, Pieter   37, 240

Erickson Beamon   36, 236, 240
Eugene   168

F
Fahrner   26, 108–9
Fashioncraft Jewelry Company   185
Felch Wehr Company   166
Fels, Jerry   150
Ferré, Gianfranco   82
Field, Patricia   37, 232
filigree jewelry   33
  Czech   212
  Fahrner, Theodor   108–9
Finkelstein, Sol   184
Fishel, Carlton   42
Fishel, Karl   40
Fleuridas, André   140
Florenza   168
Fontaine, Joan   142
Fonteyn, Margot   80
Fouquet, Georges   22
Freiler, Curt   150
Frères, Piel   25
Furst, Clifford   161

G
Gaillard, Lucien   22
Galliano, John   82, 84, 169, 236
Ganz, Victor   122
Gardner, Ava   134
garnets   11
Gaskin, Arthur and Georgina   25
Geissman, Robert   76
Gershel, Ben   192
Giardinetti   14
Gilbert, Jack   193
girdles   12
Givenchy   169, 240
Givenchy, Hubert de   89
Gone with the Wind (film)   134, 146
Goossens, Robert   82, 90, 105, 106, 107
Gorham & Co   25
Gothic jewelry   161
Gradl, Max Joseph   108
Graham, Tracy   231
Grant, George   193
Greek puzzle rings   33
Gripoix   104, 106, 170
Gripoix, Josette   82, 170
Grosse   170
Guinness, Lulu   231

H
Hagler, Stanley   32, 62–71, 209
  boutique collection   64

manipulated jewelry   62
  Shocko pieces   64
  and Wallis Simpson   62, 66
  wardrobe necklace   64
hair jewelry   19
Hale, Frank Gardner   24
Hall, Jerry   132
Hanack, Matthias   25
Har   144 5, 155
  Dragon designs   144 5
Harlow, Jean   29
Haskell, Miriam   30, 32, 52–61, 62, 188
  identifying jewelry by   54
  Japanese faux pearls   54–55, 58, 61
  and Larry Vrba   194
  Retro Line   52
Haussler, Hermann   108
Hayworth, Rita   80
Heibronner, Joseph   144
Henkel & Grosse   82, 170
Hepburn, Audrey   169
Herrera, Carolina   176
Hess, Frank   52, 54, 62, 116
Hobé   29, 134–5
Hollwood   29, 30
Hollycraft   171
Huber, Patriz   108

I
ironwork jewelry   18
Iskin, Harry   171

J
Jaffe, David   185
Jagger, Bianca   132
Japanese faux pearls   54–6, 58, 61
Jean Pierre, Roger   89
Jelly Bellies   216–17
  Coro   31, 74, 78, 216
  Trifari   40, 42, 216–17
jet jewelry   21, 36
jewelry fraud   12
Johnson, Lady Bird   192
Jomaz   140 1
Joseff of Hollywood   7, 29, 98, 103
Joseph, Larry   142
Judy Lee   174

K
Kalo Shop   25
Kamke, Ruth M.   138
Kao, Jen   234
Karan, Donna   236, 237
Katz, Adolph   74, 76, 78, 216
Kelly, Grace   31, 89

King, Jessie M. 25
Kleeman, Georg 108
Klein, Susan 144
Kling, Anton 109
Knightly, Kiera 173
Knox, Archibald 25
Korean War 114, 208
Kramer 82, 114–17, 124, 138, 164
　Amourelle 116
　Christmas themed pins 114
　Diamond Look 114
　Golden Look 114
　Kramer Sterling 116
Krussman, Leo 40, 42

L

Lacroix, Christian 34, 172, 192
Lady Gaga 236
Lagerfeld, Karl 35, 107, 173, 242
Lalinque, René 23
Landsman, Irving 185
Lane, Kenneth Jay 7, 33, 36, 126–9, 156, 164
　Big Cats pins 33, 126, 128
　cabochons 126, 129
Lang, Fritz 37, 240
Lanvin, Jeanne 173, 233, 235
Laroche, Guy 233, 235
Leigh, Vivien 146
Lelong, Lucien 80
Levitt, Edith 144
Levy, Robert 185
Lim, Phillip 234
Linsey, Loelia 214
Lisner 122 5
　Lanvin's Violet 122
　Leaves 124
　Richelieu 124
Liz Claiborne Inc. 42
Lombard, Caroline 166
Lorenz, Dana 237
Love, Diane 33, 42
Love, Pamela 234
Lucite jewelry 31
　Boucher, Marcel 96
　Jelly Bellies 31, 40, 42, 74, 78, 216–17
　Saint Laurent, Yves 187
　Lisner 122–23
　Vendôme 118

M

McCardell, Claire 142
McQueen, Alexander 240
Madonna 64, 132, 236
Maer, Mitchell 82–3
Maison Gripoix 104, 106, 170
Maltese cross jewelry

Chanel 104, 106–7
　Lisner 126
Marcher, Royal 76
Marion, Helen 118, 121
Markle, William 161
Marvella 174
Matisse 150–1
Matsumoto, Kunio 51
Mawi 238–9
Mazer 140–1
Mello, Dawn 232
Memphis Designers for ACME 154
Mendini, Alessandro 154
Middle Ages 11–12, 24
Miners, Steven 163
Minogue, Kylie 132
Miranda, Carmen 28
Mogul jewelry 27, 35
Moini, Iradj 34, 176
Molnar, Robert 236
Monet (Monocraft) 177, 187, 210
Monroe, Marilyn 81, 98, 136
Morawe, Ferdinand 108
Morris, Robert Lee 35
Morris, William 24
Moss, Kate 241
Moss, Sandy 194
mourning jewelry 18 19
Mower, Simon 239
Mugler, Thierry 192
Murano 36
Murrle, Bennet & Co 25, 109
Mylu 210

N

Nakles, Edward 62
Napier 178 9
Napoleon, French emperor 18
Native American style 33
　Castlecliff 161
necklaces
　1970s 33
　Art Deco 27, 28
　Arts & Crafts 25
　Avon 156
　Bakelite 202, 204, 205, 207
　Bengel 158
　Bijoux Heart 231
　Bogoff 159
　Butler & Wilson 131–2
　Carnegie, Hattie 142–3
　Castlecliff 161
　Caviness, Alice 160
　Chanel 104, 106, 107
　Coppola e Toppo 148, 149
　Cristobal 163
　Czech 212–3
　DeLizza & Elster 165
　Dior 81, 82, 84, 85

Eisenberg 138–9
Florenza 168
Georgian 17
Givenchy 169
Har 145
Haskell, Miriam 52–60
Hobé 135
Hollycraft 171
Jewels of India 30
Joseff of Hollywood 99, 100, 102, 103
Judy Lee 174
Kramer 115
Lane, Kenneth Jay 127–9
Lisner 123, 124, 125
Lorenz, Dana 237
Marcel Boucher 93, 95–7
Matisse 151
Mawi 37
Mazer 141
Napier 179
Regency 182, 183
Robert 185
St Erasmus 240
Saint Laurent, Yves 187
Schiaparelli, Elsa 87, 90–1
Schreiner 136, 137
Selro 189
Sherman 190
Hagler, Stanley 62,–71
Tatty Devine 241
Tortolani 193
Trifari 41, 45, 47–51
unsigned 224 5
van der Straeten, Hervé 192
Vendôme 119, 121
Victorian 21
Vrba, Larry 195
Weiss 111
Whiting & Davis 197
see also chokers; crosses; pendants
Newlyn pansy necklace 25
nineteenth century jewelry 18 21
Nixon, Pat 192
Norell, Norman 136, 142

O

Oakes, Edward Everett 24
Obama, Michelle 37, 233, 236, 240
Olbrich, Joseph Maria 108

P

Panetta 180
Parker, Sarah Jessica 37, 176, 236
pearl jewelry 13
　Butler & Wilson 130, 131
　Chanel 26, 104, 105

Dior, Christian 81, 83–5
Hagler, Stanley 62
Haskell, Miriam 54–6,58, 61
Kramer 114
Lagerfeld, Karl 35
Lane, Kenneth Jay 128
Roman 11
Vendôme 118
pendants
　Art Nouveau 23
　Arts & Crafts 25
　Avon 156
　Bijoux Heart 231
　Chanel 35
　eighteenth century 15
　Lane, Kenneth Jay 129
　Moris, Robert Lee 35
　Roman 11
　Schreiner 137
　Victorian 21
　Westwood, Vivienne 196
Pennino brothers 180
Pepper, Arthur 155
Perry, Katie 241
Petronzio, Millie 52
Philippe, Alfred 31, 40–2, 44, 45, 46, 47, 216
Phoenicians 11
pinckbeck 16, 20
pins
　1960s 33
　Art 155
　Art Deco 27
　Art Nouveau 23
　Arts & Crafts 24
　Austrian 200, 201
　Avon 156
　Bakelite 202–207
　Barclay, McClelland 175
　Beaujewels 157
　Bengel, Jakob 158
　Bond Boyd 159
　Boucher, Marcel 92–7
　Butler & Wilson 131–3
　Cadoro 160
　Carnegie, Hattie 142, 143
　Caviness, Alice 161
　Chanel 106–107
　Christmas tree 208–11
　Coro & Corocraft 31, 72–7
　Cristobal 163, 208–9
　Czech 212–3
　Daché Lilly 166
　De Rosa 167
　DeLizza & Elster 165
　DeMario, Robert 167
　Dior, Christian 80–5
　eighteenth century 15, 16
　Eisenberg 138
　Fahrner, Theodor 109
　Florenza 168

Grosse 170
Hagler, Stanley 63–71
Har 144, 145
Haskell, Miriam 53, 55, 59, 60
Hobé 134, 135
Hollycraft 171
Iskin, Harry 171
Joseff of Hollywood 7, 99–102
Judy Lee 174
Kramer 114–7
Lacroix, Christian 172
Lane, Kenneth Jay 33, 126–129
Lisner 123, 125
Marvella 174
Matisse 150–1
Mazer & Jomaz 140–1
medieval 12
mourning 19
Napier 178
Panetta 180
Rebajes 181
Regency 182, 183
Réja 184
Robert 185
Roman 11
Rosenstein, Nettie 186
Sandor 188
Sarah Coventry 162
Schiaparelli, Elsa 86–91
Schreiner 136, 137
Sherman 190, 191
Simpson, Adele 192
Stein, Lea 147
Tortolani 193
Trifari 40, 41, 43, 45–51
    Jelly Belly 216–17
    unsigned 218–22
van der Straeten, Hervé 192
Vendôme 118, 119, 120, 121
Victorian 19, 21
Vrba, Larry 195, 208
Warner 196
Weiss 110–13
Westwood, Vivienne 196
see also clips
Placco, Oscar 76
plastic jewelry 28, 32, 33, 202–7
    Lisner 122
    Stein, Lea 146
Pliny the Elder 11
plique à jour enamel 22, 25
Plunkett, Walter 98
Poiret, Paul 86
Polaris pin 151
Porter, Mrs Cole 214
portrait medallions 12
Posen, Zac 236
Presley, Elvis 146
Primavera, Victor 166
Pucci, Emilio 148

R

Radice, Barbara 154
Raimond, Massa 76
Raines, Peter 52
Randhal, Julius 25
Rebajes 181
Regency 182–3
Regina Novelty Company 182
Réja 184
Renaissance jewelry 12 13
Renoir 150 1
rhinestones 27
rings
    Avon 156
    Bakelite 203
    Bijoux Heart 231
    Egyptian hair ring 11
    medieval 12
    mourning 19
Rivers, Joan 164
Robert 185
Roman jewelry 11, 15, 18, 20
Romanticism 20
Rosenstein, Nettie 45, 186
Rousselet, Louis 186
Ruskin, John 24

S

St Erasmus 37, 240
St Gielar, Ian 64, 70
Saint Laurent, Yves 82, 90, 177, 187
Sandor 188
Sarah Coventry 162
Saxon jewelry 11
Scaasi, Arnold 126, 176, 177
Scannavino, Adrian 180
Schiaparelli, Elsa 7, 30, 86–91, 104, 122, 124, 148, 177
Shocking Pink collection 86
Schleer, William 42
Schlumberger, Jean 30, 89
Schreiner, Henry 82, 136–7
Schultz, Eugene 168
Scottish pebble jewelry 20
seed pearls
    Hagler, Stanley 62
    Haskell, Miriam 54
Seeger, Georg 108
Selini 189
Selro & Selini 189
Semensohn, Sandra 92, 94
seventeenth century jewelry 13
Shapiro, Harold 193
Shearer, Norma 142
Sherman 190–1
Shire, Peter 154
shoe buckles 15, 19
silver 12, 24
silver gilt 31

Simpson, Adele 192
Simpson, Wallis, Duchess of Windsor 62, 66, 82, 126, 160
Snow, Carmel 81
Staerk, Camilla 234
Staneskieu, Dan 160
Stein, Lea 146 7
Steinberger, Fernand 146
Strauss, Georges Frédéric 14
Stuart, Charles H. 162
Sui, Anna 236
sumptuary laws 12
Swarovski company 27, 31, 42, 46, 82, 128, 138, 144, 177, 190
    and Austrian jewelry 200
    and Bijoux Heart 231
    and Hanna Bernhard 230
    and Mawi 238
    and St Erasmus 240

T

Tassie medallions 17
Tatty Devine 241
Taylor, Elizabeth 126
Teese, Dita von 231
Thammachote, Yai 163
Tisci, Riccardo 169
Todd, Emery 25
tortoiseshell piqué 17
Tortolani 193
Toussaint, Jeanne 126
Trifari 29, 31, 33, 40–51, 140, 180
    cabochons 44, 51
    Clipmate 76, 214–5
    copyright 42
    Crown pins 40, 42, 44
    Fruit Salad/Tutti Fruitti 42
    hand set crystals 44
    Jelly Bellies 40, 42, 216–7
    Jewels of India 30
    Moghul 42
    Orientique 42
    partures/demi patures 51
    Swarovski crystals 42, 46
    Trifanium 40
Trifari, Gustavo 40, 42
Trigère, Pauline 136, 142
twentieth century jewelry 26 35
    1940s & 1950s 30–1
    1960s & 1970s 32–3
    1980s & 1990s 34–5
    see also Art Deco
twenty first century jewelry 36–7

U

United States
    American influences 29–31
    Presidential Inaugural Balls

37, 42, 45
unsigned gems 218–27

V

Van Cleef & Arpels 33, 42, 46
Van der Straeten, Hervé 192
Vauxhall glass jewelry 19
Vendôme 118 21
Verdura, Fulco di 104, 106, 177
Verrechia, Gene ("Verri") 74, 76
Viano, Blance and Aldo 174
Vici, Lou 134
Victoria & Co 178
Victoria, Queen 20–1
Vidal, Marion 242
Viking jewelry 11
Vine, Harriet 241
Vintage Fashion and Costume Jewelry Club 62
Vogue 193
Vrba, Larry 52, 194–5, 208
Vreeland, Diana 126

W

Wagenfeld, Willhelm 158
Walker, Catherine 231
Warner 196
Wedgwood cameos 17
Weinrich Bros. Co. 174
Weiss 76, 110 13, 124, 138, 164
    aurora borealis 31, 110, 111
    black diamonds 112
Welles, George 25
Westwood, Vivienne 35, 196, 231
Whiting & Davis 33, 122, 197
Whitney & Rice 178
Wilson, Patti 232
Wilson, Scott 242 3
Wilson, Simon 34, 130, 132
Winfrey, Oprah 176
Winter, Francis 81
Wolfenden, Rosie 241
Wolfers, Philippe 22
Wood, Grant 25
World War II 31, 92, 109, 116
Wyman, Jane 102

Y

Young, Loretta 166

Z

Zausner, Nat 150
Ziegfeld, Florenz 58
Zodiac jewelry 100

ACKNOWLEDGMENTS

In putting together a book like *Costume Jewelry* there are so many people who have contributed in so many ways. Firstly a thank you to all my friends in the costume jewelry world who have inspired me, including Steven and Yai from Cristobal; Chrissie Masters of The Design Gallery; Andrew and Michael from Glitz UK; Alan and Sue Poultney from Scarab; and, of course, Roxanne and Bonny.

On the editorial side, my great friend Julie Brooke—whose enthusiasm for dazzling diamanté is equal to my own—has been, in the words of my son Tom, "awesome," and this time she has been superbly assisted by Katy Armstrong. Mark Hill has always been there when we need him. Tracey Smith is the most wonderful Editorial Director—always on hand when crises threaten. Carolyn Madden and Alycen Mitchell have worked their magic on the text. Thank goodness for proof-readers, in this case Ruth Baldwin, or some horrible errors would have crept in! And when you want to use a book like this you need a good index, so thanks to Isobel McLean.

As for the beautiful look of this book—thanks, as always, to the best photographer Graham Rae. In the stunning design, Pene Parker's genius is evident: the pieces simply spring off the page. The whole design team are inspired, especially Yasia Williams-Leedham and Mark Kan, whose total commitment to the project and brilliant image choice has made the book un-put-downable.

And then Sue Meldrum and Pete Hunt in Production, who have worked their miracles, color correcting the images and ensuring that the pages look wonderful.

Books are a team effort and this team have quite simply worked above and beyond to ensure that the book looks and reads the way it does.

A sincere thank you to you all.

Additional images from:
Bridgeman Art Library Hermitage, St Petersburg, Russia 13 (3); Museum of London 13 (2), 15 (2)
Corbis Bettmann 45 (above right), 58 (above left), 62 (above left), 84 (below left) ; Hulton-Deutsch Collection 86 (center)
Getty Images AFP/Mandel Ngan 37 (above); Michael Ochs Archives 31 (above); Roger Viollet 104 (below)